The Cello

The Cello

Elizabeth Cowling

B. T. Batsford Ltd London and Sydney

*To Dudley Powers and Janos Scholz
and to the Memory of Paul Bazelaire,
Pablo Casals, and Luigi Silva*

First published 1975
© Elizabeth Cowling 1975

ISBN 0 7134 2879 1

Printed and bound in Great Britain by
Cox & Wyman Ltd, London, Fakenham and Reading
for the publishers B. T. Batsford Ltd,
4 Fitzhardinge Street, London W1H 0AH
and 23 Cross Street, Brookvale, NSW 2100, Australia

Contents

Contents

List of Illustrations

List of Music Examples

Preface

Writing this book has taught me much including how helpful people are when one must impose on their time (necessarily), either for correspondence or for interviews. I have enjoyed particularly my correspondence with my cellist colleagues, many of whom I have not met. I am indebted especially to those who were willing to send me pictures of their cellos that appear in this book. Also special thanks are due to Mr. Kenneth Jacobs of Rembert Wurlitzer for help with a number of questions. I am grateful for the interviews, from which I profited much, with Mrs. Carleen M. Hutchins, Miss Nona Pyron, Mr. Janos Scholz, Miss Milly B. Stanfield, the late Mr. Ernest Wassing, and Mr. Laurence C. Witten II. I enjoyed the playing sessions with my cellist colleagues, Mrs. Martha Jane Bishop and the late Mrs. Catherine Farley, with whom I played over dozens of continuo sonatas, and with Mrs. Mary Alicia Cox, pianist, with whom I sight-read a number of works from all periods. She has also been kind enough to proofread the book, for which I thank her.

My own university (the University of North Carolina at Greensboro) has been generous in its help, granting me a June grant in 1970 as well as a semester's leave of absence, and particularly the Faculty Research Council for a grant which allowed me to study in Europe in the summer of 1970. The university library staff has been most helpful, especially Mrs. Elizabeth Jerome Holder, Mrs. Nancy Clark Fogarty, and Mrs. Marcie Kingsley, as well as the staffs of other libraries, particularly those of the Library of Congress, the New York Public Library, the Sibley Library of the Eastman School of Music, and the University of North Carolina at Chapel Hill.

Others who have been helpful in various ways, which I acknowledge with warm thanks, are Mrs. Kathleen Bulgin, Mr. Clifton Karnes, Mrs. Anita Regelin, Mr. Kenneth Skeaping, the late Mrs. Imgard

Stearns, and Miss Martha Whittemore. Mrs. Martha Jane Bishop has been helpful in so many ways that I am quite at a loss to thank her properly.

I am grateful to Mr. Andrew Martin of our university Department of Art for drawing the cello diagrams appearing in the book, and to Dr Charles L. Schepens for his unusual kindness in helping me with my work in Ghent.

I am bound to acknowledge the Belwin Mills publishing house for for permission to print the Luigi Boccherini excerpt (ex. 14), and the Bibliothèque Nationale for the illustration of a page of Giorgio Antoniotti's Sonata 3, first movement (Plate 34). I wish also to thank Mr Janos Scholz for the charming picture, 'Il virtuoso del Sigr. De Bacqueville', which is part of his private collection (Plate 33).·

Thanks are also due to my typists, Mrs Kathryn Jett and Mrs Louise Mills (for the final typing), along with her remarkable patience. My special thanks are due Professor Amy M. Charles of the Department of English for reading the manuscript. Needless to say, all errors are, of course, mine.

I acknowledge with pleasure the owners of the following cellos, who are teachers at various universities and colleges, for the pictures of their instruments:

Professors:

Robert L Deutsch *Francesco Ruggeri cello*
Lucca Di Cecco *Lorenzo Storioni cello*
J. Robert Hladky *David Tecchler cello*
W. Howard Jones *Guiseppe Guarnerius "filius Andrea" cello*
Joanna de Keyser *Santo Seraphin cello (picture taken by Allen Madans)*
William Klenz *Joannes Franciscus Pressenda cello*
Ronald Leonard *Pietro Guarneri (of Mantua) cello*
Lucien Laporte *Matteo Gofriller cello*
Ira Lehn *Giovanni Baptista Gabrielli (Gabrielly) cello*
David Vanderkooi *Giovanni Baptista Grancino cello*
Louis A. Potter *William Forster cello*
Gabor Rejto *Domenico Montagnana cello*
Edward Szabo *Nicolo Gagliano cello*
Robert L. Stewart *Matthias Albani cello*
Stephen Stalker *Thomas Dodd cello*

Also I would like to thank Mr Laurence C. Witten II for the pictures of the Andrea Amati cello; the University of Saskatchewan for the

Preface

Girolano Amati II cello pictures; B.T. Batsford, Ltd., for pictures of the arpeggione and the violoncello piccolo; the Museum of Fine Arts Boston, for the picture of the five-string cello and the copper cello; the Smithsonian Institution for pictures of the Abraham Prescott cello; and to the following instrument houses: Jacques François, Rare Violins, Inc., for the Giovanni Battista Rogeri cello pictures; William Moennig & Son, Inc., for the G. B. Grancino cello pictures (for Mr. Vanderkooi), pictures of the Giovanni Baptista Guadagnini cello and the Tommaso Balestrieri cello; and Rembert Wurlitzer, Inc., for pictures of the Lorenzo Guadagnini cello, the Jacobus Stainer cello, the Antonio Stradivari cello and the Nicolo Amati cello. (The picture of the Francesco Gofriller is of my cello.)

Elizabeth Cowling

Greensboro, North Carolina
October, 1973

Introduction

Heretofore two books in the English language have dealt primarily with the history of the cello and its literature. The first is Wilhelm Joseph von Wasielewski's *The Violoncello and Its History*, originally printed in German in 1889 and translated by Isobella S. E. Stigand into English in 1894. A reprint of this 1894 edition was made by the Da Capo Press in 1968, with a new Preface and a few added footnotes by Robert C. Lawes, Jr. There has been no revision of the text since the book appeared in 1889, some 80 years ago. The second book, *The History of the Violoncello, the Viol da Gamba, Their Precursors and Collateral Instruments* . . . 2 vols., by Edmund van der Straeten, was printed in 1915. This book actually absorbs the whole Wasielewski book, the pioneer work, but adds greatly to it, so is the more valuable of the two. It was reprinted by Reeves in 1971. Both of these books have a defect in their beginning by devoting so much space to the viola da gamba (both about the first fifth of the book), which emphasis implies a relationship between the viola da gamba and the cello when there was no relationship. The reprint of the Wasielewski book even carries a picture of a gamba stamped on its cover. I think this emphasis has aided in the continuing persistence of the belief in some quarters that the bass gamba was the ancestor of the cello. Both books are particularly inadequate in dealing with the early history of the cello and its early literature. Therefore, I have dealt with these subjects in somewhat more detail.

Starting with the middle of the eighteenth century, van der Straeten's recital of cello performers and literature written by cellists is more complete. (He scarcely mentions any of the literature written by non-cellists in the nineteenth century, which is the more important.)

My attempt in writing this book has been to place before the reader the essential material for an understanding of the instrument, and because the instrument exists to play its literature, something of the literature itself to about the middle of the twentieth century. I have confined the discussion of the literature to the solo literature written originally for the cello. To discuss its role in chamber music (other than duos) and in orchestral music, important as it is, would require another volume. Parts of this book I consider a kind of *pasticcio*, not representing original work, but gathering together between the covers of one book material that it has taken me a considerable amount of time to collect. Furthermore, I have quoted without quotation marks from my own dissertation, *The Italian Literature for the Violoncello in the Baroque Era* (1967) whenever it suited my purpose.

Let it be said that the rank of cellists has been distinguished in the past by a number of composers, cellists turned conductors, writers, and even royalty. Among the composers the cello was the instrument of the Venetian baroque opera composer, Antonio Caldara, who wrote at least 16 continuo sonatas for cello as well as a lesson book; Christoph Willibald Gluck the great opera composer; Johann Rudolf Zumsteeg, the creator of the German pre-romantic Ballad, who wrote a concerto and a sonata or two for his instrument; Jean-Jacques Offenbach, founder of the romantic *opéra bouffe*, who wrote a number of pieces for cello; Victor Herbert, pupil of Bernard Cossmann, who wrote much for the cello, including two concertos; and Heitor Villa-Lobos (1887–1959), the Brazilian composer who has written extensively for the cello. Although the cello was not the main instrument for either Gioacchino Rossini or Arnold Schoenberg, they both studied the cello, and Schoenberg was a member of Zemlinsky's orchestra in Vienna. This may have been the basis for Schoenberg's interest in the G. M. Monn cello concerto in G minor and his transcription of a Monn harpsichord concerto in D major for cello and orchestra. Although Schubert was not a cellist, that his father was may account for his great sensitivity to the instrument, culminating in his string quintet, Op. 163, with two cellos.

The number of cellists turned conductor is impressive; but we might mention in particular Arturo Toscanini, Hans Kindler, the founder of the National Symphony Orchestra in Washington, D.C. Sir John Barbirolli, and Pablo Casals.

Among the persons more famed for their writing than their cello playing were the great lexicographer, Ernst Ludwig Gerber (1746–

2b Cello of Andrea Amati, labelled 1572 (details)

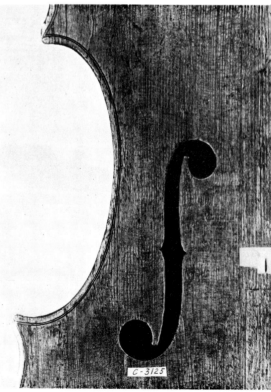

1819); Louis-Antoine Vidal, author of the important book on string instruments, *Les Instruments à archet*, 3 vols. (1876–78), and Laurent Grillet, *Les Ancêtres du Violin et du Violoncelle, les Luthiers et les Fabricants d'Archets*, 2 vols. (1901).

Among royalty, Joseph II of Austria (reign 1765–90), Frederick William II of Prussia, nephew and successor to Frederick the Great, and three Princes of Wales studied the cello: the Prince later to become George III (reign 1760–1820), the Prince, a student of Crosdill, who became George IV (reign 1820–30), and the present Prince of Wales.

This book is addressed to the student of the cello and to the interested layman. Much of the contents of the book will already be known to the teacher who has taken any interest in these matters.

Chapter 1

The Instrument

The proper name for the instrument which is the subject of this book is 'violoncello' (pronounced vé-o-lon-chêl-lo). It was named in Italy and literally means a 'little violone,' the Italian 'cello' being a diminutive. (For an interpretation of the word 'violone' see pp. 56–60). A generation or two past, it was customary to shorten the name 'violoncello' to "cello,' the apostrophe indicating the six missing letters. Only recently has it been acceptable to use simply 'cello' as the name for this instrument.

The Anatomy of the Cello (see figures 1–3):

THE EXTERIOR PARTS

The top (table, belly or front plate) is typically made of two pieces of matching spruce or pine glued together. These pieces are extremely important in determining the basic tone quality of the instrument. The inside of the top is graded from $\frac{3}{16}$ inches in the middle to $\frac{9}{64}$ inches at the edges, for a cello with a body length of $29\frac{1}{2}$ inches. This grading process is also an extremely important and delicate operation. Two graceful f-holes on the top of the instrument on each side are positioned by a proportion of 7:10 between the length of the neck and the distance from the upper edge of the top to the central notch of the f-holes, which position determines the string length. The f-holes, of course, allow the volume of sound to escape from the instrument.

The back is usually made of two matching pieces of maple (a hard wood), which are often chosen for the figuration in the wood. The back is also graded, for the normal cello from $\frac{4}{16}$ inches in the middle to $\frac{9}{64}$ inches at the edges. There are a few cellos with one-piece backs.

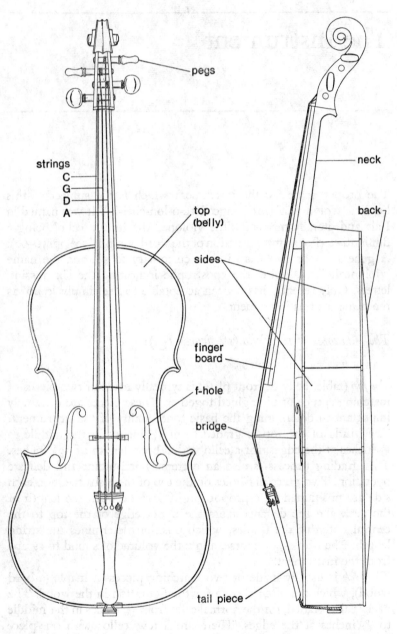

pegs

strings
C
G
D
A

top
(belly)

sides

finger
board

f-hole

bridge

neck

back

tail piece

Fig. 1

18

The neck, peg box, and *scroll* were originally shaped from one piece of maple. The necks of older cellos were shorter than today's, but because of the rise in pitch over the centuries, new, longer necks have had to be grafted on older cellos. When this is done, the peg box and scroll, a very individual and characteristic part, are kept if possible and replaced on the new neck.

The sides, or *ribs,* number six pieces of maple glued to the top and back. One piece goes from the neck to the waist, the second on the waist itself, and the third from the waist to the centre of the bottom on both sides.

The purfling is usually a triple line of narrow strips of dyed wood, the two outer ones black and a lighter coloured inner one. They are fitted into a groove around both the top and back near the edge of the instrument. These strips are not only decorative but help prevent the splitting of the edges.

The bridge is made from maple. Its two feet are set (not glued) midway on top of the instrument between the two f-holes and centred on the f-hole notches. It must be fitted very carefully so that its feet follow exactly the contours of the belly. The curvature of the top of the bridge in relation to the curved fingerboard is what enables the player to play on one string at a time.

The button, a part of the back, has the function of strengthening the joint of the neck with the body of the instrument. It is not shown in the diagrams but can be seen excellently on the Pressenda cello (Plate 22). Sometimes, for decorative purposes, it is outlined in ebony, as is the one on the Pressenda cello.

THE INTERIOR PARTS

The linings consist of twelve pieces of narrow strips of pine glued to the edge of the sides to provide a wider surface on which to glue the top and the back. Six blocks of pine are used, one each in the corners for strength, one block at the top of the instrument into which is inserted the shoulder of the neck, and one block at the bottom through which a hole is bored to accommodate the plug which holds the end pin.

The bass bar, a piece of spruce or pine which has been cut to fit the curvature of the top, is glued to the inside of the top on the left-hand side (side of the lowest string; therefore called a bass bar). The middle of the bar widthwise is placed under the left foot of the bridge. Its shaping is important and its function is to assist the top in resist-

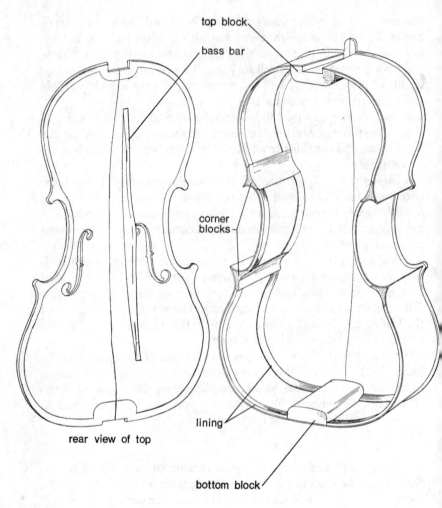

top block

bass bar

corner blocks

lining

rear view of top

bottom block

Fig. 2

ing and responding to the pressure of the bridge. It is vital in terms of structure and tone. The bass bar in the early cellos was shorter and lighter than at present; so again, because of the rise in pitch and therefore greater pressure on the top, all the bass bars in the earlier cellos have been replaced with longer and stronger bars.

The sound post is a small, cylindrical piece of spruce or pine that fits between the top and the back without being glued. It is placed just in front (lower on the instrument) of the right foot of the bridge. It is put in place by a special tool called a sound-post setter after the instrument has been assembled. Its function is to transmit the vibrations of the top to the back of the instrument. If the sound post is even slightly too long, the area around the bridge foot on the top will be weakened. If the sound post is too short, it will fall over too easily. The ends of the sound post must be shaped to fit exactly the contours of the top and back where it comes in contact with them. The perfect placing of the sound post is one of the most sensitive adjustments, and the better the instrument, the more sensitive it is to this adjustment.

THE FITTINGS

The fingerboard, fashioned from ebony, is glued to the neck of the instrument and provides the surface upon which the fingers depress the strings for the notes. In former days the fingerboard was shorter than today, as can be seen in the Bréval picture (Plate 32).

The pegs around which the strings are wound are usually made of ebony, occasionally of rose-wood, and are carefully fitted to the holes in the peg box. By turning the pegs forward, the pitch of the string is lowered; by moving them backwards, the pitch is raised.

The four strings on the cello are tuned to C-G-d-a. The top two strings were formerly made of gut and the bottom two of wound gut. Now, the gut a-string is more often replaced by a steel string; the d-string is often of aluminium-wound gut or steel; and some players use four steel strings. (This practice, however, detracts from the most beautiful quality that a fine instrument is able to produce, and steel strings are substituted purely for expediency). A steel string is fitted with a tuning mechanism fastened to the upper end of the tailpiece and adjusted by a screw.

The nut is a small piece of ebony glued to the top of the fingerboard where it joins the peg box. There are four grooves in the nut, each

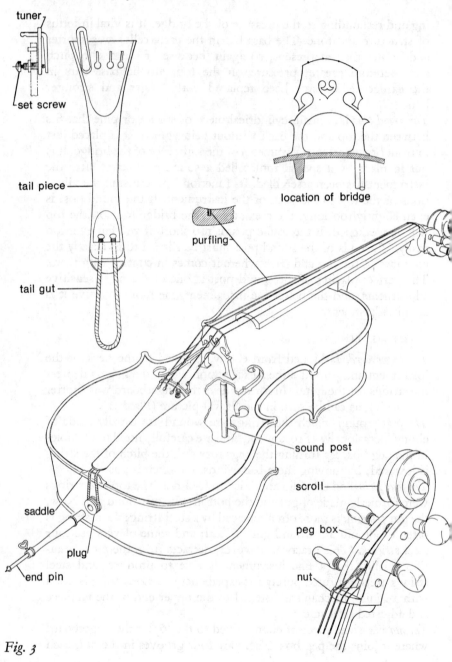

Fig. 3

string passing over its groove to its peg. The grooves regulate the spacing between the strings and also the height of the strings over the fingerboard at this point. The open (i.e. non-stopped) vibrating string extends from the nut to the top of the bridge.

The tailpiece is also made of ebony. The lower ends of the strings are attached to the upper end of the tailpiece, which is held in place by the *tail gut*. The tail gut is fastened to one side of the lower part of the tailpiece, looped around the plug and secured to the other side of the tailpiece.

The plug, inserted into a hole at the bottom of the cello is the device into which the end pin is inserted.

The end pin, the length of which can be adjusted for the convenience of the player, is held in place by a screw. It rests on the floor, its function being to provide a secure hold of the cello. End pins are detachable or, after use, reinserted into the cello through the plug.

After the instrument is assembled, a filler is applied to the wood, which is then varnished. The hues that are used are various shades of red, orange, brown, or yellow. The varnish used by the early makers has been an endless source of speculation. They used an oil varnish rather than a spirit varnish. An oil varnish takes longer to dry and is best sun-dried. It was once thought that there was some secret about the varnish used earlier and that the varnish accounted for the special beauty of the tone quality in the old instruments. This theory is now questioned, the general belief today being that the tone quality results, then as now, primarily from the choice of the wood itself and its gradations as fashioned by the maker, combined with the varnish, which both preserves the wood and consequently the tone quality and must be neither too thick nor too thin. The wood and the varnish are equally important and certainly a poor varnish can spoil an instrument.

Remarks on Some Practical Aspects of the Physics of Cello Sound

For sound to be produced on the cello, one or more of its strings must be put in vibration. This is done by the stroke of the bow, which has been rubbed with rosin to produce greater friction, or by plucking the string (pizzicato). The string, the vibrating source, has too small a surface to be able to produce the sound without amplification.

Leaḃarlanna Conṁḋae Ḋoṅclaiṅɼe

(Mrs Carleen Hutchins, a contemporary maker, put it very nicely when she likened it to the effectiveness of fanning with a toothpick.) The body of the cello, including the enclosed air, is the amplifier or resonator. The string's vibrations are communicated to the top of the cello through the motion of the bridge. The vibrations of the string (amplified) make sound waves in the outside air. The frequency of the number of sound waves per second determines the pitch of the tone. The standards of pitch have varied, but at present 440 vibrations per second (or 440 c.p.s.) for a^1 is considered standard. The various seven note segments with their notes are frequently designated in the following manner, which will be accepted in this book:

Example 1: Designation of Octaves

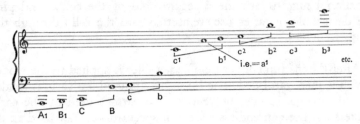

In Haydn's day the standard for a^1 was more like 422 c.p.s. and lower before that. Today's higher pitch of the strings puts more pressure on the belly of the instrument and is the reason for higher bridges and heavier bass bars than when the instruments were made. Vuillaume, for one, predicted that the higher pitch would eventually destroy the old instruments, but his prediction has not come true.

Almost all tones we hear are composite tones, being made up of the fundamental tone and its partials. For instance, on the C-string on the cello the low C is the fundamental, or the first and strongest partial, but also present in the tone are the following:

Example 2: Series of Partials

*Brackets indicate notes too out of tune to notate.

This series is infinite, but most tones above the 32nd partial cannot be represented on a staff. (Some people refer to the notes above the fundamental as overtones; small c would then be called the first overtone. Others, however, refer to all the notes as partials; small c accordingly is the second partial). It is the frequency of the number of sound waves per second of the first partial, or fundamental, which determines the pitch of the note; the number and relative strength of the other partials determine the tone quality. It was Helmholtz who first stated that tone quality depended on the number and relative strength of the partials, and that these in turn determine the shape of the vibration wave. Each instrument has its own characteristic shape of vibration wave. The number and relative strengths of the partials can be varied in several ways on the cello. They vary according to whether the string is bowed or plucked; according to the placing of the bow on the string, nearer to or farther from the bridge; and according to the speed and pressure of the bow. If the bow is placed very near the bridge, a special effect is obtained called 'sul ponticello', which is caused by altering the partials; if the bow is placed as far from the bridge as possible, over the fingerboard in fact, the effect is known as 'flautato' or 'sul tasto'. A mute, a device placed on the bridge, will sift out the higher partials, not only making the tone softer, but giving it a different quality. Vibrato also varies the quality of tone. Taste has changed in regard to the vibrato. In the nineteenth century, vibrato was used only for a special effect; now we use vibrato almost constantly, and 'senza vibrato' for a special effect. For example, the Joachim Quartet, perhaps the most famous nineteenth-century quartet, played without continuous vibrato, as did the famous cellist, Alfredo Piatti (d. 1901).

When a string on the cello is set in motion, it vibrates in 16 segments. At the end of each part is a node, where the string does not vibrate, and if one touches the string lightly at any one of these 16 spots, the bow will sound a natural harmonic. The top line of the following illustration tells where to touch the string lightly, and the bottom line shows what notes will be heard on the a-string. The notes produced in relatively the same places on the other strings are in the same relation to their fundamental as are the notes on the a-string. The fractions tell the proportion of the string that is vibrating.[1]

The different quality of the harmonics in contrast to the natural tone of the cello is caused by the cancellation of all the partials below the note sounded. There are also artificial harmonics which can be produced on the cello. If the thumb is placed firmly on any note and then the string lightly touched a perfect fourth above the thumb, the string will sound a note two octaves above the note held down by the thumb. The thumb note is a new fundamental, and lightly touching a perfect fourth above it will give the same relative note to it as that produced by note five on the chart.

Example 3: Table of Cello Harmonics

The frequency of the number of sound waves per second determines the pitch of a tone, and this frequency is on the cello actually the frequency of the first partial or fundamental tone. It should be noted further that the frequency of the number of sound waves is itself determined by the length, weight, thickness, and tension of the string. The longer, heavier, thicker string with less tension will produce the lower tone. The number of vibrations decreases as the length of a string increases (violin 'a' string = 440 c.p.s.; the cello 'a' string, twice as long = 220 c.p.s). With the stringed instruments, the player changes the effective length of the string by the fingers of the left hand. As one proceeds 'up' the cello string (the motion of the hand in space is down), the length of the vibrating string is shortened; consequently the notes are higher. For practical reasons, the strings on each of the instruments of the violin family have the same length from nut to bridge. Instead of lengthening the lower strings or making them unreasonably thick, strings are wound with silver, copper, or aluminium to compensate.

The choice of strings is a matter of great importance to the cellist. If the string is too strong or too weak, it will affect the tone. One has to experiment with strings to find the most suitable ones for his instrument. No generalization can be made in the form of a recommendation for certain makes or gauges of strings as superior to others, although in general, the better strings are the more expensive ones.

Temperature has an effect upon these instruments and their strings. If a string absorbs moisture, it becomes heavier and the pitch goes down. If it dries out, the reverse. Strings also shrink and stretch. Steel strings are not as sensitive to weather changes as gut strings, or gut-wound strings, which practicality appeals to many performing cellists.

In addition to the above conditions, the loudness, or intensity of a tone, which determines the amplitude of the sound wave (versus its shape), is important. If greater force is used to make the string vibrate, the tone will be louder. Since the human ear is capable of distinguishing a vast number of degrees of intensity, this characteristic of tone is particularly important to the musician. The ability to produce infinite shades of intensity is a very important source of expressiveness in music.

A tone is also characterized by the manner in which it is started or stopped. On the piano, for instance, the tone on being struck immediately begins to die away. An editor's mark, the < > over one piano chord in the Peters edition of Brahms' first Violoncello Sonata, 1st movement, m. 26 is, therefore, illogical. On the stringed instruments, however, the tone can be started and stopped, loud or soft, with or without attack, and can be continued relatively indefinitely with crescendo or diminuendo during any part of its duration. The length of the bow does not determine the length of the note. It takes much practice, however, to change the direction of the bow so that the fraction of a second when the bow stops before it can be reversed will not be heard. One practises to make this break imperceptible to the ear.

Early Makers of Cellos

Great instruments of the violin family are works of art as well as musical instruments. To appreciate them fully as works of art, they have to be seen. Some people are as moved by looking at a fine instrument as they are looking at a great painting or piece of sculpture. No descriptions can possibly convey a true impression of any instrument. In this chapter some description of instruments are quoted from the experts to give the reader an idea of how they talk about instruments. When judging an instrument, an expert will examine the quality of the wood, the varnish, and the thickness of the top and back plates, which cannot be done by just looking at pictures. They also study the general model, i.e., the curvature of the upper, middle and lower bouts; the scroll, which has been compared to a signature; the f-holes, their height and width, as well as exact placement; and the purfling, especially at the corners, all of which the reader may compare among the various cellos pictured. The cello, in other words, appeals to the expert first as a work of art. From a performer's point of view, the tone quality is of first importance.

According to present knowledge, Andrea Amati (*c.* 1511 – shortly before 11 January 1581)[2] of Cremona, Italy, is the first known maker of cellos, but not actually the first maker of them (see p. 52). It is not known how many cellos he made nor how many still exist. In my correspondence with various dealers in violins and with other experts in the field, the highest estimate of extant Andrea Amati cellos is six. I know of only three, two of which are in the United States.

The Andrea Amati cello, which was formerly in the Snoeck Collection in Ghent, was sold to Mr M. H. Bakaert of Belgium, who by letter (17 July 1973) informed me that he had sold it to a Belgian artist.

Of the two cellos in the United States, the first is dated *c.* 1569 and was at the time I saw it (10 September 1971) in the possession of the shop of Rembert Wurlitzer in New York. The neck and scroll are not original; indeed, the scroll is too heavy-looking and so a bit ugly. The sound holes are equal, that is, the top half is the same size as the bottom half, unlike most others in which the lower hole was made larger than the higher one. The body of the instrument has been cut down, as most early cellos have been, and now measures $29\frac{5}{8}$ inches (75·24 cm.). The body is in remarkably good condition, but the original varnish has had some colour added over it. It is an undecorated cello.

The other Andrea Amati cello is in the possession of Mr and Mrs Laurence C. Witten II. Mr Witten showed me the cello and explained what the decorations symbolize. This cello, called 'The King' (shown on Plate 2), is historically the most famous of all cellos.[3] It is briefly described as follows in the brochure *Stringed Instruments and related material from the collection of Mr. and Mrs. Laurence C. Witten* II, and was exhibited at the Rockefeller University for the Conference on Scientific Aspects of Musical Instruments on 20–24 May 1968:

Violoncello, by Andrea Amati, Cremona, not after 1574, body length 75·5 cm. (reduced from larger dimensions). Neck and fittings modern. Painted and gilded with the arms, devices, and mottoes of Charles ix, King of France. Label probably a facsimile, dated 1572.

This cello, because of its decorations, is thought to be one of the eight basses [i.e. cellos] included in the 38 instruments ordered by Charles ix of France from Andrea Amati. The paintings are on the back and the sides, and there are decorations on the peg box as well (the peg box and scroll on this cello are original). On the centre of the back can be seen a crown over the remaining outline of the royal coat of arms, on either side of which is a figure. To the right is a figure of a woman and further to the right, a column, with a crown on top, and still another crown near the bottom of the instrument. On the left side, the figure is no longer visible, and only a portion of the column remains. The figures stand for Piety and Justice. On the sides of the cello were the words 'Pietate' and 'Justicia.' On the bass side only the letters ETA remain visible from the word 'Pietate' (see Plate 2e); 'Justicia' was on the treble side. Above the 'K' which stands for Charles (Karolus) is a crown, surrounded by other decorative figures on the middle bout. In each of the four corners of the back is a fleur-de-lis, the symbol of the royal family of France. There is also a fleur-de-lis at the back of the peg box. On the peg box is a fifth peg hole that may or may not have been there originally. (There were five-stringed cellos up to the middle of the eighteenth century.) The instrument has obviously been knocked about a little, but it has been beautifully repaired and is in a healthy condition today. The overall colour is of amber. The voice of this cello is remarkable. It possesses a beautiful, full-throated sound, vigorous enough to be heard in a concerto. By studying the seven different views of this cello, one can observe that it is basically the same as ours today, although it has been cut down. In every other respect than size, Andrea Amati made cellos as they are known today.

For a span of 200 years the makers of this family working in Cremona were among the greatest in the world. The lineage is as follows:

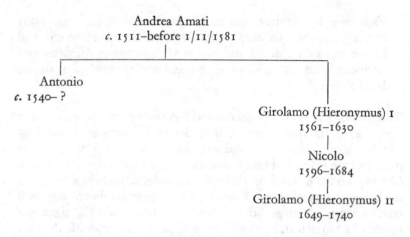

Andrea Amati
c. 1511–before 1/11/1581

Antonio
c. 1540– ?

Girolamo (Hieronymus) I
1561–1630

Nicolo
1596–1684

Girolamo (Hieronymus) II
1649–1740

The sons of Andrea, Antonio and Girolamo, worked along the model established by their father. Their instruments were usually labelled jointly, possibly even after Antonio's death. Nicolo, son of Girolamo, is the best-known maker of this family (see Plate 3). He was also a famous teacher of his craft, counting among his students his own son, Girolamo II, a fine maker who was eclipsed by his fellow-student, Antonio Stradivari. Plate 4 pictures a cello by Girolamo II Amati. Nicolo also taught Andrea Guarneri, Francesco Ruggeri, G. B. Rogeri, Gioffredo Cappa, and possibly Paolo Grancino.

For a long time Gasparo Bertolotti (1542–1609), called Gasparo da Salò after his birthplace, was given the credit for making the first instruments of the violin family. He worked in Brescia and is the first known maker of violins in that city. His claim to first place among known violin makers, however, has now given way to that of Andrea Amati, his senior by a generation, and one who was very possibly making three-stringed violins in the 1540s.[4] Da Salò is more famous for his violas and double basses, but he did make a few cellos. The one that Robert Haven Schauffler describes, however, suggests an adaptation of a viola da gamba,[5] and the one mentioned in the article on da Salò in *Grove's Dictionary* is there suggested as being a cut-down double bass. An instrument labelled as a cello by da Salò, in the Sforzesco Castle in Milan, has the dimensions of a half-sized cello (body length 23·6 inches [60 cm.]) and seems also to be a converted gamba. I have been unable to locate any bona fide da Salò cellos. Giovanni Paolo Maggini (1580–c. 1630), the most noted of da Salò's students, made a few cellos, of which only two were known in 1892[6] and these are still extant. After Maggini there was a hiatus in the production of great cellos in Brescia until the rise of the Rogeri family.

Two early families were the Ruggeri (Rugieri, Rugeri, Rugger, Ruger) and Rogeri (Rogero, Roggeri) families. These are sometimes confused and considered as one family. The Ruggeri family worked in Cremona, the Rogeri family in Brescia. Plate 5 pictures a Francesco Ruggeri cello (*c.* 1663) and Plate 6 a very beautiful Giovanni Battista Rogeri cello of 1706. Some of Rogeri's cellos, incidentally, have brought higher prices than his violins. G. B. Rogeri (*c.* 1650–*c.* 1730), born in Bologna, trained by Nicolo Amati, settled in Brescia only after his training, that is, in 1670. The hiatus in violin making in Brescia, then, lasted from the death of Maggini (*c.* 1630) to 1670. G. B. Rogeri's son, Pietro Giacomo, although not so great a maker as his father, continued making instruments in Brescia.

In Cremona, unlike Brescia, the production of great cellos was continued throughout the seventeenth and eighteenth centuries, with the founders of both the Guarneri family and the Ruggeri family students under Nicolo Amati. Francesco Ruggeri (1620–*c.* 1694) was, in fact, according to the Hill brothers, his first student and Andrea Guarneri his second. The five members of the Guarneri family were

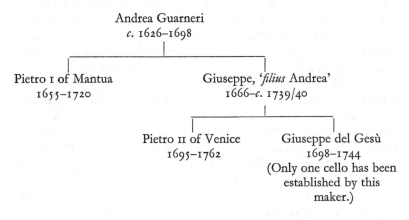

Andrea Guarneri
c. 1626–1698

Pietro I of Mantua
1655–1720

Giuseppe, '*filius* Andrea'
1666–*c.* 1739/40

Pietro II of Venice
1695–1762

Giuseppe del Gesù
1698–1744
(Only one cello has been
established by this
maker.)

It is unfortunate for cellists that Giuseppe del Gesù, generally acknowledged to be the greatest maker of this family, made no more cellos. Some of his violins are considered on a par with the best violins of Antonio Stradivari. In the handsome volume by the Hill brothers, *The Violin Makers of the Guarneri Family* (1931), there are six plates of cellos, one each in photogravure and in colour, of instruments by Andrea, Giuseppe (*filius* Andrea), and Pietro (of Venice) Guarneri, but not any of Pietro of Mantua, because they did not believe he made any. Plate 7 pictures a Pietro Guarneri of Mantua cello, certified by Emil Herrmann. The certificate, dated 23 April 1951, states 'that the Violoncello sold by me to Mr. Luigi Silva of New York City is in my opinion a work of Pietro Guarneri of Mantua and about the period of 1695. It bears a label of Andrea Guarneri, Cremona, 1694, ex. Robert Maas'. The description on the certificate reads, 'The back is of two pieces of curly maple cut on the slab [cut along the grain instead of across it] of small figure, the sides also of small curl and the scroll likewise. The top is of two pieces of pine medium wide grain in centre, somewhat broader on flanks. The varnish is of a golden-brown colour. The instrument was originally of larger dimensions and has been reduced in size; it is in a very fine state of preservation'.

A picture of a cello by Giuseppe Guarneri, '*filius* Andrea' may be seen in Plate 8. A beautiful coloured picture of this same cello may be found in the Hill brothers' book opposite page 52. The cello is unusual in that it is made of three kinds of wood; the top, spruce; the back, poplar; and the scroll, beechwood. The top, furthermore, has 'wings' at the lower bouts, that is, pieces of wood spliced on. (If the original top was not quite large enough, or if it were defective, makers sometimes did this.) The certificate for this instrument includes the statement, 'The varnish has a golden orange-red colour. This instrument is an outstanding example of the maker's work'.

The Hill brothers believed that Andrea Guarneri, about 14 of whose cellos they had seen, created the smaller model of cello, and that he did so late in life, between 1690 and 1695. His son, Giuseppe, followed him in this respect as well as his son, Pietro of Venice, for three of his six cellos. The Hill brothers possibly emphasized this point because it has often been thought that Antonio Stradivari created the smaller model, beginning in the year 1707.

Nearly all the early cellos, from Andrea Amati to, I believe, *c.* 1680, (see p. 59) and some later, were on a large model that is, about 30 inches or more, with some as large as 31¾ inches or even larger. The smaller cello, or the standard as we know it today, has a body length of 75 cm., with a little leeway either way. Stradivari adopted the smaller pattern only in 1707, but not before he had made a number of large-model cellos, all of which have been cut down

4 Cello of Girolamo II Amati

except a very few, including the one in the Institute Cherubini in Florence (79·9 cm.) and the one given to the Library of Congress. The standardization was not immediately universally adopted, so that a number of cellos made during the first half of the eighteenth century were still made on the large model, but most have been subsequently cut down.

The first demand for the smaller-sized cello does seem to have co-incided with the rise of cello virtuosi at the end of the seventeenth century. The smaller-sized cello is easier to play because the distance between the notes is not so great, lessening the tension of the left hand and facilitating greater dexterity. The tone of the two bottom strings is slightly sacrificed, but the virtuosi wanted emphasis on the top string anyway, on which the cello sings best.

Antonio Stradivari (*c.* 1644–1737) was the greatest maker of cellos as well as violins. Not very much is known about his early life. Although he came from a Cremonese family, there is no record of his birth. It is thought that perhaps the family left Cremona when the plague struck that city in 1630, and that he was born elsewhere. Neither is it known in exactly what year he was born. The knowledge that he was an apprentice to Nicolo Amati comes from only one source, a label in a violin of 1666, where he calls himself a pupil of Amati. When this apprenticeship started or how long it lasted is not known. He was twice married, and the father of 11 children, one not surviving infancy. The two sons who followed in his footsteps as violin craftsmen, Francesco and Omobono, were born of his first marriage. Recently there has been founded 'The Stradivarius Association' in Aubonne, Switzerland, whose first purpose (of 15) stated in its brochure is 'To create an International Centre to promote the studies and research on Stradivarius.'

There are 63 known extant Antonio Stradivari cellos left in the world. The three books giving the best accounts of these cellos are the Hill brothers' *Antonio Stradivari, His Life and Work, (1644–1737),* originally published in 1902, revised in 1909, and republished in 1963 (the 1902 version), Ernest N. Doring, *How Many Strads?*, and Herbert K. Goodkind, *Iconography of Antonio Stradivari, 1644–1737.* The Doring book is based on the Hill brothers' book, although the accounts do not precisely concur. Stradivari's first cello is dated from the period 1680–84 and his last in the year 1736. Most of the cellos have been given names, mostly after famous performers who owned them at one time. Among his most famous cellos are the 'Duport'

(1711), which became one of the chief models on which J. B. Vuillaume based his work; the 'Batta' (1714); and the 'Piatti' (1720). In the Doring book there are pictures of 12 of the Strad cellos and in the Goodkind book 43.

All Stradivari's early cellos, until 1701, the year he made the famous 'Servais' cello, were on the large model, that is, a body length of approximately 30 inches or somewhat over. (The 'Servais' is 31¼ inch.) Then he made no cellos until 1707, when he adopted the smaller pattern, that is under 30 inches. The 'Piatti' cello, for instance, is 29⅞ inches.[7]

The Hill brothers believed that Andrea Guarneri was the first to make the small-model cello, and that besides other members of his family, F. Ruggeri and G. B. Rogeri also made small-model cellos. Since they were all in Cremona, Stradivari must have been influenced by these makers to make cellos of a more convenient size.

Plate 9 pictures the 'Castelbarco' cello of 1697, now housed in the Library of Congress, USA. It is an uncut cello, with a body length of 30⁷⁄₁₆ inches. This is one of several Stradivari cellos which has a back, sides, and head of poplar wood, not considered as fine as maple. The cello is in an excellent condition. A letter from Rudolph Wurlitzer Company, dated 27 February 1934, quoted in the brochure *The Stradivari Memorial*, by W. D. Orcutt, states that this cello was 'formerly priced at $55,000'. Part of the stipulation of Gertrude Clarke Whitehall in giving a quartet of Strad instruments to the Library of Congress was that they were to be performed on in concerts every year. (Instruments must be played on to remain alive and at their best). For years the Budapest Quartet was brought to Washington for a series of concerts in both the fall and the spring, the concerts of course being given on these instruments. The Juilliard Quartet has continued this practice.

The Bergonzi family should also be mentioned in connection with Cremona. The founder of the family, Carlo 1 (*c.* 1683/5–1747), was the best maker of this family, but unfortunately, in spite of attributions of cellos to him in the past, he made no cellos. His son, Michel Angelo, and in turn his son's son, Nicolo, are the other notable members of this family who did make cellos. Lorenzo Storioni (1751–*c.* 1801), along with G. B. Ceruti, is known as the last great makers of Cremona. Plate 10 shows a fine example of 1794 of Storioni's late period.

There were other important families of violin makers than those associated with Cremona and Brescia that started in the seventeenth and continued into the eighteenth century or even later. The Grancino family and the Testore family both worked in Milan as did Carlo Ferdinando Landolfi. Giovanni Baptista Grancino (see Plate 11) and Carlo Giuseppe Testore were the finest workmen in their respective families. Members of the Tononi family worked in Bologna and Venice, while the Gagliano family made Naples famous as a centre of violin making for several generations. The Nicolo Gagliano cello of 1753, illustrated in Plate 12, is described in the Hill & Sons certificate (19 March 1925) as follows: '... a fine, characteristic and well-preserved example. The back, a jointed one, is of handsome wood marked by a medium curl; that of the sides matching, and the head, plain; the varnish being a beautiful golden colour. The instrument measures 29 inches in length of body ...' The Lewis & Son certificate (12 November 1947) adds, 'The top is of figured spruce of fine grain at the centre joint, widening towards the flanks ...'

Mention should be made of the very great maker, David Tecchler, who worked in Rome during the first half of the eighteenth century. One of his cellos, dated 1712, may be seen on Plate 13. The description of it on the Wurlitzer certificate (5 December 1958) reads: 'The back is cut on the quarter from two pieces of maple with regular medium width flames slightly descending from the centre joint. There is an original added wing at each lower flank. The top is cut from two pieces of spruce with slightly wavy grain, medium width at the centre and broader on the flanks. The sides are of maple matching that of the back. The scroll is of plainer maple. The varnish is a dark reddish brown colour. This instrument, somewhat reduced in size [now body length of $29\frac{11}{16}$ inches] from its original larger dimensions, is a fine and typical example of the maker's work'. The owner writes, 'The Tecchler I have is one of the very finest. I have played upon a number of Tecchlers, but this is the best. ... It is referred to as the Ex-Maurice Eisenberg Tecchler'.

Giovanni Baptista Gabrielli (Gabrielly) worked in Florence during the middle third of the eighteenth century; a specimen of his work may be seen in Plate 14. Tommaso Balestrieri (1720/40–1788/90) worked in Mantua, and although he probably was not born by the time Pietro I Guarneri of Mantua died, he is said to have been influenced by his work. He only made a few cellos, but they are fine instruments, as are his violins. Plate 15 pictures one of his cellos dated 1765. Camillo Camilli also worked in Mantua.

For cello history, an important development beginning in the 1690s was the rise of the Venetian School of violin makers. The three greatest makers of cellos of this school were Matteo Gofriller, Domenico Montagnana, and Santo Seraphin. An interesting case is that of Matteo Gofriller, because he is literally a twentieth-century rediscovery. For a long time he was practically unknown, so that his magnificent cellos were ascribed to Andrea Guarneri, Carlo Bergonzi (who made no cellos), or to Stradivari himself. It was in the 1920s that Gofriller began to be identified with his instruments and came into his own right as one of the very greatest makers of cellos. Nothing is known of his background. It is supposed that he was a Tyrolean by birth; he worked in Venice. The first known instrument by him is, interestingly enough, a viola da gamba dated 1689.[8] This was made, perhaps, in response to what must have been a certain demand for gambas in Venice at that time, for Giovanni Legrenzi on his appointment as maestro di cappella at St. Mark's Cathedral in 1685 reorganized the Cathedral orchestra, which included two violas da gamba as members of his 34 piece orchestra.[9] E. N. Doring accounts for 21 extant cellos.[10] These instruments date from *c.* 1697 to 1732. Many famous cellists have knowingly owned these cellos in the twentieth century, including Pablo Casals, whose cello was first attributed to Carlo Bergonzi. Plate 16 pictures a Matteo Gofriller cello of 1729. Matteo's brother, not so esteemed, but still a fine maker, worked in Venice and Udine. Plate 17 pictures a Francesco Gofriller cello of 1730. The Hermann certificate gives the following description: 'The back is in two pieces of bird's-eye maple, the sides to match, the scroll plain. The top is of spruce of medium wide grain. The varnish is of a deep reddish brown colour and of fine quality'. It also states that it is from the ex-Wahl collection, although it is not specifically listed in the inventory of the Wahl estate as recorded in *Violins and Violinists*, July–August, 1955, pp. 170–71.

Domenico Montagnana (*c.* 1683/90–*c.* 1750) ranks with Matteo Gofriller as one of the greatest makers of cellos, and both of these makers are know particularly for their cellos. Nothing is known definitely about his earlier life or training. His cellos are large and bold in outline, the scrolls being particularly massive. The cello illustrated in Plate 18 is tonally magnificent. The lower strings have a mighty tone, and throughout the range the tone is very beautiful. This is surely one of the great cellos.

Santo Seraphin (1665/99–1737/48) was born in Udine, Italy, and his work as a painter before becoming a maker of instruments may account for the extremely fine detail of his work. His instruments are not numerous, but particularly his cellos have been highly regarded. The tone, though beautiful, does not have the volume, for instance, of a Montagnana. Plate 19 pictures a Seraphin cello. The Wurlitzer certificate reads: 'The back is cut on the quarter from two pieces of maple with handsome flames of medium width sloping downwards from the centre joint. The wood of the sides and the scroll matches that of the back. The top is cut from two pieces of spruce with grain of medium width at the centre, broader at the flanks. The varnish is plentiful and a golden orange colour. This outstanding example of the maker's work with its original uncut dimensions is in a fine state of preservation'. (As the body length is $28\frac{3}{4}$ inches, there really would have been no need to cut the instrument down). The corners on this cello are projected in an unusually sharp manner, as can be seen in the plate.

Francesco Gobetti was also a well-known maker of instruments from Venice.

The Guadagnini family was one of the most prolific in the production of instrument makers. The family line began with Lorenzo (*c.* 1695–1745/50) and ended with Paolo (d. 1942). Several of the makers in the family during the nineteenth century made guitars either along with or in preference to making violins. The genealogy table in Doring's *The Guadagnini Family*, (1949) p. 302, should be amended according to his own later corrections:[11]

Very little is known about Lorenzo Guadagnini. Few of his instruments are extant. (Doring's book on the Guadagnini family lists no cellos in his tabulation of Lorenzo's instruments.) Plate 20 pictures one of his rare cellos. Hamma says Lorenzo's instruments are 'mostly a large wide model on spirited lines; the arching varies a great deal'.[12] The arching on this cello appears high; the model is certainly 'spirited'.

It was Giovanni Battista, however, who was the greatest maker of the family, in spite of great variation among his works. His best cellos, because of their marvellous and powerful tone, have brought very high prices.

Plate 21 pictures a G. B. Guadagnini of 1748. In his tabulation of

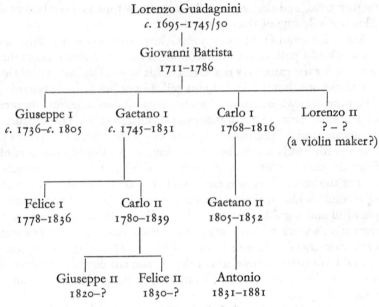

Lorenzo Guadagnini
c. 1695–1745/50

Giovanni Battista
1711–1786

Giuseppe I	Gaetano I	Carlo I	Lorenzo II
c. 1736–*c.* 1805	*c.* 1745–1831	1768–1816	? – ?
			(a violin maker?)

Felice I	Carlo II	Gaetano II
1778–1836	1780–1839	1805–1852

Giuseppe II	Felice II	Antonio
1820–?	1830–?	1831–1881

(Later members of the family are not included).

G. B. Guadagnini's instruments, Doring has listed 21 cellos, making comments on five of them from the Turin period (his last of five places of work).[13] Doring states that 'Guadagnini's determination to adhere to his own concepts establishes him as the only great maker subsequent to the passing of the Cremonese masters who gave to posterity a type of instrument completely of his own design and technique, and entirely the work of his own hands'.[14]

The only notable followers of G. B. Guadagnini in Turin were Francesco Pressenda (1777–1854) and his student, Giuseppe Antonio Rocca (1807/10–*c.* 1868). Plate 22 pictures a Pressenda cello of 1835. The owner writes: 'The back is of one piece (small "wings") fine curl maple as are the sides and head. All the maple appears to have come from the same block of wood. The top is fine grain spruce, 15–16 rays to the inch. The head is massive but graceful and characteristically outlined in black. The cello is generously covered with a rich fiery red-orange varnish'.

The seventeenth and eighteenth centuries produced hundreds of Italian makers of instruments of the violin family, of which we have mentioned only some of the more important. The best instruments

of these centuries have never been matched, for reasons as yet unknown. With all our current scientific know-how it has not been
possible to duplicate the tone of an Antonio Stradivari instrument or
that of any other of the great instruments of these centuries.

It is interesting to note that almost all the important early Italian
centres of violin making through the eighteenth century were in the
same latitudinal belt, roughly between 44° and 46°, across northern
Italy and extending from west of Milan eastward to Venice and Udine.
The chief exceptions were Rome (Tecchler) and Naples (the Gagliano
family). We shall leave the question of 'why' unanswered because it
involves too much speculation.

The founder and greatest maker of the German School of violin
making, Jacobus Stainer (1621–83), was a Tyrolean by birth but was
probably trained in Italy. One of his cellos is pictured in Plate 23.
The high arching for which he was famous should be seen. The
upper shoulders are quite widely rounded, the f-holes a little nearer
the sides, with an animal head replacing the scroll. Matthias Albani
(*c.* 1620–*c.* 1712) and especially his son, Johann Michael (*c.* 1677–
1730), were also noted German makers. Plate 24 pictures a Matthias
Albani cello of 1694. The high arching of both the back and top
reflect a Stainer influence. It is even possible that Matthias Albani
was Stainer's apprentice.

The greatest representative of the French School was Nicholas
Lupot (1758–1824). William Forster (1739–1808) and Thomas Dodd
(*c.* 1760–*c.* 1820) (the latter for his cellos only) are among the best
known English makers. Plate 25 pictures a William Forster cello of
c. 1780. The William Lewis & Son certificate for this Forster cello,
dated 27 May 1942, reads in part as follows: '. . . a plentiful covering
of the original golden brown varnish, of excellent texture. The wood
selection throughout being in two parts matching in figure excepting
the middle section of the right side which shows curving curls, the
figure otherwise straight and slanting slightly downward from the
centre joint; the sides show a wider, plainer figure; the wood of the
scroll plain. We consider the cello to be representative of the best
traditions of the English School'. Plate 26 illustrates a cello of 1790
by Thomas Dodd. In spite of some fine instruments, the German,
French and English Schools have never commanded anything like
the prices of those of the best Italian makers.

Abraham Prescott (1789, Deerfield, New Hampshire – 1858, Con-
cord, Massachusetts) was an early American instrument maker who

specialized in the large model of cello, the church bass. He was not the first maker of members of the violin family in America, since one James Joan (Juhan), a Frenchman, 'made and sold violins and bows' in Boston as early as 1768, and Benjamin Crehore (d. 1819 in Milton, Massachusetts) was a 'widely-known maker of cellos, basses, harpsichords and pianos'.[15] Prescott, however, is the best known of these early makers.

The Prescott cello shown in Plate 27 was made between 1831 and 1845. I have included a picture of this cello partly so that the reader can compare the beauty of the proportions of the great Italian cellos with a different style of cello. The aesthetic impression of the Prescott is far less satisfying. The instrument has historic interest, but it is a considerably less-than-great cello. The measurements of this cello may be compared with those of Pietro Guarneri (Plate 7) and Santo Seraphin (Plate 19).

	Pietro Guarneri	Santo Seraphin	Abraham Prescott
Length of body	30 in.	$28\frac{3}{4}$ in.	32 in.
Upper bouts	$13\frac{3}{8}$ in.	$13\frac{13}{16}$ in.	$14\frac{1}{2}$ in.
Lower bouts	$17\frac{1}{2}$ in.	$16\frac{7}{8}$ in.	$18\frac{5}{8}$ in.

The price range 30 years ago of the best Italian cellos was from about $2,500 to $40,000 or more for a few of the best A. Stradivari cellos.[16] Since prices of instruments rise with the rise in the price level, these prices are now several times as high. In the past, interested wealthy people bought instruments as investments, but the custom has been largely dropped in favour of the stock market with its ready exchange.

A number of students have asked me over the years how one knows the original maker of a cello in spite of the fact that many makers did not label their works and because of the extensive skulduggery in tampering with labels that persisted throughout the nineteenth century and even into our own. The answer to this question is that a dealer selling a fine instrument today will give the buyer a certificate of authenticity for the instrument. These certificates are mostly made out by the great experts in the world who have made a lifelong study of instruments, and they are frequently associated with the great instrument houses of Europe and America, the oldest and most prestigious being Hill and Sons in London. The firm was established in the eighteenth century. Other famous firms are John & Arthur Beare, Ltd., London; Hamma & Co., Stuttgart, Germany; Werro of Berne, Switzerland; Pierre Vidoudez, Geneva, Switzerland; Etienne Vatelot of Paris; Rembert Wurlitzer of New York; Wm. Moennig & Son, Philadelphia; and Wm. Lewis & Son, Chicago, as well as others. There are some individual experts who have their own business. The certificates stating that an instrument is made by such and such a maker will hold until proved false. The example spoken of earlier of Matteo Gofriller's cellos illustrates the point. One reason that it is safer financially to buy an instrument from one of the well-known dealers is that they will stand behind the certificate they issue with the instrument.

By the nineteenth century mass production of instruments of the violin family was under way and still exists. Important industrial centres were to be found at Mirecourt in France, Mittenwald in Bavaria, and Markneukirchen in Germany. Take, for example, the Heberlein family, working at Markneukirchen. Fairfield says, 'They are commercial makers and have made many thousand instruments and hundreds of copies of Stradivarius and Guarnerius, all very well done. Their labels are inscribed with names of different copies, such as 'Wilhelmy', [name of a Strad violin], and so on. They had a regular catalogue, listing instruments by numbers, the Stradivari models from 1 to 8, and the Joseph Guarneri models from 1A to 8A. Their own prices ranged from $50.00 to $240.00. They also made special models that sold as high as $350.00'.[17] There were dozens and dozens of makers and families associated with these centres. They often put the name of the maker they were copying, as for instance 'Stradivarius' as the label, inside the instrument. Although this was professionally understood, and quite a general practice, it resulted in a confusion in some people's minds, who upon discovering, for instance, an old violin in the attic, and seeing the label, were fooled into thinking they had found a treasure.

The greatest copyist in violins who ever lived was Jean Baptiste Vuillaume (1798–1875). For his cellos he often used the Duport Strad for his model. I owned one of these copies at one time (No. 2761 in the series of *c.* 3,000 instruments that Vuillaume made). It was a handsome, bright red cello, and always reminded me of a racehorse. The tone was very pleasant, but lacked altogether the Italian quality, the two bottom strings lacking a certain depth of tone, particularly the C-string; and the varnish was of a harder texture. The cello was not so subject to changes of weather or season as are the instruments of the great Italian makers. The tabulations in *Violins and Violinists*, the six issues of 1958, and November–December 1960 list 23 cellos by Vuillaume. Undoubtedly this list is incomplete and represents only instruments known at that time. Roger Millant says only that Vuillaume made 'relatively few' cellos.[18] Vuillaume did much trading with the Italian, Tarisio.

Luigi Tarisio (*c.* 1790–1855) who lived in Milan, Italy, was a fascinating eccentric who had a passion for collecting violins, cellos, and basses made by the Italian masters. He scoured northern Italy for them for 30 years, and in his annual trips to Paris and later to London, he is thought to have brought more than a thousand instruments back into circulation. The first great wave of appreciation for the Italian seventeenth- and eighteenth-century masters was due to Tarisio, and he undoubtedly rescued many instruments from destruction. He was trained as a carpenter, and his knowledge of woods gathered during his apprenticeship served him well. He had a natural gift for identifying fine instruments, no matter in what condition, and the accounts of his searches make fascinating reading.[19] He undoubtedly identified the makers of many of the best instruments now in circulation. He also had a mentor in the first great collector of violins, Count Cozio de Salabue, who probably helped him a great deal.

Let it be said that although the shift from craftmanship to commercialism started in the nineteenth century and still exists, and that although G. B. Guadagnini may have been the last original artist-craftsman, there were during the nineteenth century and are right up to the present, many, many fine craftsmen who do not have the commercial attitude, and continue to meet the demand for fine violins. It is simply that none of them has established a reputation to be compared with those of the violin makers of the 'Golden Age' of violin making, that is, the seventeenth and eighteenth centuries.

Variants of the Cello

There have been cellos with six strings, as well as five strings, and van der Straeten mentions a three-string cello in the William Heyer Museum at Cologne, which he said belonged to the second half of the seventeenth century.[20] Plate 28 pictures a five-string cello with a body length of 28·54 inches (72·5 cm.) and dated 1720. It is in the

Museum of Fine Arts in Boston and pictured and described in Bessaraboff, *Ancient European Musical Instruments*, as 'Back of two pieces of maple. Ribs of maple. Belly of two pieces of spruce, two holes. Peg-box integral with neck, of somewhat narrow pattern with large scroll. Five tuning pegs with unusually large heads . . . Reddish brown varnish . . .'.[21]

The violoncello piccolo is a small-sized cello with four or five strings, usually tuned G d a e^1 or C G d a e^1. The Jakob Stainer violoncello piccolo from the Dolmetsch Collection in Haslemere, Surrey, pictured in Plate 29, has a body length of 23¼ inches (59 cm.). The instrument was held in the downward position like the cello or in 'da spalla' fashion (see p. 45). It has often been confused with the viola pomposa, also a five-stringed instrument tuned approximately an octave above the violoncello piccolo (c g d^1 g^1 c^2, according to Donnington or d g d^1 g^1 c^2, according to Galpin). The viola pomposa was held in the violin position, but perhaps rather on the arm than under the chin. The J. C. Hoffmann viola pomposa in the Royal Conservatory at Brussels has a body length of 17·99 inches (45·7 cm.). This length puts it in the class of the tenor viola. (Even larger violas than this exist, as large as 48 cm., although the more normal is 39 cm.).

J. S. Bach designated the violoncello piccolo to be used in nine of his cantata scores but never wrote a score calling for the viola pomposa. The violoncello piccolo is thought by some to be the instrument called for in Boccherini's string quintets with two cellos. The Chez Janet et Cotelle edition of the Boccherini quintets carries this notice on the title page: '*La Partie de premier Violoncelle peut être remplacée par l'Alto Violoncelle*'. (Notice that Boccherini did not designate an alto cello [i.e., a violoncello piccolo]). It seems to me more than likely that the editors were put off in suggesting an alto cello to be substituted for a cello because of the use of the alto clef, not realizing that this use was a frequent practice in cello music in the eighteenth century. The first cello part in these quintets is written with the alto and treble clefs rather than the bass and treble clefs which are used for the second cello part. It should be remembered that various clefs were used very liberally in the eighteenth century, these being the ones I have found in cello music:

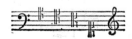

The treble clef was used in several ways: to be interpreted down an octave (as explained in Duport's *Essai*), and if used this way, the term 'in loco' or |⁸ 𝄞 was used to indicate it was to be interpreted as notated. Just when the custom grew up that the treble clef was to be interpreted as an octave lower if following a passage in bass clef and 'in loco' if following a passage in tenor clef is still unclear. The treble clef was also at times assumed to be played as notated. The four 'C' clefs (baritone clef, tenor clef, alto clef, and soprano clef) were all plentifully used in baroque cello music, but I have run across only one example of the 'C' mezzo-soprano clef (where the clef centres on the second to bottom line), which was in the first movement of Carlo Grazioni's *Six Sonatas*, Op. 11, Sonata 6, m. 47–52. Furthermore, clef changes were made not only between movements, but in some scores rapid changes are made in one movement.

The choice of clef was based on the range of a passage, to contain it within the staff as much as possible instead of adding many leger lines below or above the staff which was an expensive process if the music was printed. Thus, in the quintets where Boccherini does not write notes below small 'c' in his first cello part, the alto clef suits his purpose best. For the most part the notes do not go above c^2, although there are a few as high as a^2. When he uses the treble clef in these particular quintets, the notes are not necessarily always higher than when he uses the alto clef, but the passage fits better within the staff. Since Boccherini owned a Stradivari cello and presumably played the first cello part in performances of those quintets with the members of the Fout family in Madrid,[22] it is hard to imagine him giving up his wonderful cello for a smaller one that could not possibly match the tone of his Stradivari. And for what reason? Certainly not because these first cello parts were unusually high. Cellists before his time were quite used to playing throughout the cello range.

The sixth suite by J. S. Bach for unaccompanied cello is also thought by some to call for a violoncello piccolo because of his designation 'à cinq accordes'. It seems strange that Bach would not have specifically designated a violoncello piccolo if that is what he meant instead of a normal five-stringed cello. The most potent argument for the violoncello piccolo is perhaps the way he designates the stringing:

The bracket might suggest the basically smaller instrument, that is, one with large G as its normally lowest note to which was added a fifth string on the bottom. This was the way the fifth string was added on the violoncello piccolo. On the other hand, the low C-string would sound much better on a five-string cello of normal or of ⅞ size. We can dismiss the assumption by some that the suite was written for the viola pomposa, because there are notes called for below its range. The question may never be settled to everyone's satisfaction. Needless to say, the performance of this suite today on the normal four-stringed cello is vastly more difficult than it would be with the five-stringed one.

The name 'violoncello alto' means a small cello, and it is more than likely a synonym for 'violoncello piccolo'.

The violoncello tenor, invented by Eugen Sprenger in 1922, was an instrument made on double the dimensions of the violin.[23]

The violoncello d'amore was a small cello with sympathetic strings. Van der Straeten reports one as having been a part of Count Valdrighi's instrument collection in Modena.[24] Perhaps this cello represented an attempt to imitate the bass gamba with sympathetic strings (called bastarda). This is the only violoncello d'amore reference which I have found.

The term 'violoncello da spalla' does not refer to a kind of cello but to a manner of holding it. 'Spalla' means 'shoulder' in Italian. When cellos were used in processions, serenades, and so forth, the instrument was held against the shoulders by a strap which went through two holes made in the back of the cello and then around the player's neck; or only one hole was made, a plug inserted, and the strap attached to that. The first cello clearly referred to in print in 1556 by Jambe de Fer (see p. 55) was a violoncello da spalla with one hole and a plug.

The arpeggione could be considered a cousin of the cello, although because the body is cornerless, it actually looks more like a guitar. It has been called a guitar violoncello, a guitare d'amour, and a bowed guitar as well as arpeggione (see Plate 30). The fingerboard is fretted, and the tuning of its six strings is E A d g b e¹. The instrument was invented by G. Staufer in 1823, and as far as is known there were only two compositions written for it, a concerto by Heinrich August Birnbach (1782– ?) and a sonata by Franz Schubert; there was also a method for the instrument written by Vincenz Schuster, who first performed Schubert's sonata. According to van der Straeten, Birnbach was called to the court in Berlin in 1825 as cellist and virtuoso on the arpeggione. He also mentions that an arpeggione dated 1824 was in the Wilhelm Heyer Museum at Cologne.[25] The instrument became obsolete after its brief life in the 1820s. The sonata by Schubert has been transcribed for cello and piano and is now known as the 'arpeggione' sonata.

Van der Straeten mentions three other variants of the cello: the violoncello portatile, the harmonicello, and the cellone. He states that the violoncello portatile 'resembled an oblong box, two feet long and nine inches wide. The neck with the finger-board was detachable, and could be placed inside this box together with the bridge and tail-pin'.[26] One trusts that none other existed than this one made by Johann Wilde (d. 1770).

The harmonicello 'had five strings and ten metal strings which ran underneath but over another finger-board so that they could be played separately. We are not informed how this was made possible'.[27] This instrument was made by J. C. Bischoff in the latter part of the eighteenth century.

The cellone was a large cello tuned:

Van der Straeten tried this instrument and concluded that the lowest string was too heavy for the body of the instrument (46 in.) so that it had a muffled tone. The other strings were brighter, but he actually did not have a word of praise for the instrument, which was made by A. Stelzner. (No date is given for the cellone; Stelzner made a tenor violin which he called 'violotta' in 1891).

The violoncello-piano, known under the name 'Melotetraphone', was an instrument invented by E. de Vlaminck and Limonier in 1892. It is described as 'somewhat resembling a large keyed monochord'.[28]

Finally, today we have the porta cello, 'a light cello with retractable knee supports, a narrow, slightly rounded box body, without customary curves and bouts. The fingerboard is standard.'[29] This cello is comparatively cheap and is recommended only for school programmes, because it has serious faults; for example, the top is weak so that the bass bar side may sink or the sound post may break through it.

Changes, Improvements, and Attempted Improvements after Antonio Stradivari

Practically all the early cellos were on the large model, but as we have said, most of these cellos now in use have been cut down for the convenience of the player. These earlier instruments were built in terms of a lower pitch than is considered standard today, which is $a^1 = 440$ c.p.s. Consequently, in order to bear the increased pressure, the cello demands a longer neck (now inclined slightly backwards), a higher bridge, and a longer and heavier bass bar. A longer finger-board has also been adopted. The shorter fingerboard can be seen in Plate 32, picturing a cellist in the Bréval method of 1804. The fingerboard now has also been slightly cut down on the C-string side to accommodate the vibrations of that string.

Various shapes, sizes, and designs of bridges have always been in use. Today, a cellist will rotate the bridge at least twice a year, summer and winter (ideally four times a year, with each change in season), because of the shifting relation between string and finger-board, caused by changes in climate which necessitate a higher bridge in summer and lower one in winter.* Janos Starker has attempted to improve the bridge by boring a hole up into both feet. The rationale behind this (according to the information supplied by Mrs Starker) is that 'The conical shaped holes act as tiny ampli-fiers. The overtone reaction is heightened and thereby the quality of sound (more than quantity) is improved'.

The end pin has not always been a part of the cello's standard fittings; indeed, it has been in use only about one hundred years. It is usually assumed that the Belgian cellist, François Servais, initiated it in his 'old age'. (He died at the age of 59 in 1866). It was suggested, however, at least 100 years before by Robert Crome in the second edition of his method, *The Compleat Tutor for the Violoncello*, which was originally published *c.* 1765.

This instrument may be Consider'd as a Large Fiddle only held the contrary way, and the fourth string is next the Bow Hand, as the Body is turn'd downward, the lower part is to rest on the Calves of the Legs supported with the knees, but for the greater

---

* I am informed that bridge changing is only necessary in America because of the climate and hardly ever in Europe.

ease of a Learner we wou'd advize him to have a hole made in the Tail-pin and a Wooden Peg to screw into it to rest on the Floor which may be taken out when he Pleases.[30]

It would appear that Crome is implying that when the learner outgrew that stage and became a performer, he would no longer need the end pin. In the book the picture of the cellist (Crome?) is of one holding a cello without the end pin. Whatever the situation, the fact is that the end pin was not generally adopted until the latter part of the nineteenth century. The reader can observe the early method of holding the cello by again referring to Plate 32.

Mstislav Rostropovitch has invented a new style of end pin (which may be purchased as the 'Rostropovitch End Pin', retailing in the US at present for $35.00) which instead of being straight, bends downward at an angle of about 35°. The position of the cello, consequently, is less upright in relation to the floor and slightly more parallel to it. Some players may find this a more comfortable position.

We have already mentioned the adoption of one or more steel strings in place of gut strings and their advantage and disadvantage (see pp. 21, 27).

It remains a dream to create instruments of the violin family possessing the tone quality equal to that of the best masters of the seventeenth and eighteenth centuries. No instruments have ever been made to match the best instruments of a Giuseppe del Gesù Guarneri or an Antonio Stradivari, and nobody knows why not. Where is the secret? All the measurements of these instruments have been taken, the wood and varnish have been studied, and still no one has discovered the answer.

The most interesting experiments now being made along this line are those being carried on by Mrs Carleen Maley Hutchins, who is approaching the problem from the point of view of acoustics. Mrs Hutchins, who worked with the noted Harvard physicist, Frederick A. Saunders, from 1950 until his death in 1963, has been granted two Guggenheim Fellowships, and is continuing her research in her own home, in the basement of which is her laboratory containing all the necessary equipment and with her materials scattered throughout the rest of her house.

Cello of Francesco Ruggeri, *c.* 1663

6 Cello of Giovanni Battista Rogeri, 1706

To put the matter very simply (it is a complex affair), Mrs Hutchins is studying the problem from the point of view of wood resonances in relation to the volume of the air which is enclosed within the instrument. Although the wood has many frequencies, she believes it is practical to work with the so-called 'main wood resonance'. She has found through much testing with 'loudness curves' that on a fine violin the relation of the main wood resonance (after the instrument is assembled) and the main air resonance (determined by volume) is approximately that of a perfect fifth. On the violin this corresponds approximately to the frequencies of the middle two open strings, a^1 (main wood resonance) and d^1 (main air resonance). She has found this circumstance is not true with either the viola or the cello, both of which are smaller proportionally, for convenience, than if modelled on the ideal measurements of the violin. Their main resonances are three or four semitones higher than the frequencies of their two open middle strings. Mrs Hutchins is building a family of instruments, all of which approximate the basic relationship between the main wood resonance and the main air resonance as found on the violin. Since the larger the air volume, the lower the frequency, her baritone violin, tuned like a cello, has to be made larger than today's cello. Her instrument has a body length of 33 inches.

The family of instruments which she has already made consists of eight members:

Treble violin	g^1	d^2	a^2	e^3	
Soprano violin	c^1	g^1	d^2	a^2	
Mezzo violin	g	d^1	a^1	e^2	
Alto violin	c	g	d^1	a^1	
Tenor violin	G	d	a	e^1	(comparable to a Violon-cello piccolo)
Baritone violin	C	G	d	a	(tuned like a cello)
Small bass violin	A_1	D	G	c	
Contrabass violin	E_1	A_1	D	G	

These instruments have already been played in concerts in a number of cities in the United States and have created much interest. My main impression on hearing them was one of great homogeneity of sound which is very attractive but lacks the expressive quality of the traditional violin family. Being accustomed to the individual voices of, say a string quartet of the violin family, one misses the variety of expressive quality in an ensemble of her instruments.

I do not believe that now Mrs Hutchins intends her new family of instruments to displace the present violin family, but rather to start on a career of its own alongside the violin family, much as the viol family and the violin family existed side by side in the sixteenth and seventeenth centuries throughout much of Europe. Mrs Hutchins hopes that a new literature will be created for it.

It might be added that if anyone ever does duplicate the expressive tone quality of a Stradivari instrument and is able to market the new instrument at a reasonable price, his fortune is made.

The Bow

Nearly 600 bow makers are mentioned in Joseph Roda's book, *Bows for Musical Instruments of the Violin Family*. Only four makers are identified as seventeenth-century makers, and a very small number are from the first half of the eighteenth century. During these periods the makers of the instruments made the bows to go with them. One wonders what kind of bow was used in the sixteenth century for the Andrea Amati cellos, for instance, or what Stradivari's own bows must have been like. The earliest picture of a cello bow is found in Mersenne's *Harmonie Universelle* (1636).[31] The bow stick is straight. Although the development of the bow was not direct from the arch of the bow-and-arrow bow, to a straight stick, to the inward curve or 'cambre' or our modern bow, it was roughly so. The cambre is found in bows before François Tourte, an example from the late seventeenth or early eighteenth century being described in Henry Saint-George's book, *The Bow, Its History, Manufacture, and Use*.[32] Saint-George suggests that the bow whose nut and tip are pictured in his Plate 1[33] possibly was made by Stradivari. The reason there are so few bows left from before the second half of the eighteenth century is that they were more fragile than the instruments and because they were not respected in the same way (evident in the fact that early makers did not stamp their bows).

The great period of bow-making began with François Tourte (1747–1835), and it is the French School which excelled in this art, as the Italians did with instruments. Tourte established the classical characteristics of the bow rather than invented them. He did not invent the cambre, although he may have been the first to shape this curve by heating the stick rather than cutting it. He did not invent the ferrule and slide of the frog, but used them, as he did the movable, screw-type frog. He established the use of Pernambucco wood (a Brazilian wood) as being the finest for bow sticks because this wood best combines strength and elasticity.

The greatest French successors to François Tourte in the art of bowmaking were François Lupot (1774–1837), Nicolas Eury (fl. 1810–30), Dominique Peccatte (1810–74), and François Nicolas Voirin (1833–85). The greatest English bow-makers were John Dodd (1752–1839), the eccentric contemporary of François Tourte, who worked independently and is known especially for his cello bows; and James Tubbs (1835–1919), who made altogether some 5,000 bows. There are no comparable Italian or German makers of bows unless we consider Nikolaus Kittel, who worked in Russia, whose works are rare indeed.

A famous private collection of cello bows in the United States, that owned by Janos Scholz, includes about 200 cello bows, 36 of which were shown at the Jacques Français Exhibition at the Lincoln Center from 29 January to 31 March 1971. The earliest bow in this collection, a viola da gamba bow, is dated *c.* 1720. The earliest cello bows date from the second half of the eighteenth century.

If the reader will examine Plate 32, he will observe that the cellist is still playing (1804) with a pre-Tourte type of bow that appears essentially straight. He will also see that the bow is held farther up on the stick, beyond the frog, than it is held today. This method could only result in a very light manner of playing, a manner characteristic of the French School.

It might be mentioned that with today's interest in the subject of performance practice, that is, the attempt to recreate music as it sounded at the time it was written, there has been some interest in the reconstruction of the baroque violin and baroque cello. Since the cello was used in the baroque period so extensively as a continuo instrument, and increasingly in the late seventeenth and early eighteenth century as a solo instrument, the lack of appropriate sound in the performance of this music, that results from the use of the modern cello and (no less) its bow, is inevitable.

Needless to say, it is a desideratum to own as fine a bow as possible. I have known several cellists who said, given the choice of a fine cello and a mediocre bow or a mediocre cello and a fine bow, they would choose the latter. The importance of a fine bow can hardly be overemphasized.

Chapter 2

The Early Development of the Cello

Sixteenth-Century Beginnings to 1556

In Saronno, Italy, a town about 20 miles north of Milan, a fresco on the inside of the dome above the chancel in the church of Santa Maria dei Miracoli pictures, among other figures, an angel dressed in a luminous blue robe, playing the cello, primitive though the instrument may be (see frontispiece). The cello, along with the violin and viola that are also pictured, is of a natural wood colour. The fresco, painted by Gaudenzio Ferrari in 1535–36, provides evidence that the cello emerged some time before 1535.

One other early picture of a cello appears in Plate 16 of *Gaudenzio Ferrari, His School, and the Early History of the Violin* by E. Winternitz, where it is identified as a 'tenor violin'. To me, Dr Heinrich Besseler's monograph, *Zum Problem der Tenorgeige* (1949) based on the assumption that the tenor violin was a very large viola (pictured there as being held against the shoulder), is more convincing than Bessaraboff's flat statement that the tenor violin was the size of a child's cello (half-size?) and held like one. Besseler's assumption answers more convincingly questions regarding the tenor violin. On this basis I believe the instrument pictured in Winternitz's book is better labelled a small cello. The instrument, besides being held in the downward position (the proportional sizes of instrument and player would preclude the possibility of holding the instrument against the shoulder), appears to have deeper ribs than would be found on any viola. The picture is dated about the middle of the sixteenth century. It should be noted that both of these early cellos are of a small model. The latter of these cellos has already acquired the rounded shoulders of the violin family instead of the sloping shoulders of the Ferrari cello. These two pictures do not provide sufficient evidence that there were no large model cellos before Andrea Amati, but none are known at present.

The primary sources mentioning bowed string instruments during the first half of the sixteenth century are equivocal regarding their description of instruments that might refer to members of the violin family, and recent authorities are hesitant to identify absolutely any of them as members of that family.

The authors of these primary sources, along with their equivocal terms, first discussed in detail by Hayes (1930) and later with great insight by Boyden (1965), may be presented to the reader in chart form:

Date	Author	Book	Equivocal Terms	Possible Meanings
1511	Virdung	Musica Getutscht	—	—
1523	Judenkünig	Ain schone künstliche vnderweisung	—	—
1528–29	Agricola	Musica instrumentalis deudsch	kleine geigen	rebec or violin?
1532	Gerle	Musica teusch	kleymen geyglen	rebec or violin?
1533	Lanfranco	Scintille di Musica	violette da arco senza tasti, violette da braccio, a da arco	rebec or violin?
1536	Luscinius	Musurgia seu praxis Musicae	—	—
1542–43	Ganassi	Regola Rubertina	viola senza tasti, viola da brazo senza tasti, violone d'arco da tasti	rebec or violin?
1545	Agricola	Revised edition of above	polischen geigen, kleinen dreyseitigen handgeiglein	probably refers to violin
1549	Bermudo	Libro llamado declaración de Instrumentos musicales (also revised 1555)	—	—

Virdung's *Musica Getutscht* (1511) is the first book written to describe instruments. There is no term in it which is equivocal, and none refers to the violin, perhaps because the violin probably did not yet exist. Judenkünig's book basically deals with the lute, but he mentions that the geygen can use the same tablature. (His term 'geygen' refers to viols). The Luscinius book is 'mainly a translation into Latin of Virdung's *Musica Getutscht*'.[1] Bermudo does not refer to viols or violins, but rather to the vihuela.

It may be understood from the chart that the violin family may have been described or referred to in writing in the second quarter of the sixteenth century, but it is not clearly established.

*   *   *

What was the ancestry of the violin family? The persistence of the untrue legend that it derived from the viola da gamba family is unfortunate. Undoubtedly the emergence of the violin family was a result of a complex of influences, or as Winternitz says, 'the final product of a long and variegated process of development, a combination or fusion of many patterns and elements contributed by a number of different bowed instruments'.[2] One line of development, however, stands out with a stronger force than others, the heritage from the lira da braccio. It was Alexander Hajdecki who first pointed to the lira da braccio as the immediate ancestor of the violin. In his book *Die italienische Lira da Braccio* (1892) he sets forth his argument. Since only 300 copies of his book were printed, however, his discovery did not gain much attention, and it was not until Bessaraboff brought this discovery back into light in 1941 that it became more common knowledge. It was the body characteristics of the lira da braccio that the violin adopted, that is, 'its typical outline, including upper, middle, and lower bouts, the arched top and back supported by a sound post, the ribs, and overhanging edges. Other features are the neck as a part fixed to the body separately, a fingerboard without frets, and sound holes usually of the f-form.'[3] The disposition of the peg box and the tuning in fifths, however, were borrowed from the rebec. The violin family is not in any way related typologically to the gamba family.

The violin and the viola (perhaps in reverse order) emerged first, shortly before the cello. But when one recognizes the penchant of the Renaissance mind for making instruments in families, whether string, woodwind, or brass, he can realize that a bass instrument patterned on the violin model would sooner or later be created. And it was, although for some time it was not called the violoncello (see pp. 58–60).

Jambe de Fer's Epitome Musical *of 1556*

In the year 1556 we are on firmer ground, because it was in that year that Jambe de Fer published his *Epitome Musical*, which contains the first absolutely unequivocal reference to the violin family. He did so in describing the distinction between the viola da gamba family and the violin family in the section titled 'L'accord & ton, du violon'. Of particular interest is his statement that the Italians refer to this family as the 'Violon da braccia ou violone' and his reference to the cello as 'le Bas', the bass of the family.[4] He also states that the bottom string on the violin, the highest on the cello, and the second to bottom for the alto-tenor are tuned to 'g'. Since the tuning is in fifths, the tuning for the cello was $B\flat_1$ F c g, which is evidence that the large size of cello was early among the various sizes of this instrument.

By the mid-sixteenth century, then, the cello, without its present name, had an established existence of about a generation. No instruments, however, exist from this period: the earliest extant cellos are those made by Andrea Amati.

Sixteenth-Century Uses of the Cello and Its Rise in Prestige

The cello, along with its family members, started on the lowest rung of the instrumental social ladder. One must remember that the sixteenth century was the hey-day of the viola da gamba family in Italy, and that instrument was greatly prized and cultivated by the aristocracy and the musical élite. The violin family on the other hand was looked down upon, and Jambe de Fer refers specifically in a derogatory fashion to its use in music for dancing and for processions. If the cello were used for a procession, a hole, he said, was made in the back where a peg was inserted, to which was fastened a strap which went around the player's shoulders: in other words, it was a violoncello da spalla. Before the century was over, however, the family must have had a rapid rise on the social ladder, or how would one account for the order of Charles ix of France to Andrea Amati in the early 1560s for 38 instruments of the violin family, or the fact that it was members of that family that played two of the dances in the famous *Ballet comique de la reine* at the French court in 1581?

Presumably, the occasions in which the cello participated as a bass instrument in the sixteenth century were much the same as those for the violin: dancing (whether street, tavern, or court), various festive events like processions and ceremonies (weddings or dinner parties), and chamber music. After about 1540, a number of scores were printed with the direction 'per Cantare & Sonare d'ogni sorti de Stromenti' (or some variation of that direction) in which the instruments might double vocal parts, substitute for some of them, and undoubtedly play them in a purely instrumental version.

When the cello and its family members were brought into the church is not exactly known. At any rate, the use of the violin family was so extensive in Italy by the end of the sixteenth century that it began to replace the viola da gamba family at the beginning of the seventeenth century. This substitution took place first in Italy. First the higher members of the gamba family were replaced, and by about 1640, the cello had for the most part ousted the bass gamba.

Seventeenth Century

PROBLEM OF NOMENCLATURE REGARDING THE CELLO

It is impossible to identify the extent of the use of the cello in the seventeenth century without identifying the names under which it was called upon to perform.

The family name in the sixteenth century was viola da braccio (to distinguish it from the lira da braccio from which it primarily stemmed). And to repeat, Jambe de Fer said the Italians call the family 'violon da braccia ou violone' and referred to the cello as 'le Bas' (the bass).

Monteverdi in his score of *Orfeo* (1607) calls for cellos under the name 'basso de viola da braccio' or 'basso da brazzo'. Such terms as 'basso de viola' or even just 'basso' do not point unequivocally, however, to one instrument. The term 'violone' is, however, the most problematical of all. Praetorius in his Volume II of *Syntagma Musicum* (1619), the very important primary source on instruments, states that the violone refers to the contrabass (double bass) viola da gamba. This was undoubtedly the meaning of the term in Germany at the time he wrote. There were only three printed scores of Italian instrumental music in the seventeenth century which used the designation 'violone', none in the title of the composition, but only in the table of contents, by the year 1619, when Praetorius finished his Volume II of the *Syntagma Musicum*.[5] These Italians were probably unacquainted with Praetorius' definition. The term 'violone' is used miscellaneously in only eight printed Italian scores of instrumental music through the year 1640. We shall leave open the question of the interpretation of the term up to this date.

In addition to Praetorius' interpretation of the meaning of the term, there has been a rather widespread assumption that the bass viola da gamba (rather than the double-bass gamba) was the instrument used for the most part in ensembles during the seventeenth century. But that instrument had a name, and there would not be the same reason as for the cello to use another, less well-defined name to refer to it (i.e., violone).

Furthermore, the bass gamba was going out of fashion in Italy by *c*. 1640, as we see in the famous statement (1639) of André Maugars, the French gambist, 'As for the viole, there is hardly anyone in Italy now who excels in it, and it is even practised very little in Rome....'[6] or the quotation from a letter of Thomas Hill to his brother, Abraham, from Italy in 1657:

> The instrumental music is much better than I expected. The organ and violin they [the Italians] are masters of, but the bass-viol they have not at all in use, and to supply its place they have the bass violin [English term for cello] with four strings, and use it as we do the bass viol.[7]

An anonymous article published in 1824 (nearly 150 years nearer than we are to the century we are speaking of) says, 'the violone of 1600 was no other than our modern violoncello'.[8]

John Gunn in his method, *The Theory and Practice of Fingering the Violoncello* (1793), states:

> The instrument now called the Violoncello, was for some time after its invention called the Bass Violin, to distinguish it from the Bass Viol; and in the same manner, in French, it was called Basse de Violon, in contradistinction to Basse de Viole; in Italian it was called the Violone, the augmentative of Viola. This appears from several musical publications about the end of the last century; and particularly in the Bologna edition, of 1690, of the third opera of Corelli's Sonatas, the part expressly composed for the

Violoncello, and not intended for the organ, is intitled [*sic.*] Violone.[9]

After scale and finger exercises, Gunn has chosen 33 selections from music to start the beginner. Because the basso continuo parts of Corelli's sonatas are so good for the cellist's hand position, Gunn has chosen the first 13 pieces (each a movement) and the fifteenth from Corelli's basso continuo parts. Gunn's conviction that these parts were written for a cello is obvious.

Just at the time when the cello becomes the most important bass instrument, the term 'violone' is used consistently in scores, starting with Maurizio Cazzati, Op. 2 (1642). Cazzati, who eventually became Maestro di Capella in Bologna, uses the term in the following works: Op. 2, 8, 18, 22, 35, and 55. In the majority of these works the 'violone' is called for in the title of the work and in the others internally. For whatever reason, it appears that he established a precedent for using the term 'violone' as a synonym for 'bass'. Not only do most of the composers associated with the Bologna and Modena Schools of violin playing such as Giovanni Maria Bononcini, Giovanni Battista Degl' Antonii, Giovanni Battista Bassani, and Giuseppe Torelli use this term, but even Archangelo Corelli, as well as the cellists, Giovanni Battista Vitali and Domenico Gabrielli (Op. 1). In his monograph *Primordi dell'arte del Violoncello*, (1918), Francesco Vatielli wrote the pioneer work on the early history of the cello. In this work, he refers definitely to G. B. Vitali (Vitalini in the affectionate diminutive) as a cellist.[10] It is more than interesting that in Vitali's Op. 1 (1666), until his Op. 5 (1669) when he was cellist at St. Petronio Cathedral in Bologna, he refers to himself on the title pages of these works as 'Sonatore' or 'Musico' 'di Violone da Brazzo'. Thus when he calls for 'violone' it is undoubtedly the violone da brazzo to which he refers. This, at least, is evidence that no member of the da gamba family is implied by this term ('da brazzo' refers to the violin family unequivocally), nor, I believe, the double bass of the violin family. In other words 'violone' = 'basso', an abbreviation for 'basse da brazzo' = 'cello'.

Part of the difficulty of a composer's indicating a cello in seventeenth-century Italian music was that it did not have a generally accepted name until late in the century. The first time its name appears in print is in 1641, on the title page of a score by G. B. Fontana, where it is called 'violoncino', a diminutive name as is 'violoncello'.

The times it appears in the title of a published instrumental work before 1680 are the following:

> 1641 – G. B. Fontana (violoncino)
> 1665 – G. C. Arresti (violoncello)
> 1677 – G. B. Degl'Antonii (violoncello)
> After 1677 – G. B. Degl'Antonii (violoncello)

It appears in the table of contents but not in the title:

> 1656 – F. Cavalli (violoncino)

It appears otherwise internally:

> 1667 – G. M. Placuzzi (violoncello)

The decade of the 1680s is a turning point in the name for the instrument, because it appears at least 17 times somewhere in the scores listed by Sartori, once as 'violincino' but in all the rest as 'violoncello'. We could say that its name is increasingly accepted throughout the balance of the seventeenth century in Italy, although the term 'violone' is used about as frequently as 'violoncello'. Indeed, there are several scores that call for a violoncello on the title page and violone in another part of the score, or vice versa, indicating that the terms are used synonymously. It should be remembered that the early cello, from at least Andrea Amati's time, was a large cello, and that the designation 'violoncello' means a small violone, i.e., a small cello. It will be recalled that the Hill brothers thought that Andrea Guarneri (p. 32) created the smaller-size cello in the 1690s. From the evidence provided by scores in the 1680s which called for the cello, I believe it must have been a decade earlier. A few scores carry both names on the title page, for instance, Bartolomeo Bernardi's score (1692), 'Violoncello col Violone, ò Cimbalo' or Giovanni Frederico's score (1695), calling for 'Violoncello ò Violone'. Both scores, I believe, should be interpreted as calling for a large and/or small cello. J. J. Quantz in his *Versuch* (1752) refers even at that date to the need for two sizes of cellos: 'Those who not only accompany but also play solos on the violoncello would do well to have two special instruments, one for solos, the other for ripieno parts in large ensembles'.[11]

After one plays Corelli's basso continuos, can there be any doubt that he wrote his bass parts for the cello? He used the term 'violone' from the first edition of his Op. 1 (1681) until Op. 5 (1700). In the Amsterdam edition of Op. 1 (1690), a cello is called for. There is no designation of the bass instrument on the title page of the first edition of Op. 4 (1694) although 'violone' is named internally. In the 1695 edition of the same Op. 4 a 'violoncello' is designated on the title page. The music, of course is the same (if it were written for a different instrument, one might expect at least a few changes). I believe the name only was changed from 'violone' to the then more acceptable term 'violoncello'. On the title page of his Concerti Grossi, Op. 6 (1714?), published posthumously, the 'violoncello' is called for. (These concertos may have been heard as early as the 1680s[12]).

The *Grove's Dictionary* article on violoncello playing states: 'Corelli is said to have had a cello accompaniment to his solo performances, though his basso continuo is obviously written in the first instance for the viola da gamba' [basso or contrabasso?]. This is anything but obvious to me. Charles Burney remarks that Corelli took his cellist with him to Naples.[13] For what purpose other than to play parts written for the cello? Unfortunately, Burney does not name the cellist (as he does the second violinist). Could it have been Pietro Giuseppe Gaetano Boni, who wrote a set of 12 cello *Sonate Per Camera* and dedicated them to Cardinal Ottoboni, Corelli's patron? At the end of the dedication one reads, 'Roma il 15 Fbra 1717', and although no publisher's name appears, there seems to be little doubt that these sonatas were published in Rome. There are many similarities between these sonatas and Corelli's sonatas, which indicate that he was acquainted with Corelli's works, whether or not he played the cello parts with him.

The importance of determining the interpretation of the word 'violone' in seventeenth-century Italian music is that, if it meant the cello, it can be appreciated that the cello had a far more important role in Italian music of the seventeenth century than has hitherto been acknowledged.

SIZES AND TUNINGS OF THE CELLO[14]

The baroque cello, as we have seen, was made principally in two sizes. The large cello or church bass, often referred to in scores as 'basso' or 'violone' measured from 76 cm. to 80 cm. (29·9 inches to 31·49 inches) in body length. The smaller cello, becoming popular in the 1680s, is the instrument that was called the violoncini or violoncello. Its rise somewhat corresponds to the rise of the virtuoso cellists; it is today considered the normal cello with a body length of 74 cm. to 75·9 cm., with 75 cm. (29½ inches) the norm. There have been, however, cellos even larger than the church bass, some measuring as much as 86 cm. (33·8 inches) in body length (Prescott cello, Plate 27, 32 inches). As Mr Kinney says, the cello pictured by Praetorius and called *Bas-Geig de bracio* is undoubtedly of this largest size. Smaller-than-normal cellos existed, with measurements of $\frac{7}{8}$ size (the five-stringed cello pictured in Plate 28 of 72·5 cm.), of $\frac{3}{4}$ size (67–70 cm.), or even $\frac{1}{2}$ size (54–60 cm.), (the violoncello piccolo in Plate 29 of 59 cm.). The very earliest cellos pictured, the one at Saronno and the one referred to on page 52 as dating from *c.* 1550, are evidently the smallest size. At the same time, Jambe de Fer in 1556 refers to the cello tuning as Bb_1 F c g, indicating a large-size cello.

The four- and five-string cellos had various tunings: at first the church bass was tuned in fifths with Bb_1 as the lowest note, Bb_1-F-c-g, and later C-G-d-g or C-G-d-a. If the cello larger than the church bass had five strings (Praetorius) it was tuned F_1-C-G-d-a. The normal cello was tuned at first C-G-d-g and only a little later C-G-d-a. If it was a $\frac{7}{8}$ size with five strings, it could be tuned C-G-d-a-d^1 or C-G-d-a-e^1. If it had six strings, it was tuned like the bass gamba D-G-c-e-a-d^1, with the alternate tuning of the D down to C. The four-string half-size cello, or violoncello piccolo, was tuned G-d-a-e^1, or if five strings, C-G-d-a-e^1 (where the C string would not sound well).

INTERPRETATION OF THE CONTINUO; RÔLE IN CHAMBER
MUSIC, CHURCH MUSIC AND ORCHESTRAL MUSIC
IN THE SEVENTEENTH CENTURY

By the beginning of the seventeenth century a new style of music was created that was called the *Nuove musiche* (New Music), and although it was first used in vocal music, it was soon to be found eminently satisfactory as a vehicle for purely instrumental music. In its simplest form the new style of music was one where the composer wrote out just two lines of music, the top solo line (in a recitative character in the early vocal works) and an equally important bass line that was known as a *basso continuo* (English term, thorough-bass) or continuing bass line. Often the composer put numbers above the bass notes to suggest the chords or chord positions that could be used, in which case the bass line was sometimes referred to as the *figured bass*. The terms 'basso continuo' and 'figured bass' are then not synonyms, i.e. all figured basses are basso continuo lines, but not all basso continuos are figured basses. A keyboard instrument, or chordal instrument such as the lute (or its variants the theorbo, or chitarrone) was supposed to 'realize' the basso continuo, that is improvise an accompaniment with the written notes as the bottom notes of each changing sonority. In addition, a melodic instrument such as the bass gamba, bassoon, trombone, or cello was to play the bottom line to make it quite clear as a line in contrast to the solo line. In the earlier part of the century, the bassoon or trombone (which had a lighter tone then and blended well with stringed instruments) was called upon surprisingly frequently. The cello becomes the major continuo instrument after *c.* 1640. The basso continuo became idiomatic of all baroque music except solo lute music, keyboard music, and the seventeenth-century vestige of Renaissance music in England known as instrumental consort music, written primarily for viols (English term for Viola da gamba).

Although the new style of music was written originally for voice to take the solo line, or in another popular combination, two high voices, each with its separate line, with basso continuo (three lines of music), the texture was soon adapted to instruments. One early name for these instrumental pieces was 'sonata', which meant 'to sound' instead of 'to sing.' The word 'sonata' in its earliest use had no reference to any formal characteristics of a composition. The first use of this term for a work using violins was in 1610, when G. P. Cima used it for a solo violin sonata (violin and violone) as well as for the first trio sonatas (three lines of music, SS/B).

As the seventeenth century proceeded, two types of 'sonatas' were created in Italy, the *sonata da chiesa* (church sonata) and the *sonata da camera* (chamber sonata). All the baroque cello sonata literature discussed in Chapter III is cast in one or the other of these forms, or a cross between them. As a form the *sonata da chiesa* was a variable group of movements, often four but by no means always, which were usually all in the same key but were contrasted in tempo and style. There is such a variety of contrasts that it is hard to generalize, but a frequent arrangement, in four movements, was slow-fast-slow-fast (SFSF). The tempo marks were frequently the only names the movements had. The slow movements were more singing in style, although the first movements tended to be more polyphonic than the third movements; the fast movements were often built on imitation. Each movement was based on a spinning out of one or more ideas set up in succession at the beginning, but without essential contrast between the ideas. The use of the device of sequence was a popular one for spinning out the material. The last movement of the group was often based on a dance rhythm without identification of the dance derivation. These sonatas were played in church. There was a need for this string instrumental church music, because up until the time of Frescobaldi's death in 1644 the organ had supplied the major instrumental church music. With this great organist's death, there was a slump in Italy in the cultivation of this instrument, which was accompanied by a great flourishing of string instrumental music, which gradually supplanted a portion of the organist's role in the music of the church in Italy.

The *sonata da camera* was essentially a series of dances with contrasting tempos and rhythms. The series of dances became known in Germany as a suite. This suite of dances had no standard order in seventeenth-century Italy, nor were all the movements necessarily dances. An examination of, for instance, just the works of Corelli (1653–1713) will show that the usual textbook definitions of these two types of sonatas were frequently not borne out by the music. The dances which were composed were originally functional dances, that is, actually danced, but the Italian composers wrote their works as 'ideal' dances, that is, retaining only the essential characteristics of the dances. They were chamber music to be performed in a room of some palace or nobleman's house. The dances that were written were very numerous, including among them the Allamanda, Corrente, Sarabanda, Gavotta, and Giga. Each of these dances had its typical tempo, metre, manner of starting, and rhythmic characteristics. All the dance movements were in binary form (two-part form), with the following plan:

	‖:	:‖:		:‖
Major Key	T	D	Key	T
Minor Key	T	RM	Excursions	T

'T' stands for tonic key; 'D' for the dominant key; and 'RM' for the relative major key. If when the tonic key returns in the second half, the original material is restated, the form is referred to as a 'rounded binary'. In many of these sonatas the second part begins with the original material, in which case the form is called a 'parallel binary'.

Even in the *sonata da chiesa*, if the movements were dances, though without being so named, they were in binary form.

The instrumentation of these two types of sonatas varied, but the *sonata da chiesa* was composed mostly for the violin family. If the composer wrote two lines of music, the solo part was most frequently for violin, and the continuo part would be 'realized' by organ (in church) or harpsichord (in chamber music) to which was added a melodic bass instrument, so frequently designated as 'violone' in seventeenth-century Italy after *c*. 1640. There was also a comparatively small number of sonatas that called for a cello as the solo instrument in the seventeenth century in Italy. (See p. 81). If the composer wrote three lines of music, the top two were solo lines, usually in the soprano range and calling for two violins, with the usual basso continuo realization.

Among the most important seventeenth-century Italian composers of these solo sonatas (two lines of written music), trio sonatas (three lines of music), or sonatas from four to eight parts were the seventeenth-century violinists Marco Uccellini, associated with the Modena court from 1645 and becoming Maestro di Cappella there in 1654; G. B. Fontana, with only one publication, in 1641 (the first to designate 'violoncino'); Giuseppe Colombi; G. B. Vitali (cellist); G. M. Bononcini; G. B. Bassani; G. Torelli; and A. Corelli. Several organists also contributed to this genre: Maurizio Cazzati, Maestro di Cappella in Bologna from 1657 to 1671, and in Mantua from 1673 until his death in 1677; Giovanni Legrenzi; and G. B. Degl'Antonii.

Near the end of the century the baroque concerto types were created, the concerto grosso, the solo concerto, and the orchestral concerto. The concerto grosso was the first and in many ways the most typical; it was based on the concertato principle, with the basic contrast between the full orchestra (*tutti* or *ripieno*) and a small group of soloists (*concertino*; with Corelli, the instruments for the trio sonata, two violins and a cello). Of Corelli's 12 concertos, eight are *da chiesa* and four *da camera*; they may be considered orchestrated sonatas. In the concerto grosso, the cello was often featured as one of the *concertino* group, with a second cello playing the basso continuo in the *ripieno* orchestra.

The solo concerto in which the soloist is pitted against the whole orchestra (*tutti*), established by Torelli (the last six of Op. 8) was carried to its fullest heights by Antonio Vivaldi and J. S. Bach. Vivaldi wrote an amazing number of concertos, at least 454 of which

8 Cello of Giuseppe Guarneri, *'filius Andrea'*, 1721

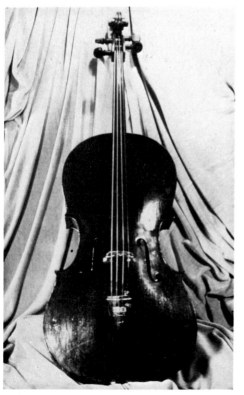

9 Cello of Antonio Stradivarius,
'*The Castelbarco*', 1697

27 were for solo cello. The orchestral concerto was not so popular, perhaps because of the fact that no soloist was featured.

The role of the cello in the opera orchestra should be mentioned. Since the rooms in which the operas were performed were larger than those for chamber music, the cello was from the beginning in Italy preferred as the opera orchestra's bass voice, that is, the instrument to play the continuo, because it was louder. As has been mentioned, Monteverdi in his *Orfeo* (1607) called for both cellos and bass violas da gamba. Landi in *Il San Alessio*, called for 'violoni'; but most scores designated only 'basso' or 'basso continuo'.

THE RISE OF THE FIRST SOLO VIRTUOSI

The first cello performers who can now be identified by name are several associated with the S. Petronio Cathedral in Bologna, Italy, in the latter part of the seventeenth century. According to Vatielli, they were Angelo Bovi, Dominico Maria Marcheselli, Benedetto Zavatteri (about these three absolutely nothing is known), G. B. Vitali, Petronio Franceschini (the first paid cellist at the Cathedral), Domenico Gabrielli, and Giuseppe Jacchini. So far as is known, these performers were only locally known and none became a travelling virtuoso. It is in the eighteenth century that this new role was created. Giovanni Bononcini, for instance, was an early travelling cellist whose travelling took place in the early eighteenth century. To this list perhaps two other names could be added as early cellists, that of Francesco Todeschini of Mantua, who called himself on the title page of his collection of dances (1650) '*Musico, & Sonatore di Violino & di Violone* [cello?]' and Clemente Monari of Bologna, who referred to himself on his score (1686) as '*Musico di Violone*'.

In summing up the role of the cello in seventeenth-century Italy, we could say it was not only important in the performance of basso continuo parts in the Italian opera orchestra starting early in the century, in the church sonatas and in chamber music from at least *c.* 1640, and in the orchestral music of the latter part of the century, where it was sometimes employed as one of the soloists in the concertino, but also as soloist perhaps as early as the 1660s (see pp. 78–80).

The first known reference to a cello in France is Jambe de Fer's *Epitome musical* (1556), which was published in Lyons. There was a famous instrument maker (living in Lyons at that time, Gaspar Duiffoprugcar (German, Tieffenbrücker). He was primarily a lute and viol maker, but that he made instruments with some violin characteristics may be seen in his well-known portrait engraved in 1562 by Woeriot. There are two instruments in this portrait that resemble a violin (they are hybrid instruments), but on this basis some writers in the past have claimed that he was the first violin maker. There is no instrument of a cello size shown. The first known reference to cello performance in France is in the orchestra of the *Ballet comique de la reine* (1581). In the seventeenth century the violin family was the one used in the Vingt-Quatre Violons du Roi established by Louis XIII (reign 1610–43), and later cellists took part along with gambists in Lully's orchestra. The first dated French chamber music score to call for the violoncello was in 1705, a set of trio sonatas by Jean-François d'Andrieu.[15] In England the violin family did not come into favour until the reign of Charles II and was not popularized until the 1730s. Sufficient information is not yet available to form a picture of the German situation. Van der Straeten mentions only two German cellists, who scarcely could have begun their careers in the seventeenth century, Gregor Christoph Eylenstein (born 1682) and Gottlob Hayne (born 1684). Fred. Leopold Pückl was employed at the Imperial Chapel, Vienna, from 1686 until his death in 1711. It would seem that E. F. Dall'Abaco was one of the first important cellists (he was also a violinist) in Germany, having accepted a post at Munich in 1704, where he served with some interruption until his death in 1742.

*   *   *

Italy, then, was the dominant country for the development of the violin family in the seventeenth century, for the production of the instruments, for their employment, and for the creation of their first literature.

The Eighteenth Century

THE SPREAD OF THE POPULARITY OF THE CELLO TO OTHER COUNTRIES

The spread of the popularity of the cello all over Europe and even to America late in the century is one of the phenomena to be observed in the history of the instrument during the eighteenth century. This dispersion resulted partly, of course, from travelling cellists who visited other countries.

The most famous of these earliest cellists was the legendary

Franciscello.[16] He was not really a travelling virtuoso in our sense, because there are records of his being heard only in three cities – in Naples, where he was born, in Rome, and in Vienna, where he was employed as cellist at the Imperial Chapel from 1726 until his death. Not much has been known about him until the last decade or so. It has been established that his real name was Francesco Alborea, that he was born in 1691 and died in 1739.[17] He entered the Loreta Conservatory in Naples at the age of ten and was a student there for 12 years, after which he was employed in the Royal Chapel until 1726, when he went to Vienna. It is possible that he performed in Prague, since two sonatas attributed to him are to be found there in the library of the National Museum.[18]

If it had not been for several contemporary impressions of Franciscello's playing, he might have slipped completely into oblivion. But he impressed A. Scarlatti, F. Geminiani, J. J. Quantz, and Franz Benda. Charles Burney repeats what he heard from Geminiani:

> The violoncello parts of many of these cantatas by A. Scarlatti were so excellent, that whoever was able to do them justice was thought a supernatural being. Geminiani used to relate that Francischilli, a celebrated performer on the violoncello at the beginning of this century, accompanied one of those cantatas at Rome so admirably while Scarlatti was at the harpsichord, that the company, being good Catholics and living in a country where miraculous powers have not yet ceased, were firmly persuaded it was not Francischilli who had played the violoncello but an angel that had descended and assumed his shape.[19]

J. J. Quantz commented on Franciscello's performance:

> The first church composer in Naples [1725] was the Oberkapellmeister and knight, Alessandro Scarlatti, under whom the present Oberkapellmeister of Saxon music, Herr Hasse, was studying counterpoint. The others were Mancini, Leo, and Feo. The orchestra was fairly good. There were no outstanding instrumentalists except for the incomparable violoncellist Franchiscello, who later joined the Imperial service.[20]

He also said:

> In honour of Count von Lichtenstein, who was in Naples at this time with his wife, several concertos were performed by the greatest musicians of the country. Besides Hasse, Farinelli, Tesi,

and Franchiscello, I too had the honour of being invited to play.
...[21]

Benda relates:

> In Vienna I was recommended to Count von Uhlefeld, who later
> was ambassador to Constantinople. He learned the violoncello
> with the famous royal violoncellist Francischello. Thus several
> times I had the opportunity to hear this particularly skilful man,
> whose ability surprised me.[22]

The legend of Franciscello was so great that he was credited with
teaching musicians he never met. Fétis records that Barrière, one of
the founders of the French School, was in Italy from 1736 to 1739
and studied with Franciscello. As the latter was in Vienna at this
time, Fétis was undoubtedly wrong. It was Gerber who created the
myth that J. P. Duport studied the cello with Franciscello in Genoa.
Since Franciscello died in 1739 and J. P. Duport was born in 1741,
there is no longer any doubt of the fiction of that tale.

London was unusually hospitable to foreign artists, and many of
them visited there during the eighteenth century. A number of
cellists found their way there, an early account being given by
Charles Burney:

> The elder Cervetto [1682–1783] is now [1739] first mentioned as
> just arrived; and this worthy professor, who remained in England
> till the time of his death, at above a hundred, with Abaco, Lan-
> zetti, Pasqualini, and Caporale, about this time brought the vio-
> loncello into favour, and made us nice judges of that instrument.[23]

Other cellists to visit London were, for instance, Giovanni Bononcini, Stefano Galeatti, G. B. Cirri, Carlo Graziani, and Jan Stiastný
(Stiasny).

Cellists even reached Russia. The two brothers Domenico and
Giuseppe Dall'Oglio, the former a violinist and the latter a cellist,
arrived in St Petersburg in 1735 and stayed at the Russian Court
until 1764. Both were fine virtuosi on their respective instruments.
The first German to travel to Russia mentioned by van der Straeten
is one Riedel. Van der Straeten states that he went to St Petersburg
in 1727, where he became the cello teacher of the Czar, Peter II,
as well as the fencing master at court.[24]

The Italian cellist, Jean Baptiste Stuck (i.e. Batistin) spent his
career in Paris, from 1709 to 1755. Several Italian cellists gave

début concerts in the Concert Spiritual series in Paris or settled there for their careers. The Concert Spiritual series was an important series started in 1725 and lasting until 1791. Success at these concerts could be compared to a successful Town Hall or Carnegie Hall recital in New York, a Wigmore Hall recital in London, or an Usher Hall recital in Edinburgh today. The Italian cellists Carlo Ferrari (1758) and Boccherini (1768) gave concerts there, as well as a number of French cellists. Nochez, an Italian cellist who lived in Paris, became the first cellist of the Concert Spiritual Orchestra *c.* 1763.

Luigi Boccherini (1743–1805) spent the major part of his career in Spain, from 1769 until his death (he may or may not have been in Germany some time during 1787 to 1796, for nothing is known about him during those years). (See pp. 116–117).

Antonio Vandini was Tartini's cellist and went with him to Prague in 1723–1725. Was the first known Czech cellist, Johann Cermak (*c.* 1710–*c.* 1790) inspired by Vandini? One does not know. The strings must have been cultivated to some extent, especially in the second half of the eighteenth century, in Bohemia (now part of Czechoslovakia), because some remarkable players came from there, though for the most part they sought employment elsewhere, usually in Austria or Germany. Among the most distinguished of these were J. W. Stamitz, and the cellists Wenzel Himmelbauer, A. T. Stamitz, Anton Kraft, J. B. Mara, the brothers Bernard and Jan Stiastný, and Joseph Reicha (an uncle of Anton Reicha). The Czech cellist (also oboist) Joseph Fiala travelled a good deal, visiting Poland and Russia. A Mr Werner was a cello teacher in Prague in the eighteenth century, teaching among others Anton Kraft. When Charles Burney made his grand tour of Central Europe and the Netherlands in 1772, he visited Prague and wrote, 'The best, and indeed, the only violoncello player in this city is M. Hetes . . .'[25]

Once the cello got a foothold in Germany, many German cellists not only toured their country, but also beyond its borders. Johann Baptist Baumgartner toured as far as Norway and Sweden; later J. G. Rauppe travelled to Denmark and Sweden. There was one native cellist in Stockholm in 1783, a Mr Cloos, as well as several foreign cellists. Ernst Hausler settled in Zurich, Switzerland; Ernst Jager toured as far as Hungary, and Johann Daniel Braun to Poland. The cellist Wolfgang Schindlocker is mentioned as touring America.[26]

Foreign musicians even began coming to the New World to live after the American Revolution, that is, after 1783. Among them was the cellist J. George Schetky, who perhaps came over in 1786 with his uncle Alexander Reinagle; Schetky, according to Sonneck, played cello in Philadelphia as early as 1787.[27] (According to Baker's *Biographical Dictionary*, however, Schetky did not come over until 1792, in which case he may have come with Reinagle's teacher, Raynor Taylor, who came to the United States in 1792). Sonneck reports two cello concertos performed during the 1790s, a concerto by a Mr Phillips played by him on 4 October 1792, in New York, and one composed and performed by the cellist Mr Demarque in Baltimore on 15 July 1795. Sonneck reports that neither of these concertos has come to light.[28]

THE BATTLE WITH THE GAMBA IN FRANCE

In no other country was the battle between the cello and the bass viol more dramatic than in France. The preference at the French court of Louis XIV was for the viola da gamba, and French taste was dominated by that of the court. Louis XIV's reign (1643–1715) was just beginning when the cello ousted the bass gamba from the orchestras and chamber music ensembles in Italy *c.* 1640. The rise of the great French virtuosi on the gamba from Maugars, Hotman, and Sainte-Colombe down to the next generation of Marin Marais (1656–1728), Antoine Forqueray (1671–1745) and Louis de Caix d'Hervelois (1670–*c.* 1760), was in response to the French taste for the instrument. (When Forqueray as a youth played the cello for Louis XIV, he ordered Forqueray to exchange the cello for the gamba).[29] Le Blanc's *Défense de la basse de viole contre les entreprises du violon et les pretentions du violoncel* (1740) is a famous diatribe against the violin family, and illustrates how bitter the battle was between the two families in France:

> *Le Violoncel, qui jusques là s'étoit vu miserable cancre, haire et pauvre diable, dont la condition avoit été de mourir de faim, point de franche lipée, maintenant se flatte qu'à la place de la basse de viole, il recevra maintes caresses; déjà il se forge une félicité qui le fait pleurer de tendresse.*[30]

[Free translation: The violoncello who up until now has considered himself a miserable scoundrel, hated, and a poor devil whose condition would have to be to die of hunger without real appreciation, now flatters himself that in the place of the bass

viola da gamba, he is going to be treated kindly, already imagining
for himself a happiness that makes him weep tenderly.]

This *Défense* was a cry in the night, because the battle was already
being won by the cello, partly just because it was louder, which
capacity was needed in the larger concert rooms.

A word should be said about La Borde's *Essai sur la musique
ancienne et moderne* (1780). Jean Benjamin de La Borde was a violinist
and a student of Rameau in composition. The *Essai* is first of all the
original source of information that Charles IX gave the order to
Andrea Amati for the 38 instruments, including eight cellos (1, 358).
It should also be mentioned that this book contains an essay on cello
playing (1, 309–323) which, according to Fétis and repeated by
Wasielewski, was written by the cellist Nochez. The essay is of interest
only historically. For instance, it gives the credit to Tardieu for
inventing the cello in 1708. It mentions a few French cellists as perfecting cello technique (Berteau, Duport, and Janson), proceeds to
describe the cello as based on the Stradivarius model, and ends with
about a dozen pages on the technique of the instrument.

THE END OF THE SYSTEM OF PATRONAGE

The patronage system which had existed from early times (the
church was the early patron of music, until at least the fifteenth century, when it divided the responsibility with the nobility) came to an
end as a system with the close of the eighteenth century. One of the
last great patrons and one particularly important for cello history
was Frederick William II of Prussia, a cellist and nephew of Frederick
the Great, who succeeded him on the throne in 1786 and ruled until
his death in 1797. Early in the year in which he was crowned he
had given the cellist Boccherini the title of 'Composer of our
Chamber'. It is still uncertain whether Boccherini actually went to
Germany. Frederick William II had first studied cello with Graziani,
but while still Crown Prince he began study with the great French
cellist, Jean Pierre Duport, whom his uncle had employed in 1773.
J. P. Duport was associated with the Prussian court until his death.
His brother, the even more famous Jean Louis Duport, joined the
Prussian court when Paris was in the turmoil of the French Revolution in 1789, but he returned to Paris in 1806. Both of the Duport
brothers were in Berlin when Beethoven stopped there in 1796,
carrying with him his first two cello sonatas (Op. 5) which he

composed for this visit. He played them at court with Jean Pierre Duport in the presence of the King. Beethoven's dedication of the two sonatas of Op. 5 reads, '*Dem König Friedrich Wilhelm II. gewidmet*'. Haydn's string quartets, Op. 50, and Mozart's last three string quartets (K. 575, 589, and 590) were likewise dedicated to the King of Prussia. In the Mozart quartets the cello is given the chance to state many of the themes first and altogether the role of the cello is exceptionally important. Also the cellist, Peter Ritter, appeared at the Berlin court and played for the King, who was greatly impressed by his performance.

EIGHTEENTH-CENTURY USES OF THE CELLO

During the eighteenth century the cello continued to be used in all the ways it had been used in the previous century, but with certain differences because of the change in the style of music. It continued in the opera orchestra, but by mid-century it had supplanted the viola da gamba in all countries. A role that became popular was that of the art of accompanying recitative or aria. Actually Domenico Gabrielli (d. 1690) was the first to write cello accompaniments to arias, which he did in *Flavio Cuniberto* and *Muarizio*. In the eighteenth century the cellist was expected to improvise part of what he played as accompaniment. Several instruction books explained how to do this, the most detailed account being found in Baumgartner's method (1774) and the Baillot-Levasseur Catel-Baudiot method (1804), but actually by this time the art was dying out because cellists were no longer trained in the realization of the basso continuo. Some cellists were particularly noted for their ability to accompany, such as Friedrich August Kummer, J. G. C. Schetky, or the English cellist Robert Lindley, who was principal cellist of the London Opera for more than 50 years (1794–1851): '. . . his accompaniment of recitative was in its way perfection, though his style was wholly unsuited to recitative secco'.[31]

The classical orchestra created by the Mannheim School continued to be written for by Haydn, Mozart, and Beethoven. In the new conception of orchestration, all the inner parts were written out so that there was no longer any need for a basso continuo. (That Haydn still played and conducted from the harpsichord for his London concerts in the 1790s was not because of necessity but because of habit).

In chamber music, although the continuo sonatas continued to be written throughout the century for solo music, the trio sonata was displaced by the string quartet. The string quartet and the piano trio were established (not created) by Haydn, and the major repertoire for the cellist in classical music was his part in the string quartets of Haydn, Mozart, and Beethoven. The rise of the string quartet particularly opened up a new profession for the cellist, which flourished in the nineteenth century and continues today.

CELLO METHODS AND THEIR PROLIFERATION

Just when the first cello method was written is not really known. It has often been stated that the first one was by Michel Corrette, his *Méthode, theorique et pratique, Pour apprendre en peu de tems* [sic] *le violoncelle dans sa perfection* (1741). This work of 46 pages is not a comprehensive method at all, but it does contain more verbal description than the methods referred to below which may be earlier. Corrette was not a cellist but an organist. He apparently perceived a lack of instruction books for various instruments and wrote one each for most of the instruments of his time. There are some quaint things about his cello method, such as his statement that Bononcini (d. 1755) invented the cello; that some cellists hold their cello by placing it on the floor (Sigr. De Bacqueville was not the only one then! – see Plate 33); and that in his fingering patterns, he never used the third finger.

A method discussing 'elementary theory and rudiments of playing the violin and violoncello' by Sebald Triemer is mentioned by van der Straeten as having been published in Amsterdam in 1739. This may possibly be the first published method for cello.

Two works that could be considered methods of one kind or another, which are impossible to date, may have preceded Corrette's method. They are in manuscript, to be found in the Nationalbibliothek in Vienna: an anonymous set of 98 short 'Lexione' (lessons) and 'Lexione' of 44 short pieces by Antonio Caldara, a cellist as well as opera composer. Neither of these has any verbal explanations, nor are they graded studies. Since Caldara died in 1736, his set of 'lessons' naturally preceded Corrette's method. Caldara's are the more interesting. Each lesson, accompanied by a figured bass, uses some of the techniques current at that time. The collection represents a partial summary of the various devices used by cellists in the early eighteenth century. The ingenuity of the multitude of figures used within the narrow range of d–g^1 could, I believe, have been thought of only by a practising cellist. A third anonymous method of 100

'Lezioni' is also to be found in that library. These studies, however, are much more carefully organized and more advanced; all in all, it seems of a much later date.

There are two works both in manuscript by the neglected, probably Neopolitan composer, Francesco Scipriani (1678–1753), which should be of great interest to the cello world. The one is *Principij da imparare a suonare il Violoncello e con 12 Toccate a solo*; the other, *Sonate per 2 Violoncelli e Basso*. These works are to be found in the Conservatorio de Musica, S. Pietro a Majella, in Naples. The *Principij* is indeed close to a method for cello. It is undated, but may have preceded the Corrette method. It starts with two pages of explanation of music fundamentals (note values and their equivalent rests, keys, clefs, tempi, signatures, accidentals, and so on). Following this explanation are two pages of fundamentals appropriate to the cello (scales, up and down; tetrachord segments, broken thirds up and down, broken fourths up and down, octaves on the notes of the C major scale, and a four-line passage mixing various interval leaps and including some chromaticisms). After the drill in getting acquainted with the instrument, there follow 12 'Toccatas' which are very fine exercises on the instrument in various metres, note values, and patterns. The ninth Toccata, written in $\frac{3}{2}$ metre, uses white eighth notes, a practice that is found occasionally in this period.

The *Sonate per 2 Violoncello e Basso* (three lines of music) consist of 12 one-movement works, each called 'sonata'; because the last one was left incomplete by the composer, we may presume the set to be a late work. The top line of the first ten 'sonatas' has a skeleton melody, while the middle line consists of written-out divisions on the skeleton melody. This work illustrates excellently how a baroque composer would elaborate on a given melody. In the eleventh 'sonata' the parts have changed places, that is, the more elaborate part is on the top line. In the incomplete twelfth sonata, broken off at m.22, only the top solo line and the basso continuo had so far been written, the middle line being blank. The divisions are composed largely of arpeggiated figures, string-crossing patterns, double stops, and scale fragments. In fact, those 'sonatas' are in reality a series of exercises for the cello, but on an advanced level. They cover well the range from C–d^2 and offer varied and excellent studies in cello technique, including thumb position. It is in the sense of their being études that they are particularly fascinating, for they contain a repertoire of various devices and illustrate the stage of advancement technically that is little realized today as that of the closing years of the baroque. These offer a challenge to today's performers. This work reflects a composer fascinated with the technique of the cello, and it seems more than possible that Scipriani may have been a cellist.

An example may indicate the stage of development in the late baroque period:

Example 4: Scipriani. Sonata No. 7 per 2 Violoncellos e Basso.

After the Corrette *Methode* there are no published methods until the 1760s, with one curious exception, if one wants to call it a method, *The Gamut*, printed by Henry Waylett in 1745 or 1746. It is one page long and gives fingerings for the C scale, the chromatic scale, a little lesson in binary form in C major, and another in D major going to a¹. The most interesting thing about it is the recommendation of the fingering 1–2–3 for first position in the C and G strings (a fingering that Casals often used).

The proliferation of cello tutors somewhat before and after the turn of the nineteenth century would certainly indicate an accelerated interest in the cello. (See Chart p. 76). Many of these tutors would presumably have been addressed to the amateur, or as he styled himself, the dilettante. By far the most important of these is Jean Louis Duport's *Essai sur le doigtes du violoncelle et la conduite de l'archet, avec une suite d'exercises*. In this work, Duport establishes the modern method of fingering. The discussion is followed by 21 exercises, the sixth being by Berteau, the eighth and tenth (the latter from Sonata No. 5, Op. 4, 3rd movement) by his older brother, Jean Pierre; the rest are original. These 21 exercises have appeared in several modern editions and are standard fare for the student today.

French

c. 1764	Tillière
c. 1768	Cupis, Le Jeune
1797	Raoul
Before 1800	J. C. Miné
1802	Bideau
1804	Bréval
1804	Baillot-Levasseur- Catel-Baudiot*
1805	P. E. O. Aubert
c. 1805	Hus-Desforges
c. 1806	J. L. Duport†

German

1774	Baumgartner
c. 1780	J. G. C. Schetky, Lessons (As he lived in Edinburgh, the text is in English).
1788	F. Kauer
c. 1800	J. Alexander
1810	J. Froehlich

Italian

c. 1749	Geminiani, *True Taste*
Before 1770	Lanzetti‡
17—	Caperolli
1780	Nochez
	(*Essai* in Laborde)
c. 1802	de Benito (It.?)§

English and Scottish

c. 1765	Crome
c. 1785	Hardy
1793	John Gunn, *Theory and Practi*

TUTORS WITH TITLE, *New Instructions*

1784–95	Pub., Longman & Herron
c. 1795	Pub., Cuhusac & Sons
c. 1800	Pub., Messrs. Thompson

TUTORS WITH TITLE, *New & Complet
Tutor*

c. 1785	Pub., Preston & Son
c. 1800	Pub., Bland & Weller

TUTORS WITH TITLE, *New & Comple
Instructions*

1787	Pub., G. Goulding
c. 1795	Pub., Longman & Broderip
c. 1800	Pub., Clementi *et al*

STANDARD TUTOR

c. 1800	Pub., Addison & Hudson
c. 1800	Riley's Preceptor
1801	John Gunn, *An Essay*
1811	McDonald
?	Robert Lindley, Op. 4
1823?	Joseph Reinagle
1826	Crouch

Belgian

c. 1800	Müntzberger

Czech

c. 1812	Stiastný

* Baudiot wrote his own method *c.* 1830
† Heron-Allen dates this method *c,* 1790
‡ Not 1736, the date of his first sonatas
§ One edition was published in Madrid, Spain

Chapter 3

About the Literature
for the Cello

The Earliest Literature

Three composers are presently acknowledged to be the first three to
write solo literature for the cello: Giovanni Battista Degl'Antonii,
Domenico Gabrielli, and Domenico Galli. The one composition for
cello by Antonii, *Ricercate/Sopra Il Violoncello/o Clavicembalo*, Op. 1
was published in 1687. It is a set of 12 unaccompanied ricercari. The
term 'ricercar(e)' (ricercata) in the sense used here means an instructive piece or an étude. In the title '*o Clavicembalo*' – literally 'or Clavicembalo' – suggests that this score could be used as a bass upon which
the harpsicord player could make improvisations (Antonii was an
organist). Seven of the 12 ricercari have figured bass symbols that
could be of aid in such improvisations. Because of the nature of the
music a third alternative, that of accompanied ricercari, was probably
not intended. All but the middle section (26 measures long) of No. 8
are in the perpetual motion style of running eighth or sixteenth
notes. Mr Kinney has made the ingenious suggestion that these
ricercari call for a cello with six strings, tuned like the bass viol,
with the alternate tuning for the lowest string depending on the key,
C (or D) G c e a d^1.[1] Although the works can be played on the cello
with four strings and normal tuning, his suggestion is very persuasive
because the notes are better under the hand with the above tuning.

Domenico Gabrielli, the second composer, has left a manuscript
collection, fortunately dated, 1689, and two additional undated
manuscript continuo sonatas in the keys of G major and A major.
The title of the collection reads:

Gabrielli Domenico = Bolognese = /Ricercarj per violoncello
solo, con un Canone a due Violoncelli e/alcuni Ricercari per Vllo
e B. C./ In tutto pezzi 11/. Gabrielli un detto Mingain/dal Viulunzeel.

('Mingain' is an affectionate diminutive in Bolognese for Domenico, and 'Viulunzeel' is Bolognese dialect for Violoncello). Above the staff on the first page of music is found the date '15 genaro 1689'. The manuscript contains seven ricercari for unaccompanied cello, a canon for two cellos, and four ricercari with basso continuo accompaniment – all of which adds up to 12 pieces instead of the 11 stated on the title page. The canon is inserted between ricercar no. 5 and no. 6 without number and was perhaps omitted in the counting. The four pieces with continuo accompaniment were revised and prove to be the first version of the four movements of the above-mentioned sonata in G major. Gabrielli, obviously, is using the terms 'ricercar' and 'sonata' as synonyms. The instrument for which Gabrielli's compositions were written was a four-stringed cello tuned C G d g.

Domenico Galli, the third composer, wrote one work for cello. The title page and dedication are printed, but the notes are in manuscript. The title is *Trattenimento Musicale Sopre Il Violoncello A' Solo*. The date at the end of the dedication is 1691. The word '*trattenimento*' here means simply 'entertainment' (not a method). This is a collection of 12 unaccompanied 'sonatas'. The term 'sonata' is used in its early meaning of an instrumental piece and has no reference to form. The tuning called for by this work is $B\flat_1$ F c g. Frankly, these sonatas are disappointing to play because of their lack of structural coherence, and remain of historical interest only.

In addition to these three composers, there are three problematical composers who should be considered as possible candidates for early cello works: G. B. Vitali (*c.* 1644–92), Giuseppe Columbi (1635–94) and Antonio Giannotti (fl. in Modena some time during the reign of Francesco II, 1660–94). These three composers were all associated with Modena, but G. B. Vitali had worked in Bologna before moving to Modena. Bologna and Modena were two important Italian centres of musical development in the second part of the seventeenth century. Don Marco Uccellini became maestro di cappella of the Modena Cathedral in 1654, and the most brilliant years musically in that city were during the reign of Francesco II, a member of the renowned Este family and an enthusiastic patron of music. Maurizio Cazzati established the Bologna School in 1657.

The works of these three composers are for violone (G. B. Vitali), basso solo and violone (Columbi), and basso solo in the title but violon(e) internally (Giannotti). The undated manuscript by G. B. Vitali is in two parts:

Partite sopra diuerse Sonate/di Gio: Batta: Vitali per il Violone and
Partite sopra diuerse Sonate/di Gio: Batta: Vitali per il/Violino.

Both sets are unaccompanied. The *Partite* for violone consist of ten pieces from 17 to 124 measures. All of the pieces in the *Partite* are variations, even the capritios, except for the opening toccata. The word 'sonate' as used in the title again harks back to the earlier meaning of the term, simply pieces suitable for instrumental music. The tuning for this instrument would seem to be B$\flat_1$ F c g, the old cello tuning.

If the term 'violone' on this manuscript was used as a synonym for 'basso' (violone da brazzo = basso da brazzo), the most likely instrument designated by the score is a cello. As has been mentioned, the research of Vatielli makes it quite clear that Vitali was a cellist. I think it is highly likely that these are early cello works. G. B. Vitali was a performing cellist from 1666 to 1763, and it seems reasonable to assume he wrote these *Partite* during this period rather than later, when he became involved in duties as an administrator.

One of G. B. Vitali's colleagues when he went from Bologna to Modena in 1674 was Giuseppe Colombi, a violinist. There are three unaccompanied manuscript works of Colombi which are probably for cello: *Chiacona a Basso* solo, *Toccata a Violone solo* (unfinished), and *Balli Diversi a Basso solo*. The *Chiacona* is a theme and variation, and is undoubtedly for an instrument tuned B$\flat_1$ F c g because the score calls for a B$\flat_1$. It is an interesting piece. The *Toccata* is a curious work consisting of a consecutive series of more than one hundred sequences (with much repetition of sequential figures here and there throughout the piece). The work is a study book of patterns appropriate to the instrument; in this sense the word 'toccata' is used as a synonym for 'ricercar'. The *Balli diuersi, a Basso solo* is a collection of 81 very short and very primitive pieces, primarily dances. It is impossible to tell the tuning for this instrument from the music, but if Colombi used the old tuning for the *Chiacona*, he probably did for the *Balli* and the *Toccata* as well.

Antonio Giannotti has left a manuscript, perhaps autograph, entitled, *Balli e Sonate a 2 Violoni e Basso,/ a Violino e Basso ed a Basso solo,/ con B. C.* The manuscript consists of 30 pieces for two violins and basso continuo, two pieces for one violin and basso continuo, and one solo for basso and basso continuo. Unfortunately the basso continuo part for the bass solo is missing. Internally the *Basso solo con B. C.* is identified as 'Sonata a Violon Solo'. Here, Giannotti is using the terms 'Basso' and 'Violon' as synonyms. The work is a sonata in four movements, none of which has a tempo designation, but the order is apparently S-F-S-F. It is impossible to determine the tuning of the instrument by any internal evidence. The range called for is C–e^1; the tuning may be C G d g ('g' instead of an 'a') because this was an earlier tuning.

The works of these last three composers, if for the cello, as I believe they are, probably all pre-date the Antonii and D. Gabrielli compositions. They seem to be much more tentative works and perhaps laid the foundation for the works we know composed in 1687 and 1689.

The first published continuo sonatas are by Giuseppe Jacchini. He wrote four of them; two appear as Nos. 7 and 8 in his Opus 1 (before 1695), and two as Nos 9 and 10 in his Opus 3 (1697). (His fourth sonata appears again in a slightly modified form in a collection entitled *Sonata A Tre Di Vari Autori* [*c*. 1700]).

Two other works from the seventeenth century should be mentioned. The first is Luigi Taglietti's Opus 1, *Suonate/ Da Camera/A tre due Violini, e Violoncello, con alcune/aggiunte a Violoncello Solo (1697)*. The '*alcune aggiunte a Violoncello Solo*' indicated in the title (i.e., some additional pieces for violoncello solo) are named *Capriccio* in the score. There are eight of them for violoncello and basso continuo, and they are interspersed throughout the score, which otherwise consists of ten trio sonatas. Perhaps Taglietti inserted these for variety in texture for his work, but one of them is followed by a da capo direction, indicating that it is an integral part of that trio sonata. The others are complete in themselves. At the beginning of one of these is a direction for tuning that he calls '*discordatura*' and illustrates by

indicating that this older tuning is already out of fashion. These short capriccios are quaintly charming.

The other is Angelo Maria Fioré's (*c*. 1660–1732) only known published work, the title of which is *Trattenimenti Da Camera/a Due Stromenti/Violoncello, E Cembalo E Violino, E Violoncello/*. It was first published in Lucca, Italy in 1698. A second edition was published in

12 Cello of Nicolo Gagliano, 1753

14 Cello of G. B. Gabbrielly, 1756

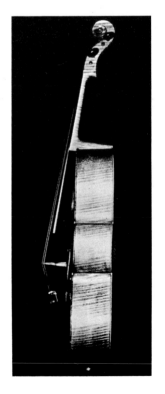

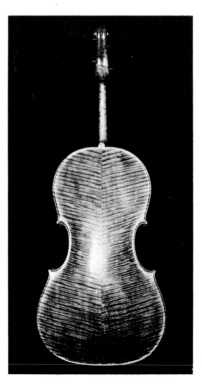

Amsterdam, with the pieces in a different order (*c.* 1705) and is here called Opus 1. There are 14 parts to this work, ten sonatas da camera for violin and continuo, three sonatas for cello (alternate viola) and continuo, and the last trattenimento (No. 14), a piece in three parts: 'Minuet, a Violoncello solo, Canone all 'Unisono a due Violoncelli, and Allegro' also in canon for two cellos. The cello range for these works is C–a^1, and I believe the tuning was C G d a, which is more convenient for the several double stops. These works of Taglietti and Fioré at least furnish further examples of the very sparse repertoire of solo cello writing in the seventeenth century.

The continuo sonata, which we have already described, was a very important vehicle for cello literature before Beethoven's first cello sonata (1796). As a generalization it could be said that all cello sonatas before Beethoven were continuo sonatas. There must be more exceptions to this generalization than I have been able to find, because I know of only one, de Leaumont's *Duo Concertant Pour le Clavecin ou le Forte Piano et Violoncelle* (1787). This work is a true duo and not a keyboard sonata with cello obbligato, which is a transitional type of composition about which we shall speak later (pp. 127–8). The composition of cello continuo sonatas starts unequivocally with the last four pieces in D. Gabrielli's manuscript of 1689 (where the four movements are referred to as ricercari). Equivocally it could have started with a 'sinfonia' for cello by G. B. Vitali (referred to by Vatielli as lost)[2] or with the sonata for violon(e) by Giannotti, if it is for cello. The only other seventeenth-century continuo sonatas in addition to those by Gabrielli are the three by Fioré and the four by Giuseppe Jacchini.

The D. Gabrielli sonatas – the G major sonata in its revised version, the revision consisting primarily of an entirely new fourth movement and certain refinements in the other movements and the A major sonata – are available in modern editions. They would seem really too mature to be the first groping efforts of cello solo writing.

Since there had not been any solo gamba music in Italy since the first part of the century, these were not in imitation of gamba music, but from the first modelled more on violin music. The harmonic vocabulary used in these sonatas was that of most composers of cello music during the baroque: the triads with inversions; seventh chords; altered chords used as secondary dominants modifying all triads except VII, and also V, VII, and N$_6$. Modulations are to nearly

♭$_3$ ♭$_1$

related keys except in one sequential repetition. These sonatas are, of course, historically very important; furthermore they are interesting musically and acceptable for programming today. The Jacchini and the Fioré sonatas have a quaint charm and also are historically full of interest.

The Eighteenth-Century Continuo Sonata to 1750

The continuo sonata of the eighteenth century is, of course, a continuation of the seventeenth-century Italian composition in this genre. A great deal of progress was made during the first half of the eighteenth century in understanding the instrument and adapting it to the medium of the continuo sonata. By far the majority of the composers during this time were Italians, regardless of where they worked, whether in Paris, in London, or in several of the German courts. This study accounts for 56 Italian baroque composers who wrote cello continuo sonatas with a few more than 300 such works to their credit. (See Appendix A). Naturally, we can discuss only several of these composers with the hope that their compositions will give an insight into the others. The choice of those to be discussed will necessarily be somewhat arbitrary.

The fine set of continuo sonatas by Pietro Giuseppe Gaetano Boni, twelve *Sonate Per Camera* Op. 1 (1717) dedicated to Cardinal Ottoboni, Corelli's patron, are musically under the influence of Corelli. The sonatas have three or four movements. Of the 41 movements in the work, only six are not in binary form. Although Boni calls these sonatas 'Per Camera', not a single movement is given a dance title, although many of the fast movements and a few of the slow ones suggest dance patterns. Their key signatures are as follows:

Example 5: Signatures in Boni's Sonatas

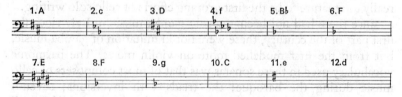

Many baroque scores have incomplete signatures, a circumstance that may represent a vestige of modal writing: major keys lacking the last sharp were mixolydian in pattern; minor keys, phrygian; major keys lacking the last flat were lydian; minor keys, dorian. When the modal inflection was not wanted, the composer simply added the accidental in the text.

Large expressive leaps characterize a number of Boni's movements. He has a penchant for the upward leap of a minor seventh and ninth. These large leaps often involve the use of the lower two strings, which give a greater resonance to many of these movements than is achieved by most of the other composers of this period. The range of the sonatas is from C–b^1, which is fairly standard for the period, but his greater use of the C and G strings distinguishes them. The harmonic vocabulary is essentially that of Gabrielli; his sense of cello sonority is superior to that of most of his contemporaries. The solo line is unusually flexible, the shape of the movements convincing; and the variety of rhythmic patterns, the flow of the music, and the presence of the quality of bel canto all combine to make the sonatas full of interest.

The three sonatas by Alessandro or Domenico Scarlatti (a manuscript copy in the Biblioteca Conservatorio G. Verdi in Milan is a possible holograph by Alessandro, but the same sonatas in a much neater hand, and possibly a copy, are to be found in the Biblioteca Communale in Bologna, attributed to Domenico), and one sonata each by Nicola Antonio Porpora, Francesco Scipriani, and Giovanni Battista Pergolesi[3] should be singled out as beautiful examples of bel canto writing. This quality is not unique to these composers but is rather a characteristic quality of the Italian baroque instrumental composer; consequently these works, though simple, have a charm that is lacking in the later eighteenth century, when composers became fascinated with developing the technique of the instrument.

Two sonatas found in the library of the National Museum in Prague are attributed to the legendary Franciscello. (See pp. 66–8). Surprisingly, there is nothing very unusual about these sonatas. The Sonata in D major has three movements, Amoroso, followed by an Allegro in binary form, followed by a Menuet in binary form. The Sonata in G major is in four movements: Adagio, Allegro (binary form), Adagio (6 measures long, all double stops), and a binary Menuetto. The range of the sonatas is C–d^2. The devices contained in these sonatas are broken chords (some crossing three strings), string-crossing figures, double stops, sequences, a few pedals, some expressive leaps, very little use of the C string, and few dotted rhythm patterns. The music is neither better nor worse than that of dozens of other sonatas of the period.

A remarkable music library in Wiesentheid, Germany, which is just becoming generally known, is housed in the Schönborn Castle in that town (about 30 miles east of Würzburg). There is a fine collection of cello music in this library, no doubt the result of the fact that Count Rudolf Franz Erwein von Schönborn (1677–1754) was an enthusiastic amateur cellist and collected as much cello music as he could. It is interesting to note that Lord Clark in his book *Civilisation* (p. 229) states, 'The Schönborn family, one of whom was responsible for the Residenz, [Würzburg], were really great patrons whose name should be remembered with the Medici'.

The whole library is being microfilmed, and the microfilms will be available at Deutsches Musikgeschichtliches Archiv in Kassel. The cello works are mostly in manuscript, and the filming of the manuscripts has not been completed. (For the Italian continuo sonatas contained in this library, see the composers marked with an asterisk in Appendix A). There are also 20 cello concertos by Platti and seven by Vivaldi, and there may be others. In addition there is a published opus from that library, an interesting work by the German Jacob Klein Le Jeune, *VI Sonates à une Basse de Violon & Basse Continue, Op. 1, Bk. III* (Nos. 13–18, which are in scordatura, with the cello tuned:

and *VI Duetti a due Violoncelli*, Op. 2 (only the sixth duet is in scordatura):

Of the Italian sonatas which I have seen from this library, Platti's are the best. There are 12 sonatas autographed 1725. According to Newman, Platti (*c.* 1690/1700–1762) was in Würzburg from 1722 until his death and was a virtuoso 'on the oboe, violin, cello, cembalo and flute and as a tenor';[4] Torrefranca, the Italian musicologist, was the first one to rediscover Platti, and he hailed him as an important pre-classicist. Although that may be true of his cembalo sonatas, these cello sonatas are early works and strictly baroque. They sound excellent with only two cellos – the proof of a good continuo sonata – and they should be given a modern edition.

Giorgio Antoniotti (*c.* 1692–*c.* 1776) was an Italian theorist who was born in Milan but spent about 20 years in London. His only known composition, *XII Sonate/le Prime Cinque/à Violoncello Solo e Basso/e le Altre Sette/a due Violoncelli Overo due Viole di Gamba/*Op. 1, was published in 1736. In spite of the indication in the title that the last seven duets could be played alternately on the gamba, these sonatas were definitely conceived in terms of a cello with normal tuning. It was not unusual for composers of that time, or publishers, to indicate that a certain set of pieces was written for alternate instruments, a practice inspired by the hope of increased sales. Some of the double stops and the broken chord figurations are idiomatic only to the cello. In three of his 'duets', Antoniotti does make a difference (from his solo sonatas) by making the continuo pattern more important in one or more movements. He does this by imitation. Antoniotti's sonatas are particularly instructive because they were written by a theorist, and they are soundly typical baroque sonatas in the following respects: (1) in being relatively short, (2) in using a limited tessitura with a sparse use of the two lower strings (range from C to $\flat^1$), (3) in lacking any technical requirement that could be labelled virtuoso, and (4) in fufilling the requirement of the day that the music was 'to move and please'. These sonatas do not require thumb position, but a few passages could be made smoother by its use.

The kinds of figuration used in these sonatas sum up the repertoire of figuration at this time: scale passages, string crossing figures, arpeggios, broken chords with or without pedal, some being bariolage (i.e. the pedal is an open string), string-leaping figures (not many), sequential patterns (many), diminutions (i.e. filling the space between two main notes with many notes of smaller value), and double stops meant to be broken into figurations. These sonatas are interesting enough to be published as a set with profit to the young cellist.

Plate 34 pictures the first movement from Antoniotti's Sonata No. 3. It will give the reader an idea of his style as well as illustrate what an eighteenth-century printed score of a continuo sonata looks like.

The Bononcini collection has been of some problem to lexicographers who have not been able to examine the work. The title reads *Six/Solos/For Two/Violoncellos/Compos'd by/Sigr. Bononcini/and other eminent Authors.* This is a set of six sonatas, only the first of which is by Giovanni Bononcini. The others are one each by Pasqualini St Martini, Caporale, Spourni (German?), and Porta. (The

St Martini in this case, was, I think, most probably G. B. Sammartini's brother Giuseppe, an oboe player and composer who lived in London from 1727 and knew Bononcini). The title of the work emphasized Bononcini's name because he was famous at the time. His instrument was the cello, but he became particularly well known as an opera composer, being called to London in 1720, where he was inevitably compared to Handel, not too favourably. He stayed in London for a decade or so.

This set of sonatas is conservative, with nothing particularly original about them. Although the British Union Catalogue carries the date of 1748 for this set, there would be nothing to preclude their having been written before then, and since Bononcini left London permanently some time between 1732 and 1735, they possibly were. Four of these sonatas have appeared in one or more modern publications, with Bononcini's, half a dozen times. The Bononcini name probably gave rise to these publications rather than any special merit of the sonatas themselves.

The Benedetto Marcello sonatas were the first baroque cello sonatas to be given modern publication. The first edition of these, by Piatti in 1874, marks the beginning of the revival of the baroque cello sonatas. Marcello's were the first because, of all the baroque composers of cello sonatas, he was probably the best known in the late nineteenth century. There is some reason to believe there was an edition of these before the Walsh edition of 1732 (Op. 2). A later edition by Le Clerc was printed in Paris in 1735, but given the Opus number 1. The key sequence of these sonatas is F, e, a, g, C G. Kolneder suggests in the preface to his edition of these sonatas (1960) that the set may have first been published in Venice between 1712 and 1717.

The problem of whether these sonatas were written alternately for the bass gamba naturally suggests itself because of passages in the text. A number of short passages are more easily played on the gamba. It is interesting to note that Marcello wrote a set of trio sonatas with alternate instrumentation, *VI Sonata/e Tre/ Due Violoncello/o/Due Viole di Gamba/e/Violoncello o Basso Continuo*, (Op. 2) published in Amsterdam. The truth of the matter is, the works sound better on the gamba, and Nathalie Dolmetsch's claim that they were written 'for viola da gamba or the violoncello' may prove correct if the first edition is eventually discovered.

For sleuth work the most interesting problem to present itself concerning these baroque cello sonatas was to try to answer the question, 'Who was Sigr. Martino?' His publication, *Sonate/Da Camera. A/ Violoncello Solo./Col Basso Continuo./*Opus 1, consists of five sonatas da camera for cello solo and basso continuo and one trio sonata for two cellos and basso continuo (three lines of music). The work is to be found in two libraries, the Civico Museo Bibliografico Musicale in Bologna and the British Museum in London (the first two pages of this score are missing). In the British Union Catalogue the date given is *c.* 1745. Sonata 3 of this collection is the *Urtext* for one of the best-known cello sonatas from the baroque period, the so-called G. B. Sammartini Sonata in G major, which has come out in several editions and is one of the few baroque cello sonatas to be recorded. A. Moffat published the first edition (Schott, 1911) and is the one responsible for equating Signor Martino with G. B. Sammartini of Milan. To be sure, the variants of Sammartini's name include 'Martino', as well as Martini, St Martini, St Martino, and so on,[5] but there is reason to doubt that this sonata is Sammartini's.

Candidates for the authorship of this work could be, besides G. B. Sammartini (1701–1775), his brother, Giuseppe (*c.* 1693–*c.* 1750, the oboe player); Padre G. B. Martini of Bologna (1706–1784); his brother Giuseppe (d. 1779), a cellist who succeeded Jacchini at the San Petronio in Bologna; Francesco Martino (i.e. François Martin), mentioned with a question mark as the composer in the Bologna Catalogue; Signor Martino (i.e., Martino Bitti) whose known compositions, which date from *c.* 1704–15, probably disqualify him as being too early; and Fillippo Martino (Martini), identified in the British Union Catalogue as the author. To make matters worse, Denis W. Stevens in his article on G. B. Sammartini in *Grove's Dictionary* (VII, 396) says, '. . . and one well-known cello sonata in G major is still published as the work of Sammartini, though it forms one of a set of twelve written by Giuseppe Dall'Abaco'. This is the sonata under discussion. Giuseppi Dall'Abaco was a cellist, son of Evaristo Felice Dall'Abaco. He was born in Brussels and was taught by his father. He was associated with the chapel orchestra at Bonn from 1729 to 1753, although during this time he spent some time in London and apparently visited Vienna. In 1753 he went to

87

live for the rest of his life in Verona. Most of his compositions are for cello, and the majority are in manuscript in the British Museum. Among these is a set of *XII Sonate Per il Violoncello, e Basso* attributed to Dall'Abaco and dated *c.* 1760. This manuscript is not signed, as are all the other Dall'Abaco manuscripts in the British Museum. Sonata No. 7 of this set is a version of the Martino Sonata in G major. The first movement is a paraphrase of Martino's first movement; the second movement is entirely different; the third movement is practically identical, and the fourth movement is omitted. This sonata could not have been composed first if Martino had published his some 15 years earlier. (It should be noted that both the dates of Martino's published work and this manuscript were assigned to these works rather than appearing on them). It seems far more likely that a printed work would be copied than that Martino published someone else's private manuscript. Therefore I think Dall' Abaco can be discarded as a candidate.

The reason for believing this sonata is not by G. B. Sammartini is based on stylistic grounds. Mishkin says: 'Whereas the G. B. Sammartini sonatas are in the typical three-movement structure of the new Neapolitan sonata, the sonatas attributed to Giuseppe are in the old-fashioned four-movements (slow-fast-slow-fast) with many of the Allegros in vigorous Baroque counterpoint. ...'[6] There are four movements to this sonata, but there is no counterpoint; the bass is a typical baroque basso continuo. One argument against Giuseppe, G. B. Sammartini's brother, is that he had already had an Op. 1 (trio sonatas for two flutes and basso continuo) published by Le Clerc in Paris; but this is by no means a final argument. It is fairly unlikely that any of Padre Martini's works would be published under the name 'Signor Martino', because he was exceptionally famous, and one would suppose that a publisher would be flattered to acknowledge such authorship. It is even now supposed that any pieces for cello that might have been attributed to him were written by his cellist brother. The set of Martino's sonatas is written so idiomatically for the cello that it is a persuasive thought that a cellist wrote it. Francesco Martino (identified by Fétis, 2nd edition, V, 474, as the French composer François Martin) did publish some cello works, an Op. 1 and an Op. 2. After examining his Op. 2, I have come to the conclusion that the style of this work is so drastically different from Martino's that the same person could not have composed these and the sonatas in question. Nothing is known about

Fillippo Martino except that he appeared in Germany as an instrumental composer of the eighteenth century. Although no final judgment can be made, my candidate for the composition of the sonatas under discussion is the Padre's brother, Giuseppe Martini, the cellist.

Although the title of the score reads '*Sonate da Camera*', only one movement is given a dance title, Siciliana. Of the total of 19 movements, 17 are in binary form; the other two are a theme and variation and a rondeau (the fourth movement of the G major sonata). The three most outstanding characteristics of these sonatas are the use of the higher range, calling for thumb position, the extensive use of double stops, and the use of harmonics. The harmonics are used in two movements which are not in binary form (II–4, the variations 3 and 6; and III–4). There is a page of preface which says:

Advertissement/Lorsque d'on recontrera des Chevrons brisés dessus et dessous les Nottes, par Exemple:

il faut placer les doigts naturellement comme les nottes sont marquées en les présentant très légèrement sur les Cordes, et en tirant de grands coups d'Archet, ce qui, forme les sons harmoniques.

(When one shall encounter the broken stripe [i.e., as on a soldier's sleeve] above or below the notes, for example, (ill.) it is necessary to place the fingers naturally as the notes are marked, pressing them very lightly on the strings, and by drawing long bow strokes, the harmonics are formed).

The following illustrates his use of harmonics:

Example 6: Martino. Sonata 2, 4th Movement, Variation 6

Double stops are a feature of the score. Undoubtedly such a series as the following should be broken up into a pattern:

Example 7: Martino. Sonata 1 – 2nd Movement

The other special feature of Martino's sonatas is his use of the higher ranges of the cello. The range of these sonatas is from C to a♭², and all the sonatas call for thumb position. Martino uses four clefs, the bass, the tenor, the alto (used more than twice as often as the tenor clef), and the C-soprano clef, which is used for the highest ranges.

Example 8: Martino. Sonata 5 – 3rd Movement

The kinds of figuration that Martino uses are repetition of patterns, sequential patterns, batteries with pedals, string-crossing figures, arpeggios, scale passages, repeated note figures, and pedal points, which are all idiomatic for the cello.

There is no doubt the composer was interested in effects, but that he could also write attractive music is evidenced by the popularity of the Sonata No. 3 in G major.

Salvatore Lanzetti (*c.* 1710–*c.* 1780) was a Neapolitan cellist who spent a considerable time in London. He came to London no later than 1739 and perhaps stayed to *c.* 1760, about the year of his last English reprint. When he returned to Italy he served as a cellist in the royal chapel at Turin, where he died. (His cello method is referred to on page 76).

The number of cello sonatas Lanzetti wrote is obscured by the number of reprints made of some of his sets. His first publications are French and number at least three, Op. 1 (12 Sonatas), Op. 5 (6

Sonatas) and Op. 6 (6 Sonatas). The five English reprints of these three sets offer only one new sonata (the Sonata No. 5 of Cooke's reprint, which brings the number of his printed sonatas to 25). There are in addition six manuscript sonatas in the Bibliothèque Nationale in Paris and four manuscript sonatas in the Westdeutsche Bibliothek at Marburg/Lahn, Germany, attributed to S. Lanzetti. These four sonatas have less rhythmical variety and a less varied texture than the published ones. His published sonatas Op. 1 and Op. 5 call for the kind of technical ability that was rather rare in his day. Many of the movements sound busy, and in them one senses a cellist exploring his instrument. The technical effect is often the dominant one.

Example 9: Lanzetti. Op. 5, Sonata 3, 3rd Movement

His Op. 6, however, offers more concentration on creating effective music rather than showing off the resources of his instrument. There are elements of the *galant* style in his music; the regular phrasing in many movements (especially the third) and the extensive use of triplets, with more frequent designation of dynamics and greater use of qualified titles expressing more nearly what he required for the interpretation.

Antonio Vivaldi's cello sonatas represent the culminating works in this genre during the baroque period. Actually he wrote eight sonatas, but chose to publish only six of them. There is a manuscript copy of three of his sonatas in Naples, but the first of these is the first in his published collection also. The two that he did not publish are not nearly so good as the six published ones, and it would do no good to his name if someone brought them out in a modern edition.

The delayed appreciation of Vivaldi's works (he is a twentieth-century rediscovery) is reflected in the modern publication of his cello sonatas. There was only one modern edition of his set of six sonatas before 1955, Marguerite Chaigneau's of 1916. Consequently these sonatas were not so generally known in the first half of the twentieth century as, for instance, the Marcello sonatas. Then suddenly there were four different editions from 1955 to 1960:

1. Leonard Rose, with revision and realization of the figured bass by Luigi Dallapiccola, with preface, published by International Music Company, 1955.

2. Walter Kolneder, with solo part edited by Klaus Storck, with preface, B. Schott's Söhne, 1958.

Kolneder states in his preface that he had access to the original eighteenth-century publication, lent him by Prunière's widow.

3. Nikolai Graudan, with Preface, published by G. Schirmer, Inc., 1959. For these sonatas Graudan used the original manuscript copy in the Bibliothèque Nationale in Paris.

4. Diethard Hellmann, violoncello part marked by Walter Schulz, without preface, published by Edition Peters, 1960.

The realizations of the basso continuo by Dallapiccola, Kolneder, and Graudan are very different. The Hellmann edition is similar to the Kolneder edition for its realization. Dallapiccola's realization is very interesting, very imaginative, and full of vitality, but an occasional mid-twentieth century sonority creates a startling effect. He seems to have delighted in his task and to have been challenged by it in spite of his famous saying about Vivaldi, 'the composer not of six hundred concertos but of one concerto written six hundred times over'.[7] The Kolneder edition is a very careful one but is perhaps too restrained. The Graudan edition is an excellent one, and the continuo part seems to have been written more with the cello solo line in mind than the other. Unfortunately this edition was printed on such poor paper that it does not stand up well with normal use.

The figuration in the Vivaldi sonatas is interesting and very well adapted to the cello. The great variety of figuration includes string-crossing figures, or string-leaping figures, scale passages, broken thirds, dotted rhythms, triplets, expressive leaps, with many of the fast movements containing figures propelling the rhythm, examples of Vivaldi's 'insistent rhythm'. His slow movements contain the element of bel canto. Altogether these sonatas seem to me to represent the best of the Italian baroque violoncello sonatas. To quote Graudan's preface, 'The sonatas deserve a high place in the cellists' concert repertoire'.

The publication of cello sonatas during the baroque period by composers other than Italian was sparse. No English composer to my knowledge published any until the 1760s, a small number of French composers, and only several Germans.

The French composers published the following works:

1726–37	Joseph Bodin de Boismortier. 5 books of sonatas, 2 for cello, Op. 26 (5 sonatas) 1729; and Op. 50 (6 sonatas), 1734; alternate duets for bassoon, cello, or viol. Op. 14 (1726), Op. 40 (1732) and Op. 66 (1737).
1733–40	Jean Barrière. 4 books of sonatas.
1733?	Michel Corrette. Op. 20 (6 sonatas). Also his *Method* published in 1741 contains a cello duet.
1736–44	J. B. Masse. 4 books of cello duets (Op. 1–4).
1746	François Martin. Op. 2 (6 sonatas). His Op. 1 is given the date 1760.
1749	Patouart. Op. 1 (6 sonatas). His Op. 2 was published c. 1754–61.

I have not included in this list works by Italian composers who lived in Paris and published works there during this period. (See Appendix A for J. P. Guigon, Alexandre Canavas L'Aîné, and Fedeli Saggione).

The German composers and others published the following works:

c. 1720	Jacob Klein Le Jeune – vi Sonatas, Op. 1, Bk. 3, Nos. 13–18; and Op. 2 (6 Duets).
c. 1745	Johann Sebald Triemer (d. 1761) – Op. 1 (6 Sonatas).
1746	Johann Ernst Galliard (1687–1749) – 6 sonatas (in a collection of xii Solos for the Violoncello, vi of Sigr Caporale & vi Compos'd by Mr Galliard (a preface identifies the composer as Johann Ernst) and Six Sonatas for the Bassoon or Violoncello (n.d.).
1740 (?) (a German?)	Wenceslaus Joseph Spourni – one sonata in the Bononcini collection. (He wrote other cello sonatas, Op. 4, 12, 13 & 14, but these are probably of a later date).
c. 1716–50	One Dutchman, Willem de Fesch (1687–1761) published several sets: 6 Sonatas in a collection of 12 Sonatas, the other 6 being for violin; Sonatas for two violoncellos (Op. 1 & 2); Sonatas for violoncello (Op. 4, 8 & 13).

Several points may be made in summary of the cello continuo sonata to the middle of the eighteenth century. With very few exceptions these sonatas were written in a score of two staves, the solo part on top and the basso continuo part on the bottom. The clefs used were the bass clef, the tenor clef, the alto clef, the soprano C clef, and the treble clef, the latter interpreted as notated and as an octave lower than notated. The terms used to identify these works were sonata, sinfonia, solo, trattenimento, divertimento, concertino, and duet (and later in England, lesson). They were all used as synonyms and furnish another example of the loose nomenclature in the baroque period.

The range of these sonatas shows a climbing to the higher notes as the period moves on. D. Gabrielli goes to g^1, but since his highest string was tuned to small g, it is equivalent to the position of a^1 today; Antoniotti goes to b^1, Scipriani (in his Sonate for 2 Violoncelli) to d^2, Martino to $a\flat^2$, and Lanzetti to b^2.

Among the bowing signs, the slur was common (⌒), but the détaché, symbolized by a stroke or a wedge (|,'), and the staccato (·) were used much less often although they were certainly known. Actually these signs, the détaché and the staccato, were often used interchangeably to mean what we today call staccato. Boyden says: 'In the late seventeenth century dots and strokes usually meant the same thing, but if both occurred in the same piece, the stroke generally meant a more vigorous and pronounced degree of separation than the dot'.[8] I believe this same interpretation also held for a number of the cello sonatas in the early eighteenth century. The stroke and the dot were also used occasionally in combination with the slur.

In only a few scores are dynamic marks sufficient and consistent enough to convey the composer's intent. A great deal must inevitably have been left to the taste of the performer.

Most of the scores contain figured bass symbols to a greater or lesser degree, with later scores using them more profusely. The notational survival, the custos sign, is used in almost all the scores.

Save for a very occasional sonata in five or even six movements, the sonatas are generally made up of three or four movements, with a great range in length among them. About 60% of the Italian sonata movements are in simple binary form, parallel or non-parallel, with or without recapitulation, binary forms with da capo, double binary patterns, and an occasional triple binary form. Other forms used are the rondeau (some of these are crossed with a double binary form), ritornello, three-part form, theme and variations, ciacona (chiacona), caccia (chasse), and canon. The remaining movements are in free form, that is, ones in which the continuous expansion does not create formal shapes.

Most of the movements have tempo names only. Comparatively few have dance names, though many are obviously dances. If named, the Minuetto (Minuet) is used most frequently, with others being Allemande, Saraband, Gavotta, Borea, Giga (Gigha), and Siciliana. Names used that are not dances include Canzona, Capriccio, Aria, Amoroso, Fanfare, Pastoralle, and Musetta.

The keys used are overwhelmingly in major, and very few scores employ keys of more than three sharps or flats. Many of the scores lack their full signature, so that many accidentals are supplied in the text that would otherwise be unnecessary. They also had some idiosyncrasies in using accidentals, i.e., a sharp sign was used to neutralize a flat or a flat sign to neutralize a sharp, or a bar line was not consistently considered as cancelling an accidental.

The limitation of the range, with the noticeably small use of the bottom two strings, and the average tessitura going to about a^1 naturally limits the style of these sonatas. Many, however, have a singing line that makes them attractive. The characteristic types of figuration are broken chord figures, almost all involving string crossing, figures in which two strings are used alternately (the French called them 'batteries'), and some arpeggios. A number of passages contain a pedal, scale fragments, and double stops. Many of the double stops were meant to be broken up into figurations, and occasionally the composer wrote out a measure or so of the kind of pattern he expected the performer to follow in breaking them up.

The embellishments were indicated mostly by $^+$, but also by t, $\mathcal{M}$, and tr. The choice of the embellishment to be used with the sign, $^+$, was left to the performer. The main performance practice problems presented by these sonatas, many of which are faced by an editor, are the realization of the continuo, the styles of bowings to be used, the interpretation of the double stops, the interpretation of the embellishments, certain rhythmic problems (i.e., dotted rhythms in certain contexts), and whether or not three methods of performance are available to the cellist: to be played by two cellos (the best sonatas sound well performed so), to be played by cello and keyboard – they were originally accompanied by harpsichord, or to be played with cello and keyboard plus a second cello playing the continuo line. The first two are accepted possibilities. It was a common practice in the baroque, even an ideal practice, to have two instruments realize the continuo, the harpsichord and usually a cello, at least after 1640. It is known that violinists had their cellists perform with them either with or without the keyboard. Tartini, for instance, took the cellist Vandini with him on his travels, and Corelli had his cellist. To my knowledge there is no record of a cellist's having done so. It seems logical that the third possibility would be available to the cellist. In the sonatas that I have heard with this arrangement, however, with the three instruments, the general effect is a little muddied because of the closeness in range of the two cellos. There is no reason to be dogmatic: the matter may be left to the taste of the performer.

Johann Sebastian Bach Suites for Unaccompanied Cello

The J. S. Bach suites hold a unique place in the literature of the cello. Written about 1720, they had no prototype in the cello literature of the time. The unaccompanied works by the Italians, Antonii, Gabrielli, and Galli, are stylistically so different from the Bach suites that they would not have offered a model for Bach even if he had known them, which in all probability he did not. It is not known exactly for whom they were written, but tradition has it, because of Spitta, that they were written for Christian Ferdinand Abel, a gambist and cellist at Cöthen. The cellist Christian Bernhard Linigke, is also known to have been a cellist in the orchestra at Cöthen during the time Bach was there, but his name has never been particularly linked with these suites. The first published edition did not appear until 1825, slightly more than 100 years after they were written. There was no performance tradition to guide the first editor, H. A. Probst, who followed the Westphal copy. His edition was obviously not considered an authentic interpretation, especially of the phrase articulation, which constitutes even today one of the major problems in the performance of these suites. Thus a number of editions, including several with piano accompaniment (i.e., Grützmacher, Piatti, Robert Schumann – the last never published), with their multitude of interpretations have been developed since Probst's and continue to be published. The first listing of these was by Altmann in *Die Musik* for December, 1922; the second, by Kinney. The following list incorporates these and brings them up to date:

16 Cello of Matteo Gofriller, 1729   17 Cello of Francesco Gofriller, 1

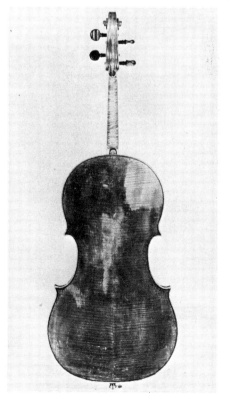

19 Cello of Santo Seraphin,
1732

1825 – H. A. Probst
1826 – J. J. F. Dotzauer
1866 – Friedrich Grützmacher
1879 – In the Bach *Gesellschaft*, vol. xxvii, ed. Alfred Dorffel
1888 – Alwin Schroeder
1897 – Norbert Salter
1898 – Robert Hausmann
1900 – Julius Klengel
1907 – Jacques van Lier
1911 – Hugo Becker
1918 – Joseph Malkin
1918 – Fernand Pollain
1919 – Cornélis Liegéois
1919 – Percy Such
1920 – Paul Bazelaire
1929 – Diran Alexanian
1933 – Paul Bazelaire – entirely revised edition
1939 – Fritz Gaillard
1941 – Enrico Mainardi
1944 – Paul Grümmer
1950 – August Wenzinger
1954 – Gino Francesconi
1963 – Marie Roemaet Rosanoff and Lieff Rosanoff
1964 – Dimitry Markevitch
1970 – Daniel Vandersall – an unedited copy of the suites
1971 – Janos Starker
1972 – Pierre Fournier

The Vandersall 'edition' was probably inevitable since everyone is more or less his own editor.

There are three contemporary manuscript copies remaining of these suites, none in Bach's handwriting. The most readily accessible is the copy made by Bach's second wife, Anna Magdalena, which can be found reproduced in the Diran Alexanian edition or in the Paul Grümmer edition. Another manuscript copy was by Johann Peter Kellner, at least a student of Bach's works. That on the title page of this copy the instrument designated is 'le Viola de Basso' (in this instance, referring to a cello) may be the reason that Wasielewski remarks that these suites may not have been written originally for the cello. A third copy is by Westphal.[9] None of these copies has very many or very precise bowing marks, and they differ from each other in many details. The spareness of bowing marks in the three early copies would seem to suggest a far greater use of detached notes than we find in today's performance. One theory, which is probably true, is that the German method of holding the bow at that time was gamba-style (palm up). This position turns the strong beats into up-bows, just the reverse from the cello-style, where the strong beats are typically down-bow. Perhaps the German method of holding the bow accounts for the difficulty in interpreting the articulation when modern cello bowing is used.

The first four suites are written for a normally strung cello of four strings. The fifth suite is written in scordatura; here the 'a' string is tuned down a whole step to 'g'. The sixth suite is written for a five-stringed cello, C G d a e^1 – whether for a violoncello piccolo or a five-stringed cello is still an unresolved question; but the balance of favour is for a normal-sized five-string cello. (There is a later version of the fifth suite, transposed from c minor to g minor, for lute.)

The six suites are all written on the same basic plan: Prelude, Allemande, Courante, Sarabande, a pair of dances, and Gigue. The pair of dances inserted between the Sarabande and Gigue are the type called 'Galanterie'; two Menuets da capo in Suites I and II, two Bourrées da capo in Suites III and IV, and two Gavottes da capo in Suites V and VI. All the movements in each suite are in the same key, except in the first three suites, in which the second of the pair is in the corresponding key. All the movements are in binary form except the Preludes. The characteristic features to note in these dances are their typical metres, the manner of beginning, the note values used, the predominant rhythmic figures, and so on. The tempos offer a performance practice problem, and contemporary performers vary greatly in their interpretation of the tempos of some of the movements.[10]

These Bach suites are unique not only because they are an isolated phenomenon in cello literature, without prototype and without offspring, not only because such great music could be wrought out of one line of music, with a few double stops (although the suites were considered as études in the nineteenth century and only with Casals and his interpretation were they first recognized for their worth), but also because they offer kaleidoscopic possibilities for interpretation. They are intriguing because there are so many ways to interpret them, many quite convincing, but none definitive. Thus the quest for the ideal interpretation continues.

The Early Concerto

In the baroque period there was no clear distinction between chamber music and orchestral music. We think of the chief distinction as being based on the number of players for each part. If there is more than one player on one or more parts, it is orchestral music, although if there is a small number of players in all, we call it a chamber orchestra. In the baroque period there was frequently an optional number of players on each part, so that the same score could be used (in our sense) for chamber music or for orchestral music.

When the baroque composers were first writing concerted instrumental music, forms and terminology had not become set. One of the confusing words was 'concerto'. One style of music labelled 'concerto' was an ensemble in which there was an obbligato part, not a *bona fide* concerto in our sense, although there were also many works which we would recognize as concertos, i.e., a virtuoso solo part as part of the texture of the orchestral score.

The first cello concertos are generally considered to be contained in Giuseppe Jacchini's Op. 4, *Concerti Per Camera/A 3. e 4 Strumenti, con Violoncello/Obbligato*, published in Bologna in 1701. The indication, à 3 or 4, refers to the number of parts Jacchini composed rather than to the number of instruments required. Actually Jacchini wrote out in each concerto five lines of music, first violin, second violin, viola (which he calls 'alto Viola'), violoncello, and basso continuo. (It was customary not to count the basso continuo line when designating the number of parts.) In about one-third of the movements, although Jacchini wrote out both parts, the second violin part is in unison with the first violin part (with some exceptions, lasting only a few measures), thus reducing the number of actual parts to three.

This Op. 4 consists of ten 'concertos', all in three movements, except No. 6. Three of the concertos have no cello obbligato parts (Nos. 3, 6 and 7), and therefore are not in any sense concertos. Of the other seven, none has an obbligato part in the second movement (except No. 5, for six measures), and Nos. 5 and 8 have no obbligato part in the first movement. The composition in the works is very primitive, and the cello writing, not yet very far advanced, would scarcely challenge a beginner today. To take just one example, in the first movement of Concerto No. 1, the obbligato appears four times, for four measures each time, with repetition of material:

Measures 11–14 (a)
Measures 31–34 (b)
Measures 39–42 (b, transposed)
Measures 46–49 (a)

Example 10: Jacchini. Op. 4, Concerto 1, 1st movement

These works prove to be ensemble music, with some cello obbligato writing. They are not concertos, really; it would seem that because Jacchini used the equivocal word 'Concerti' in the title, people who obviously had not examined the music were put off by the term and assumed that these works were concertos.

Another work is also cited as an example of the early cello concerto, Concerto No. 11 in a set of 12 concertos by E. F. Dall'Abaco, *Concerti a Quatro Da Chieso/Cioe due Violini Alto Viola Violoncello e Basso Continuo/ . . .* Op. 2 (1712–14). The Concerto No. 11 is the only one in the set with 'con il Violoncello obligato'; it is in three movements (FSF). In the first movement the cello part is largely that of steady sixteenth notes. The solo part enters in measure eight, and although it is interrupted three times by rests, it is in a quasi-perpetual motion style. The short second movement, ten measures long, is somewhat more lyrical, while the third movement is mostly continuous eighth notes, not too different from a running basso continuo. The range of the cello is D-g^1, but more use is made of the second, third, and fourth positions than in the Jacchini 'concertos'. The fabric is made up of sequences, broken chords, scale lines, and a few pedals; all three movements are shaped by repetition of motives and by a recapitulation. The fact that the cello plays a much more active role in this 'concerto', and that the outer movements are longer and more developed than in Jacchini, marks this concerto as closer to our idea of a concerto than any of Jacchini's.

It is Antonio Vivaldi, rather, to whom we can look for the first bona fide cello concertos.

Antonio Vivaldi's 27 solo cello concertos are housed in the following libraries today: the Biblioteca Nazionale in Turin, the Sachsische Landesbibliothek in Dresden, and the Schönborn Castle library in Wiesentheid, Germany. In the Turin library there are 19 concertos for one cello, one concerto for two cellos, and a concerto for cello and bassoon, more like a cello concerto with the bassoon acting as basso continuo. (According to *Grove's* Vivaldi also wrote one for one violin and one cello, two for two violins and one cello, one for one violin and two cellos, two for two violins and two cellos, and two for four violins and one cello). My inquiries have led to the information of one solo concerto housed in the Dresden library and seven in the Wiesentheid library. The contents of the Vivaldi collection in the Turin library are listed in a catalogue made by Antonio Fanna, who has divided the works into various classifications, with the cello concertos listed under F. III. Although they number 20 in all, the F. III n. 2 is the concerto for two cellos. All of these works are now available in score in the Ricordi edition under the direction of Francesco Malipiero.

It is well known that Vivaldi wrote many of his concertos, and possibly all of his cello concertos found today in Turin, for the young women in his orchestra at the Conservatorio dell'Ospedale della Pietà in Venice where he was employed irregularly from 1704 to 1740. These cello concertos are consequently student works, and many of them do not make serious demands on the part of the soloist. Most of them are what could be called 'occasional pieces', written in a hurry, intended for one performance and then to be forgotten. If Vivaldi's total concerto composition averaged one concerto a month, it would have taken him about 38 years to write his 454 concertos![11] It is no wonder, then, that we find in these cello concertos a sort of formula for their composition. Of the 19 concertos in the Malipiero edition that I have examined, all are in three movements (F-S-F). Typically the first and last movements are written in the ritornello style. This means that the opening orchestral passage (tutti), containing the main musical ideas, usually several in number, returns typically four or five times with reference to one or more of the ideas first heard in the opening tutti. It is a rondo-like scheme with the final return always being in the tonic key. In a schematic diagram these tutti passages are referred to as 'R' (ritornello). The solo passages coming between these are usually made up of the following figuration: scale passages, arpeggios, string-crossing figures, bariolage (a special effect produced by bowing back and forth between an open string and a stopped string), and the ubiquitous sequences. There are a few examples of double stops and pedals. There is a great wealth in the variety of the decorative ideas in the solo passages, and a great variety in the bowings demanded by them, in contrast to the Jacchini and Dall'Abaco concertos, in which the bowing is predominantly détaché. The slow movements are typically an accompanied solo, several being in binary form. The F. III–I is the only one with a ritornello middle movement. Several have the shape of tutti-solo-tutti, where the material in both tuttis is the same. (In a ritornello form there have to be at least two returns of the tutti). To illustrate the Vivaldi ritornello form, we may take as an example the following:

1st Movement of the Vivaldi concerto, F III–I

R I c minor (a and b motives)

S   c minor (triplet figure)

R II g minor /E♮ major (based on b)

S   E♭-f-A♭-c (vigorous figuration, sequences, return to the figuration, somewhat altered; accompaniment contains 'a')

R III c minor (based on a)

S   f minor–A♭ (varied triplet figure)

R IV f minor (based on a)

S   c minor (broken chord figure featuring string crossing, triplet figure)

R V c minor (based on b; six beats from the end is found a Neapolitan sixth chord)

The following illustration is the last solo (S) indicated above:

Example 11: Vivaldi. Concerto in C minor, F III-1, 1st movement

Copyright 1947. Permission G. Ricordi & Co., Milan, Italy

However simple some of the concertos are from a musical point of view, Vivaldi had an unerring sense of the sound of the cello. The reader should be warned that many of the Vivaldi concertos now available on record are transcriptions of his sonatas. They sound perfectly good, actually, and perhaps the reason they are frequently performed in transcription is that the worth of the musical ideas in the sonatas is on a higher level on the whole than in his concertos, so filled with figurations *per se*.

We may perhaps assume that Vivaldi began writing his cello concertos early in his first years at the Ospedale, that is, in 1704 or soon after, that their composition was scattered throughout his career at the Ospedale, and that their differences in range of difficulty was in response to the stage of progress of the particular student for whom he was writing at the time. The concerto in a minor, F. III-4, has been one of the best-known Vivaldi cello concertos.

I have never been able to locate the concerto mentioned by van der Straeten as written by Domenico della Bella and published in 1705.

A fine set of six cello concertos (one entitled Sinfonia Concertata) was written by Leonardo Leo (1694–1744). He is best known as a

Neapolitan opera composer, but his patron, like Pergolesi's, was the Duke of Maddaloni, an amateur cellist, which fact probably accounts for his interest in writing these works. They are dedicated to the Duke. The original manuscript of these concertos is to be found in the library of the Conservatorio della Pietà in Naples, and three of them have so far found modern publication (one a Russian edition). Five of the concertos are dated either 1737 or 1738; the other (in f minor) may be presumed to be of the same time. All are in three or four movements. The fast movements do not contain the rhythmic vitality so characteristic of Vivaldi: it is as if the singing master shows through, for every movement is pervaded by a singing quality, characteristic only of the slow movements in the Vivaldi concertos. The musical ideas of the Leo concertos are interesting, and the balance is easily maintained between soloist and orchestra, the latter composed only of two violins (often in unison) and a basso continuo.

Other early Italian cello concertos are one each by Nicola Antonio Porpora (manuscript in British Museum), Carlo Perroni (manuscript in Rostock, Germany), Giovanni Perroni, cellist, and Pietro Paolo Canavasso (both manuscripts in Nationalbibliothek, Vienna) and Antonio Vandini, cellist, (manuscript in Schwerin, Germany). Giovanni Platti (performer on many instruments, including cello) wrote 20 cello concertos (manuscript in Wiesentheid, Germany).

As examples of this early style of cello concerto writing, quotations from Porpora and from Platti may suffice:

Example 12: Porpora. Concerto in G major, 1st movement

Permission G. Schirmer, Inc.

Example 13: Platti. Concerto in C major, 1st movement

Permission of Count von Schonborn, Wiesentheid, Germany

The more important later eighteenth-century Italian composers of cello concertos include Giovanni Baptista Cirri, cellist, (Op. 9; Op. 14), Luigi Boccherini, cellist (certainly nine concertos, perhaps ten or even eleven; see Gérard, pp. 527–543; 661–662), Carlo Graziani, cellist (one concerto, reported in Eitner; five reported in Weber), Luigi Borghi (two concertos in D major one dated 1788), and Domenico Lanzetti, cellist (five manuscript concertos in Marburg/Lahn; Eitner reports six; van der Straeten in *Grove's* says ten concertos). I have not been able to verify whether any of the three Giuseppe Tartini concertos played by cellists today was originally written for the cello rather than the bass gamba.

A special word should be said about the fate of Boccherini's cello concerto in B♭. The Grützmacher edition of the Boccherini Concerto in B♭ (Gérard, Cello Concerto No. 9) is the one most of us were brought up on and the edition that is still played most frequently. It is more a work of Grützmacher than a work of Boccherini. Grützmacher substituted the second movement of another concerto (Gérard No. 7), and changed so many passages in the first and the last movement that it reminds one of the parody technique of the latter fifteenth and sixteenth centuries in which a composer based his own composition on another composition of his own or of someone else. The reader who is interested to compare the original version with Grützmacher's may conveniently do so by comparing the Grützmacher edition with the Edition Eulenburg No. 780, which is a miniature score and easily accessible.

For examples of cello writing in these works, we may quote from Boccherini and Borghi:

Example 14: Boccherini. Concerto in D major, Gérard #10, 1st
movement

Arranged and edited by Luigi Silva
Copyright 1964 by Belwin-Mills Publishing Corp. (formerly Franco Colombo).

Example 15: Borghi. Concerto (1788) in D major, 1st movement

Permission of Guglielmo Zanibon, Padua.   This edition revised Bonelli-Mazzacurati.

The earliest French cello concertos were four by Berteau, reported by van der Straeten, but apparently now lost. Among the important later eighteenth-century French concertos are those by Jean Baptiste Cupis, Le Jeune (two concertos, lost), Jean Baptiste Janson (Op. 15, six concertos, 1799, not yet found), Jean Pierre Duport (concerto in A major), Jean Louis Duport (perhaps six concertos), Jean Tricklir (seven concertos), Jean Baptiste Bréval (seven concertos in the Bibliothèque Nationale, Paris), and Daniel François Auber (four concertos published under the name of J. M. H. de Lamarre, but actually written by his friend, Auber, the composer of opéra-comique works).[12]

A quotation from Bréval's Concerto No. 1 may represent this list:

Example 16: Bréval. Concerto in G major, 1st movement

Permission Delrieu & Cie, Nice, France.

The English school is represented, according to Weber, by Joseph Reinagle (one or more concertos), Robert Lindley (four concertos), John Garth (six concertos, 1760), James George (one concerto) and Hargrove (five concertos for bassoon or cello).[13]

A quotation from John Garth, Concerto No. 2 in B♭ major may be taken as an example from this group:

Example 17: Garth. Concerto No. 2 in B♭ major, 3rd movement

Permission Hinrichson Edition Ltd., London.

The German Austrian School was somewhat scattered, but the main centres were at Mannheim, Vienna, with north Germany represented mainly by C. P. E. Bach.

The chief representatives in the Mannheim School for this subject are Ignaz Holzbauer (one concerto, Berlin); Anton Filtz, cellist (four concertos, two in Gesellschaft der Musikfreunde in Vienna, two in Berlin); Karl Stamitz (four concertos, Eitner); Franz Danzi, cellist (two concertos, Zurich, Switzerland); and Peter Ritter (ten concertos, Library of Congress).[14]

A quotation from Peter Ritter's d minor concerto will illustrate this group (*see overleaf*).

Example 18: Ritter. Concerto in d minor, 1st movement

Courtesy of Mrs Martha Jane Bishop.

C. P. E. Bach left three cello concertos, which he also wrote in a flute version. Indeed, the B♭ major concerto was probably a third version of it, because it was originally a harpischord concerto.[15] The keys of the concertos are a minor, B♭ major, and A major. A quotation from the a minor concerto will illustrate his style:

Example 19: C. P. E. Bach. Concerto in a minor, 1st movement

Permisson Schott & Co., Ltd.

Several cello concertos of two early Viennese composers should be mentioned. Georg Matthias Monn (1717–50) wrote an original cello concerto in g minor (which he later adapted as a harpsichord concerto), for which Arnold Schönberg realized the continuo part and made a piano reduction of the orchestral score. This concerto was first published in Volume 39 of the *Denkmaler der Tonkunst in Österreich* (1912). Schönberg also made an adaptation of Monn's Harpsichord Concerto in D major for the cello in 1932, which he dedicated to Casals. This adaptation is very elaborate and frankly not very convincing for style. The following is a quotation from the g minor concerto:

Example 20: Monn. Concerto in g minor, 1st movement

Permission Universal Edition.

Georg Christoph Wagenseil's (1715–77) two cello concertos were brought to light only in 1953, when their autographed scores turned up at an auction sale in Vienna. The Concerto in A major, composed in 1752, was given its first performance on 7 June 1956 at a music festival in Vienna, with Enrico Mainardi as soloist. He also became co-editor of the first printed edition, published by Ludwig Doblinger in 1960. The second concerto, in C major, composed in 1763, was given its first performance in 1962 by Mainardi, also the co-editor of the Ludwig Doblinger publication of 1963. A quotation from the slow movement of the concerto in A major will offer an example of Wagenseil's cello writing:

Example 21: Wagenseil. Concerto in A major, 2nd movement

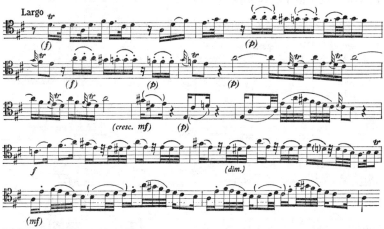

Permission of Musikverlag Doblinger, Vienna.

The Krafts, father and son, both cellists, were important Viennese composers of cello music. Anton Kraft (1752–1820), a Bohemian by birth, was employed as first cellist by Prince Esterházy, 1778–90, during Haydn's tenure there as Kapellmeister. For a time Haydn taught Kraft in composition. There has been a considerable amount of polemic about whether Anton Kraft wrote the famous Haydn Concerto in D major. The argument started in 1837 with Schilling's article on Kraft in his *Encyclopaedia* published that year. In this article he stated that Kraft wrote this concerto, presumably obtaining this information from Kraft's son, Nicolaus. The whole controversy is reviewed in the Introduction (by Josef Marx) to the publication of Anton Kraft's Sonata Op. 2, No. 2 for Cello and Piano or 2 Celli alone (McGinnis & Marx, 1948). The best I can make out of it all is that it is possible that Anton Kraft gave a sketch of this concerto to Haydn during the short time in 1779 when he was his composition student, which sketch was not returned, and that Haydn finished it for some reason, not known, in 1783. In Baker's *Biographical Dictionary* one reads: '. . . but it is now generally agreed by specialists that it is an authentic work by Haydn'. It was published under Haydn's name, while he and Anton Kraft were both living, by J. André à Offenbach in 1805. Only one cello concerto by Anton Kraft is known, a concerto in C major, published by Státní Hudební Vydavatelství in Prague in 1961. The three movements are Allegro aperto, Romanza, and Rondo alla Cosacca. The following quotation is from the third movement:

Example 22: Kraft. Concerto in C major, 3rd movement

Nicolaus Kraft (1778–1853), Anton's son, was also a famous cello virtuoso. When Prince Esterházy died in 1790, the Krafts moved to Vienna, where Nicolaus became the cellist for a time in the Schuppanzigh Quartet. Nicolaus later studied a year with J. P. Duport in Berlin, and eventually settled in 1814 in Stuttgart. He is credited with five cello concertos.

Joseph Haydn appears to have written six cello concertos, of which only four have so far been found. A concerto in C Major was discovered in 1961 in the Radenín castle collection in the National Museum in Prague and first published by Státní Hudební Vydavatelství in 1963. It is thought that this is an early work, perhaps his first cello concerto, dated *c.* 1765. Another concerto in C major first appeared in an edition by David Popper 'after a sketch', undated, and appeared again in 1959 in a Russian edition. Besides the famous concerto in D major, Op. 101 (1783), there is a second concerto in D major. The famous D major concerto was first published in an edition by F. A. Gevaert, the Belgian composer and musicologist who became head of the Brussels Conservatoire. This is the edition that is the best known even today. In making his edition, Gevaert took many liberties with the original score. He cut the first movement in three places, changed the figuration and the rhythm in some

Cello of Lorenzo Guadagnini, 1741

places, changed a few passages completely, and added 16 measures in the third movement. He did not do so much damage to the original solo part, as Grützmacher did with the Boccherini concerto in Bb. The original scoring for most of the early cello concertos had been a string accompaniment, but in the later eighteenth century two oboes and two horns were added, sometimes *ad libitum*. To this original scoring of the Haydn concerto Gevaert added flutes, clarinets, and bassoons; and in all it is his orchestration that alters this score most from its original form.

The following is a quotation from the C Major concerto, recently discovered:

Example 23: Haydn. Concerto in C major, 1st movement

With the concerto literature of the eighteenth century, obviously I have chosen to let the music speak for itself. Since the concerto has always been the main vehicle for displaying the capabilities of an instrument, the technical command of the instrument as understood by the various composers can be appreciated by looking at passages from their music. It is hard to judge from fragments the musical worth of a composition, but all of the examples are from composers of merit.

The Continuo Sonata from 1750 to 1800

In the second half of the eighteenth century, not only did Italians continue to compose continuo sonatas, but interest in writing them spread throughout various countries in Europe, with France and Germany in the lead. To represent the Italian composers of this period, of which there were about 30, we may take for examples Carlo Graziani and Luigi Boccherini. Graziani was typical, whereas Boccherini was not only a great cellist but also the most important composer for the cello in this period.

Not much is known about Carlo Graziani (d. 1787) except that he was born in Italy, that he was J. P. Duport's predecessor as cello teacher to the then Crown Prince, Frederick William II, in Berlin, and that he was active for a time in London. He published Op. 1, 2, and 3, each a set of six sonatas, c. 1760–70. He still used the bass, tenor, alto, and soprano C clefs (indicating an Italian training). His sonatas have a rather stereotyped formal design: all the first movements are in a binary form, with recapitulation (rounded binary); most of his second movements are short, with a statement of the main material, a modulatory section, and a return to the main idea in the tonic key; and the third movements rondeaux, minuettos, some combined with variations, a few binary forms, an aria with variations, and a caccia, also in binary form.

In deciding whether to label Graziani a pre-classicist or a classical composer, one should look for three features of classicism in his rounded binary forms, particularly in his first movements: a second theme in the first part at the point of modulation, or perhaps a theme derivative of the first theme (so frequent with Haydn) instead of simply figuration; a true development of the stated themes, instead again, of figuration; and a recapitulation of the second theme as well as the first theme. None of the sonatas fulfils all these requirements.

For instance, he has a true second theme in the first movement of sonata Op. 2, No. 6, which recurs in the recapitulation; but after he begins the development with a three-measure reference to the first theme, the rest is just figuration. Some of his development sections have elements of a true development; they come close to that in a classical form, but they are on the borderline, and I believe it would be more accurate to label him still as a pre-classicist. Graziani represents the Italian group as still retaining a singing quality in their works. That his Op. 3 was printed with a realization by Giacomo Benvenuti as Vol. 15 of *I Classici Musicali Italiani* attests to a contemporary interest in Graziani as one of the neglected but worthwhile composers of his period. As this edition supplies suggestions for the interpretation of many of the small notes and embellishments, it offers the student a practical reference in these matters.

Luigi Boccherini's name, at least, is well known among musicians today even if the layman knows practically none of his music. The formerly much played Boccherini *Minuet* is scarcely ever heard now, leaving the violoncello concerto in B♭ major, as mutilated in the Grützmacher edition, his most frequently performed composition today. Actually, in his own day his name had been more often associated with his string quartets and quintets, which did not survive him in performance more than a generation because of the change in musical taste from classical to romantic music.

Until recently it was not even common knowledge among cellists, and may scarcely be yet, that Boccherini wrote 28 or 29 cello sonatas, two duets (but one a duplicate of a sonata), and certainly nine, and perhaps ten or eleven cello concertos. The six Boccherini sonatas edited first by Piatti and the above-mentioned Grützmacher version of the B♭ major concerto were all of his work known to cellists in the earlier part of this century. The research undertaken in the last few decades, however, has altered this state of knowledge.

Boccherini was a cellist himself and, because of his particular patronage, continued as a practising cellist for much of his life. He represents in the history of the cello the only high-class talent as a composer combined with the talent as cello virtuoso. The great quantity of literature during the last two centuries written by cellists has faded into oblivion because none of it represents great literature – the composing talent was not there, only craftsmanship. Boccherini's works, on the other hand, may enjoy a revival because of the worth of the music. The present interest in them is augmented by the recent biography by Mme. Germaine De Rothschild (1965) and the definitive catalogue of his works by Yves Gérard (1969).

Boccherini was born in Lucca, Italy, son of a double bass player who also played the cello. After early instruction on the cello by his father, he was placed with the Abbate Vanucci in Lucca and later with G. B. Costanzi in Rome. His first position was as first cellist at the Imperial Theatre in Vienna, to which city he returned twice for employment. Although he came back to Lucca, thinking to settle there, it was not long before he moved on to Milan, where Sammartini was the attraction. He returned to Lucca once more, where he joined Manfredi, the violinist, for a joint tour. They arrived in Paris in 1767, and Boccherini made his début at the Concert Spiritual in 1768. While they were there, the Spanish Ambassador persuaded them to go on to Spain where, after some difficulty, Boccherini was employed by Don Luis, the brother of the king. His employment began in November 1770, and lasted until Don Luis' death in 1785.

It is pleasant to read that for these 15 years Boccherini was appreciated and in comfortable circumstances. He composed constantly and performed in the chamber concerts as soloist and in the cello quintets (2 violins, viola, 2 cellos) for Don Luis' establishment. The sympathetic patronage reminds one of Haydn's situation with the Esterházys, although Haydn's tenure was almost twice as long. Boccherini's music belonged to the king, by contract, so that until Don Luis' death in 1785, he was not free to compose for others. Yet a concert given in Madrid in 1782 or 1783 for the Ambassador of Frederick the Great helped to change the course of Boccherini's life. This concert included on its programme Boccherini's Op. 33. The Ambassador, knowing that the Crown Prince Frederick William II was an amateur cellist, sent him the score, with Don Luis' permission, and Frederick William II became a convert to Boccherini's music. Finally, in 1786, after Don Luis had died and Frederick William II had become king, he made Boccherini 'composer to the King' and paid him well. Whether or not Boccherini ever actually went to the Prussian court still remains an open question. Nothing is known about the years of his life from 1787 to 1796. Some biographers assume he was in Germany for part of that time, but according to Mme. Rothschild there is not one single piece of evidence for this assumption; rather, several negative facts indicate that he was not.

(The one 'signed' letter dated 30 July 1787, written in Breslau, is not now considered authentic). At Frederick William's death, Boccherini's patronage at the Prussian court ceased. Then in 1796 Ignaz Pleyel in Paris became his publisher. This arrangement lasted into 1799, but it was a relationship frustrating to Boccherini, as the letters quoted in Mme Rothschild's book indicate. Boccherini's health, never strong, was deteriorating by 1799. Unfortunately, both his wives had predeceased him, and only two sons of his five or six children survived him. He died on 28 May 1805.

Possibly the reason that it is these particular six Boccherini sonatas that all cellists know is that Piatti, who made the first edition of them, would have had access to an eighteenth-century copy of them in the British Museum. Probably no others were known to him. Of the six, the A major sonata is by all odds the one most frequently performed. In fact, it is one of the few frequently performed eighteenth-century sonatas. A seventh sonata by Boccherini was published in 1961 by Schott and Company. It is Gérard No. 565, and oddly enough much of the sonata is based on the same material as the B♭ concerto. The foreword of the Schott edition claims that Grützmacher based his edition of the concerto on this sonata, but why on this sonata rather than Boccherini's concerto in B♭ is not clear. It seems more likely that Gérard comes nearer the truth when he states that the sonata was probably Boccherini's sketch for his own concerto. There are many sonatas among the other 21 that are as good as the known six sonatas and the seventh one, and an edition should be made of the complete set.

Boccherini favours the three-movement plan of F-S-F, although several of the sonatas exist in two versions, with one version conforming to the F-S-F plan, the other in two movements. The majority of the movements are in binary form, with about one fifth in other forms.

A word should be said about the use of the treble clef in these sonatas. In general the treble clef is to be interpreted as one octave lower when following a bass clef and as notated when following a tenor clef or when starting a movement or immediately following a double bar (even if the bass clef is used just before the bar), but occasionally it must be interpreted as notated even if following a bass clef (Sonata No. 24, 3rd movement m. 40, 59).

There is nothing one can point to that distinguishes these sonatas in any technical way from others of the period. Boccherini uses the same types of figuration, the same devices, and the same forms that other composers use. The difference between these and other sonatas is simply the level of inspiration – that intangible component. He does use a great variety of formal patterns. Unlike Graziani, for example, who is fairly stereotyped in his use of the binary form, Boccherini uses a great variety of such forms; his favoured one (more than 30%) is a parallel binary with only the second theme area recapitulated. It comes close to Domenico Scarlatti's plan. Although D. Scarlatti died in Madrid in July 1757, and Boccherini did not arrive there until the end of 1768 or perhaps the beginning of 1769, one wonders whether Boccherini might have been influenced by D. Scarlatti's music.

These sonatas were not the only ones written by a fine cellist, but they reflect an unusually comprehensive understanding of the potential of the cello, as understood in the late eighteenth century.

As representative of the late eighteenth-century French school, we may take J. P. Duport and J. B. Bréval. (See Jean Shaw's dissertation, 'The Violoncello Sonata Literature in France During the Eighteenth Century').

Jean Pierre (*l'aîné*) Duport (1741–1818) was a pupil of Berteau, the founder of the French school of cello playing, and was himself an important teacher of the cello. His students included his younger brother, Jean Louis Duport, who acknowledges that fact in the Preface to his *Essai*. J. P. Duport's career was launched with his successful *début* at the Concert Spiritual in 1761. During the next 12 years he was an orchestral player (Prince de Conti's orchestra) and performed in England and Spain. In 1773 he went to Berlin at the invitation of Frederick the Great (d. 1786) and stayed there the rest of his life, though he retired in 1806. Duport taught the king's nephew and successor, Frederick William II, the cello amateur of whom we have already spoken.

Four sets of sonatas by J. P. Duport are known today, one set of which is for cello or violin. The *Six Sonates/Pour la/Violoncelle/ Dediées/Au Roi de Prusse/Frederic Guillaume II./* . . . in the Berlin and Amsterdam edition, 1788 (there is also a French edition of this work [1800] which is called Op. 4) may be chosen as offering good examples of the late French eighteenth-century cello sonatas.

To describe the shape of these J. P. Duport sonatas is to describe typical pre-classical forms. The sonatas are all composed of three movements, F-S-F, except the last movement of Sonata No. 1, an andante with variations. The first two movements of each are in binary form, most parallel binary with or without recapitulation. In the first half of the binary forms there are two key levels but without a second theme. After the double bar there is no development section but rather figuration, though several different keys are lightly touched upon. Where the tonic key is re-established, the original thematic material is not necessarily refered to again. The third movements are variations or rondos except in Sonata No. 5, a parallel binary. This is the movement that is quoted as the tenth of the 21 exercises found in Part II of J. L. Duport's *Essai*. The more regular phrasing, the slow harmonic rhythm, traditional modulations, use of triplet and rocket arpeggios, all point to the preclassical school.

The range of the solo part in these sonatas is from $C - a^3$. It should be noted that Duport frequently writes the cello solo in the treble clef, to be interpreted as transposed down an octave; when he indicates 8 va—, the notes are played as written; followed by 'loco', they are transposed down the octave. Other directions in the score are 'arpeg'. to indicate that the written block chords are to be played as arpeggios; 'segue', that the written block chords are to be broken into the pattern just established; and 'armonique', indicating that the passage is to be played with harmonics. The embellishments, called 'agréments' in France, are tr and ᴧ : respectively, trill and type of mordant; there is a scattering of small notes. There are a number of holds in the score (⌒), some inviting improvised cadenzas. The types of figuration used are scale passages, arpeggios, broken chords, batteries (fast passages in which the bow changes strings on alternate notes), wide leaps, and double stops. There are few sequences, and some repetition of figuration. The writing is not spun out, but more controlled, compact, and regular. Various bowing marks appear, calling for many types of articulation.

These sonatas do not make more demands on the performer's technique than many previous sonatas, but they offer a typical conception of the understanding of the cello by a French virtuoso of the late eighteenth century. The musical ideas are for the most part conventional, but Duport's sonatas had a fascination in their day that must have been prompted largely by the technical display of the music. Mozart borrowed Duport's Minuet theme for his variations, K. 573:

Example 24: Mozart. Nine Variations on a Minuet of Duport, K. 573

The reader may compare a sample of Duport's composition with one of Antoniotti's (see Plates 34 & 35) as an illustration of how the conception of cello writing changed in the 50 years, from the 1730s to the 1780s. The Duport basses are no longer baroque basso continuos but are only a harmonic support for the solo. The consistently higher tessitura is typical, and the Duport solo line is no longer a singing line, the bel canto of the baroque period.

Jean Baptiste Bréval (1756–1825) studied cello with Cupis and had his main career as cellist with the Paris Opera orchestra (1781–1806) and as professor of cello at the Paris Conservatory (1796–1802). He was a prolific composer and, among other instrumental works, published the following for cello:

Op. 2   – 6 duets for 2 cellos (*c.* 1770?)
Op. 12 – 6 solos for cello/b.c. (*c.* 1800)
Op. 25 – 6 duets for 2 cellos 'for the easy study of the different clefs'
      (*c.* 1790; later editions)
Op. 28 – 6 solos for a cello/b.c. 'made easy and agreeable' (*c.* 1790)
Op. 40 – 6 sonatas *'non difficiles'* n.d.
7 concertos
A method: *Traité du Violoncelle* ... Op. 42, which contains 12 sonatas (3 attributed to others) and six duos as well as many other etudes.

He is a little better known than some of his French contemporaries because six of his sonatas have had modern publication, two having been available for a number of years, the C major (Op. 40, No. 1) in several editions and the G major (Op. 12, No. 5) as well as two of his concertos. The five 'Concertinos' as edited by Feuillard for the Delrien Company are simply sonatas chosen from among his various opera numbers, i.e., Concertino 11 is the Op. 40, No. 1 in C major.

His sonatas (including duos) range from easy to difficult, and it is more than likely that the easy sonatas were written for students, to give them something of musical worth to play at the beginning stages.

A look at a set of six sonatas (Op. 12 in the Preston edition, London; same set identified as Op. 28 in the Longman & Broderip edition. A different set of six sonatas is contained in the Paris edition of Öricheler as Op. 28), may give some insight into his style. The solo line is written in the treble clef (with the exception of five spots where he uses the bass clef) to be played down an octave except when the sign ⌐8⎯ appears. Dynamic marks are not liberal. In Sonata No. 2, 1st movement, he uses the term 'rinf.' (rinforzando) in four successive measures, followed by *ff* in the fifth measure, which is duplicated in the recapitulation. Since he uses the term 'cres.' in Sonata No. 3, 1st and 3rd movements, one is left a little puzzled how to interpret the exact meaning of Bréval's 'rinf'. The only embellishment sign is 'tr,' and the score is not overburdened with them. There are a few small notes ♪ or ♪ or ♪ , where the small note gets half the value of the note. The relatively few bowing signs include the slur, staccato under the slur 𝄐♫♫ , the dash, and a combination of these three bowing styles, ♫♫ ♫♫ , as well as the slurred dash. There are several holds which may imply an improvised cadence cadenza, although Bréval has actually written out his own cadenza in three instances.

The range of these sonatas is C to d^3, although the tessitura is more like c to c^2. All the sonatas have three movements: the first movements are all binary forms; the second three-part forms or, as in Sonatas Nos. 5 and 6, through-composed, albeit with a short reference to the opening measures in the dominant key shortly beyond the middle of the movement; the third movements include a three-part Minuetto, two Presto movements in binary form, and three Rondos. Bréval was not partial to the three-movement scheme, however: four of his sonatas in Op. 28, all of the sonatas in Op. 40, and two of his own sonatas in Op. 42 were in two movements, while eight of his own sonatas in Op. 42 are in one movement.

Bréval's technical passages involve the usual scale passages, arpeggios, double stops, and many string-crossing figures. In the fast movements he invariably writes passages of figuration in eighth or sixteenth notes that convey a lively and attractive sense of motion, and his slow movements are not without lyricism. The cello sounds well in these sonatas, which require a good technical command of the instrument, at least in performing the more difficult ones. One does not have the impression that here, as in so much of the French cello music of the time, it is virtuosity for its own sake.

In Germany in the second half of the eighteenth century there was an accelerating activity in the composition of continuo sonatas. The basic research in this field has not been undertaken and there is a need for a doctoral dissertation covering the subject. In both France and England there is one central library, the Bibliothèque Nationale (which now also houses the Paris Conservatoire library) in Paris and the British Museum in London where one can find the majority of works composed in those countries, but there is no comparable central library in Germany. Before World War II Berlin was a centre with its Preussische Staatsbibliothek (formerly Königliche Bibliothek) and the Königliche Hausbibliothek. It is my understanding that the Preussische Staatsbibliothek was divided into three parts after the war, one third being in East Berlin and known as the Deutsche Staatsbibliothek, one third being in Marburg/Lahn, named Staatsbibliothek der Stiftung Preussischer Kulturbesitz, and one third in an unknown part of Polish-occupied German provinces. About one third of the Königliche Hausbibliothek was destroyed in the war; the rest was removed by the Soviets to an unknown destination. Many of the cello works, therefore, listed in Eitner's Quellen-lexikon are no longer to be located.

Anton Kraft may be taken as an example of the height of the German eighteenth-century school continuo sonata development. In addition to the Concerto in C, which we have already mentioned, Kraft published (relevant to our subject) Op. 1, *Trois Sonates/Pour le/Violoncelle*; Op. 2, *Drei grosse Sonaten/für das Violoncell mit Begleitung eines Basses*; Op. 5 and 6, Grand Duos for 2 cellos, and without opus number a Divertissement for cello with bass.

An examination of Kraft's Op. 1 and Op. 2 reveals a very able cellist, but a less than great composer of the pre-classical vein. If Luigi Boccherini and Anton Kraft are selected as perhaps the most talented composers among cellists of the late eighteenth century, Anton Kraft suffers considerably from the comparison. His works are bland and lack the spark of real genius, though they are composed intelligently. They are too much padded with cello figuration for its own sake, often going from one figuration to another without conveying any sense of inevitability. Especially in his longer sonatas the third sonata of Op. 1 and the three sonatas of Op. 2, a reaction of tedium sets in despite many attractive spots and some interesting figurations, which altogether exploit many of the technical resources of the cello. The works, in short, are verbose. The six sonatas are all cast in three movements, F-S-F, without any innovations in their formal structure. The works are interesting to the historian, as representing a high point in the German conception of the late continuo sonata, but I doubt that the sonatas will ever find their way back into the current repertoire.

Anton Kraft's son, Nicolaus (1778–1853), was an exceptionally fine cellist also, and for a time a member of the first famous string quartet, the Schuppanzigh Quartet, which gave the *première* performance of many of Beethoven's quartets at Prince Lichnowsky's palace. Nicolaus' compositions include five concertos, a *Scène pastorale* for cello and orchestra, a *Fantasy* for cello and string quartet, and a number of cello duets, eight of them called *Divertissements progressifs*.

Raynor Taylor (*c.* 1747–1825) was born in England, but lived for a time in Edinburgh, where he knew J. G. C. Schetky and his son J. George Schetky, both cellists, and also Alexander Reinagle, who was his student there. Taylor went to the United States in 1792, living first in Baltimore, then Annapolis, and then settling in Philadelphia, where he died. Reinagle preceded Taylor, going over to the States in 1786, and was active in both New York and Philadelphia; and J. George Schetky also went to the USA, possibly in company with Taylor, and also settled in Philadelphia. These three musicians were important figures in the musical life of America in the late eighteenth and early nineteenth centuries.

The 'Six Solos for Violon Cello' by R. Taylor were probably composed for one of the Schetkys. That the manuscript score of this work is now in the Library of Congress does not mean that he wrote the work in the United States. (By the way, Taylor's sonatas were not listed in the card catalogue at the time I came across them. They are to be found attached within the same binding following a set of six sonatas written by J. G. C. Schetky in the 'case' collection, the volume being designated as a gift by Hans Kindler on 25 April 1936).

The R. Taylor sonatas are delightful. Two of them, Nos. 4 and 6 were recorded in the 1950s by Luigi Silva, cellist, and Arthur Loesser, who was playing on a Challis piano, English model, *c.* 1795. The de Leaumont duo in Silva's edition is recorded on the other side. The realizations for the Taylor sonatas were made by Silva, and these could be taken as a model for others wishing to make realizations that are stylistic and therefore bring out the inherent beauty of these continuo sonatas. This record is a collector's item for cellists.

The sonatas, with the limited range of C to b^1, are in three movements; half of them start with a slow movement, with a fast second; the others vice versa. The third movements are dances, except the Allegro Moderato in the fourth sonata. The third movement of the sixth sonata, which is a Giga, is not in binary form as one might expect, but a three-part form, with a novel middle section, designated as rolled chords and giving an organ-like effect.

Two points should be made in summary about all cello continuo sonatas, of which my studies have disclosed more than 1,000. We may assume that there are more than that.

First of all, the generalization may be made that these cello continuo sonatas were, I believe, originally written for the cello and not for the bass gamba and then transcribed, as claimed by two writers, Paul Grümmer in the introduction to his *Viola da Gamba Schule* (1928) and Eugenio Albini in his article on Domenico Gabrielli in *Revista musicale italiania* (1937). To review the main arguments of my article on this subject in the *Journal of the Viola Da Gamba Society of America* (Vol. v, 1968): Grümmer states: 'The following Sonatas und [*sic.*] Suites were written originally for the viola da gamba. Though transcribed, most of them are available for this instrument. All they want are the double-stopping (thirds and sixths) here and there, which can easily be restored. (The following compositions are published by B. Schott's Söhne, where they may be had)'. Then follows this list of composers:

 J. B. Bréval
 G. Cervatta [Cervetto senior]
 J. B. Loeillet, i and ii
 G. B. Martini [G. B. Sammartini]
 G. B. Grazioli
 Francesco Guerini
 Quirino Gasparino [Gasparini]

G. Pianelli, ɪ and ɪɪ
S. Lanzetti, ɪ and ɪɪ
Hervelois, Suites ɪ and ɪɪ
Marais
J. B. Forqueray
G. B. Tillier [J. B. Tillière]
Bertau [Berteau]
Galeotti [Stefano Galeotti]
B. Galuppi, etc. [the implication being all of the sonatas.]

Of the six French composers on the list, Hervelois, Marais, and Forqueray were gambists, and the literature they wrote was for their instrument. No one has claimed that they wrote for the cello. Of the other three, Berteau was the founder of the French School of cello playing. He was originally a gambist but changed to the cello, giving his cello *début* recital in Paris in 1739. The cello concertos and sonatas by him referred to by van der Straeten in the *Grove's Dictionary* article on Berteau have not been available for study, but it seems highly improbable that Berteau, having been converted to the cello, would write for the instrument that was being outmoded in France during the time of his cello career. The two other Frenchmen were cellists, Tillière and Bréval; indeed, each wrote a cello method. There is no doubt at all that their works were originally for the cello. Loeillet is the only other composer on the list who was not Italian; he was a Belgian flutist and oboist. There is no evidence that he ever wrote for gamba. His cello sonata in the Cello-Bibliothek series, No. 16, is a transposed transcription of his flute sonata, Op. 3, No. 5. Of the nine Italian composers, not one is from the first generation of Italian composers of cello music (*c.* 1689–1720). If we remember that the gamba went out of fashion in Italy about 1640, it would have been highly unlikely that even the first generation of Italian composers would have written for the gamba and then transposed their works for the cello, especially since so many of them were cellists. It is even less likely that succeeding generations of Italian composers of cello music would do so. I have examined most of this music, and have come to the conclusion that Grümmer's statement (undocumented) was irresponsible. The one set of sonatas (not specifically mentioned by Grümmer) that did seem to me possibly written originally for gamba was the set by Marcello (see pp. 86–7). Albini mentions for the illustration for his statement of this theory the composers

Gaspare Visconti, F. Guerini, and S. Lanzetti, and gives an illustration from S. Lanzetti, which does pose a problem:

Example 25: Lanzetti (?). Sonata in A major

He claims that the version in this sample is the original gamba version of a Lanzetti A major sonata, and that the chords were changed as indicated in the cello transcription. This sonata is not among the 35 cello sonatas of Lanzetti that I have been able to locate (see pp. 90–91). B. Schott's Söhne did publish this work as Lanzetti's sonata in A major with the chords as indicated above for cello (second movement, mm. 15–16). I found it interesting that I stumbled on this very sonata in a collection of six published sonatas for violin by Francesco Guerini, *Sonates A Violino con Viola Da Gamba o'Cembalo*, Op. 1; it appears as the second sonata in this set, is transposed to B♭, and reverses the last two movements. The chords are as they appear in the cello version. Until the original version of this sonata is found, I fear the matter will have to rest here.

The second generalization of prime importance is the obvious fact that since the composer wrote only one line for the bass, the basso continuo line has to be realized by some editor in order to be performed today. When modern editions of these sonatas began to be published in the late nineteenth century, the editorial attitude was apparently that they would have to be 'dressed up' to be palatable to the contemporary audience; consequently the sonatas were given accompaniments of romantic harmony, which of course created works with a stylistic disunity. The pieces were not convincing, and not many of them found their way into the accepted repertoire. I do not think it would be an unfair statement to say that practically all of the pre-World War II editions are unstylistic. With the explosion of knowledge about Baroque music in the third quarter of this century, the situation has improved, and there are some very good contemporary editions of a few of these works. The largest number of these sonatas have been published in a continuing collection called Cello-Bibliothek, with various editors. Past editors which the reader should be particularly warned against are such as Grützmacher and J. Salmon. For instance, the Grützmacher edition of a Geminiani sonata has adapted it so:

Grützmacher Edition	*Geminiani's set of Six Sonatas*
Introduction, Poco lento	Sonata No. 6, 1st Movement
1st Movement	Sonata No. 6, 2nd Movement
2nd Movement	Sonata No. 5, 4th Movement
3rd Movement	Sonata No. 3, 3rd Movement
4th Movement	Sonata No. 3, 4th Movement

This is known as a pasticcio; Grützmacher similarly mutilated the famous Boccherini Concerto in B♭.

In his editions of these sonatas Salmon often changes the key, changes the register (puts parts higher), exchanges movements, and so on. The above remarks are intended to warn the young cellist that he must be rightly aware of the edition of the early sonatas he performs.

The Transition to Beethoven: The Pre-Classical Piano Sonata with Cello ad libitum or obbligato

The last quarter or so of the eighteenth century saw the beginnings of piano literature, although the instrument itself had been invented towards the beginning of the century (Cristofori's first piano dates from 1709). At first the violin sonata was adapted to the keyboard, taking the top part in the right hand and the bottom in the left. Many of these early piano sonatas are in only two parts. The violin, when it was reintroduced, and later the cello, or both, first as ad libitum instruments and then as obbligato instruments, established the foundation for the media of the classical violin sonata, cello sonata, and piano trio. In the piano sonatas calling for violin or cello those with ad libitum setting were not real duos, because the piano part

was obviously more important. A real duo implies an equal importance to both parts, and in cello sonata literature, this development
practically starts with Beethoven. Even in the obbligato settings that
I have seen, the cello part is scarcely independent of the right hand
or the left hand parts of the piano. At the end of the eighteenth
century, there were then two styles: the cello continuo sonata and the
new style with the piano part written out and the cello ad libitum or
obbligato. The writing of continuo sonatas simply ceases *c.* 1800,
and the future development is worked out in perfecting the duo. It
is a curious custom that we have of labelling the duo by the name of
the instrument other than the piano, hence a duet (duo) for piano
and cello becomes known as a cello sonata. The etiquette in performing duets is for both players to use music. If only the pianist
uses music, it gives a visual impression of a soloist with accompaniment. I have seen cellists with the music properly placed on the stand
nearby, turning the pages at all the wrong times (really playing from
memory), but behaving politely toward the pianists.

Ludwig van Beethoven

Beethoven fell heir to the classical sonata form (architectural blue-
print for one movement) and the classical sonata cycle or simply,
sonata, (the group of, usually, three or four movements constituting
the work), as perfected by Haydn and Mozart and their contemporaries. The classical sonata is shaped in the following manner:

Movement I Sonata Form.

Introduction (optional)

Exposition: Theme i, bridge (or transition) for the purpose of
modulating from the tonic key, in which the work
begins, to a new key. If the work is in major the new key
will be the dominant key, if minor, frequently the
relative major; Theme ii, new key; closing section (in
the new key).

Development: Parts of one or both of the themes announced in the
exposition are developed and changed to give them new
meaning. Several modulations are characteristic of this
section.

Recapitulation: The exposition is reviewed from beginning to end with
certain modifications, all unique to each individual

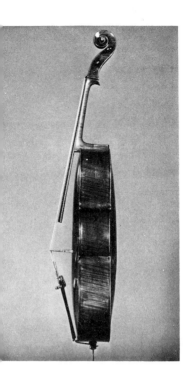

24 Cello of Matthias
Albani, 1694

25 Cello of William Forster,
c. 1780

work. One modification that is general is to put the second theme in the tonic key, hence changing the bridge passage.

Coda (optional)

Movement II   Choice of forms. It may also be in sonata form. Other choices available are three-part form, variation form, sonatina form, first rondo form, etc. This movement is usually the relatively slow movement. In classical times a typical tempo was Andante. The movement tended to become slower in the romantic period.

Movement III   If there are four movements to the cycle, this will be a double binary form with da capo, i.e., minuet and trio or with Beethoven, frequently a scherzo and trio. If there are only three movements, this movement will be omitted.

Movement IV   Choice of forms. A rondo scheme, either ABACA or ABACABA, was a frequent choice. Other choices were a rondo-sonata form (a cross between one of the rondo patterns and the sonata form), a sonata form, infrequently a theme or variations, and so forth.

As will be seen, Beethoven did not choose to adhere closely to this classical scheme for his cello sonatas, but he uses the sonata form for each of his first movements, with the freest use being in the fourth sonata.

The works that Beethoven wrote for the cello consist of five sonatas and three sets of variations. He also made a cello version of his horn sonata, Op. 17, a charming work that ought to be performed more often. (His triple concerto – piano, violin, and cello – is one of the few compositions in that genre. The cello part is difficult). The five sonatas as a group stand at the apex of the solo cello sonata literature even today. As a generalization it can be said that they are practically the first duo cello sonatas in the literature. They then represent a curious phenomenon that the greatest works are written at the beginning of a new development. Unlike his violin sonatas, these five give us examples of each of the three periods in Beethoven's life; the first period, the two sonatas of Op. 5 (in F major and G minor); the second period, Op. 69 (A major); and the third period, the two sonatas of Op. 102 (C major and D major). When the first two sonatas are labelled duo sonatas, it is with a certain qualification. They could rather be considered as culminating works in the accompanied sonata genre, because they are piano sonatas with obbligato violoncello. The original edition carried the title 'For Harpsichord or Pianoforte with Violoncello Obbligato'.

The two sonatas of Op. 5, written in 1796, are each two-movement works, somewhat curious for that time. Both movements are fast, and the first movement of each is preceded by a long, slow introduction. By the year 1796, when Beethoven wrote these, he had many models of the classical sonata cycle. Haydn, one of his teachers, had written all his symphonies and all his string quartets except the last nine, which Beethoven could have used as formal models; yet he did not choose to.

The first movement of each sonata is in sonata form, and the development section of the first sonata in F is very loose; the coda of the first movement of the second sonata is a fine example of Beethoven's so-called terminal development – a coda that strongly resembles the development section itself. The second movement of each sonata is in rondo form, uncomplicated, and with strong contrasting sections. Both sonatas contain many passages reflecting Beethoven's impetuous character; they are full of feeling and often high spirits and have a spontaneity about them that gives them away as youthful works. The second sonata has a peculiarly expressive quality that is unusually appealing, perhaps partly because of the key, g minor, although it is more often the key of c minor that elicits this type of expressiveness from Beethoven. The form of these sonatas is not so tight as that of the later three, but they are exuberant and charming works. Beethoven wrote these sonatas for the elder Duport, and played them with him at the Berlin court.[16] Beethoven dedicated these two sonatas to King Frederick William II, the enthusiastic cello amateur.

The third Beethoven sonata, in A major, Op. 69, completed in 1808 and dedicated to Baron von Gleichenstein, is probably the most frequently performed sonata in the literature for this instrument. It has that equipoise between form and expression that is the hallmark of works of Beethoven's second period. The first movement is in sonata form; the second movement is a Scherzo; and the final third movement, also in sonata form, is preceded by a brief slow introduction. This lovely slow passage is in a way extremely tantalizing; it is so beautiful and pithy that Beethoven could have created a whole slow movement out of it, but he did not. Of course, as it stands, it is a gem.

The last two sonatas, Op. 102, written in 1815, are more intellectual. They were written for the cellist, Joseph Lincke (Linke), who was at the time visiting Beethoven's good friends, the Erdodys, and the dedication of the sonata was to the Countess Marie von Erdody. Every extraneous idea is carved away, and only the minimum essential material remains. The first movements of both are short and concentrated. The fourth sonata is composed of only two movements, each of which is preceded by a slow introduction. Interpolated between the Adagio introduction of the last movement and the last movement itself is a seven-measure reference to the Andante introduction of the first movement. The first movement is in sonata form; the second has a curious structure. After the exposition there is no double bar, and the part that is really development is repeated at the end of the recapitulation, after which there is a coda. Perhaps it could be called a free conception of a sonata form.

The fifth sonata is distinguished by containing the only bona fide slow movement among these sonatas. The first movement is a very clear sonata form in the tempo of Allegro con brio. The second movement (in d minor), the very beautiful slow movement, is a three-part form. The cello has the theme at the beginning, the only time it has it, because the piano takes it in the third section. The middle section is in the corresponding major key (D); the third movement is a four-voice fugue in which the cello has one of the voices.

Beethoven's three sets of variations are Twelve Variations on the theme 'See, the conquering hero' from Handel's *Judas Maccabäus* (1796); Twelve Variations, Op. 66, on 'Ein Mädchen oder Weibchen', from Mozart's *Magic Flute* (1798); and Seven Variations on the duet 'Bei Männern, welche Liebe fühlen', also from the *Magic Flute* (*c.* 1801). Of these the set of seven variations is by far the best.

Beethoven's Contemporaries

There were a few other composers writing for cello during Beethoven's time. Bonifacio Asioli, well known in his day, but now forgotten, composed a Sonata in C for cello and piano as well as a divertimento for cello and orchestra; J. N. Hummel, a great concert pianist in his day, had been a pupil of Mozart and Clementi in piano and Salieri and Albrechtsberger in composition; he was also a one-time friend of Beethoven. His best-known composition for cello (with alternate instrumentation) was his sonata, Op. 104. Both this sonata and the Asioli are transitional works, with early romantic characteristics. Hummel's sonata, facile but typical of his day, would make a nice item on a historical cello recital.

W. A. Mozart unfortunately wrote no works for the cello. He did leave an incomplete (34 measures) Andantino in B♭ for cello and piano (K. 374g), which has been completed, quite differently, by two people, Ernst Lewicki and Felix Schroeder. Of the several children born to the Mozarts, only two sons survived. One, Franz Xaver Wolfgang, became a musician and the other, Karl Thomas, a diplomat to Milan (where he studied with Asioli at the recommendation of Haydn). Franz Xaver Wolfgang, who later adopted his father's name and was consequently known as Wolfgang Amadeus Mozart *Fils*, is also a forgotten composer. His work *Grande Sonate/pour le Pianoforte/avec Accomp.ᵗ d'un Violon obligé ou Violoncelle*, was first edited for cello by Grützmacher, where the reading is quite romantic and out of style for the period in which it was written. A more authentic edition has been made by Wolfgang Boettcher for Schott's Söhne (1969).

George Onslow, another little-known French composer, wrote three cello sonatas (alternate viola), Op. 16. Ferdinand Ries, a German pianist, was born at Bonn and studied with Beethoven there. He wrote an early book about Beethoven, in 1838, *Biographische Notizen über L. van Beethoven*, which is one of the primary sources about Beethoven. Ries wrote three cello sonatas and another for alternate violin. Joseph Wölfl wrote a Grand Duo, Op. 31, an attractive sonata available in the Hortus Musicus Series, No. 111. Carl Maria von Weber wrote several works for cello and orchestra only, the best-known being *Grand Potpourri* for Cello and Orchestra, Op. 20.

The Schubert Arpeggione Sonata in a minor, written in 1824, holds a special place in the repertoire, as it was not originally written for the cello but for the Arpeggione (see pp. 45–6 and Plate 30). After the Arpeggione became obsolete, the sonata was transcribed for a number of different instruments but was found to be most effective for cello. It is in three movements which are permeated with the Schubert magic. Benjamin Britten has expressed this quality perfectly in his monograph, *On Receiving the First Aspen Award*:

> It [greatness in art] is the quality which cannot be acquired by simply the exercise of a technique or a system; it is something to do with personality, with gift, with spirit. I quite simply call it magic: a quality which would appear to be by no means unacknowledged by scientists, and which I value more than any other part of music. It is arguable that the richest and most productive eighteen months in our music history is the time when Beethoven had just died, when the other nineteenth century giants, Wagner, Verdi and Brahms had not begun; I mean the period in which Franz Schubert wrote his *Winterreise*, the C major Symphony, his last three piano sonatas, the C major String Quintet, as well as a dozen other glorious pieces. The very creation of these works in that space of time seems hardly credible; but the standard of inspiration, of magic, is miraculous and past all explanation.[17]

To be sure, the Arpeggione Sonata was written several years before this final outburst of Schubert's, but it still possesses a good component of the Schubert magic. The only comment that Newman makes on this sonata is that it was 'hastily written',[18] a comment that implies that it was written without proper care. The fluency, however, with which Schubert wrote is common knowledge. It is, of course, a piece of chamber music, and the Cassado arrangement of it for cello and orchestra entirely misfires. The sonata is not easy to perform, as works never are which were written for instruments with higher open strings than the cello.

Romantic Nineteenth-Century Literature

The literature for the cello ranging from good to first-class is surprisingly small in the romantic period. Little has survived in the current repertoire from this century, and perhaps for this reason it is frequently thought that the cello repertoire is very small, especially since little pre-Beethoven literature is performed either. Actually, the cello repertoire, excellent to indifferent to poor, is extensive. The nineteenth-century composers included many virtuosi cellists who wrote quantities of music for their instrument. The following list will at once present the great nineteenth-century virtuosi as well as some of their most important works:

German Cellists and Composers	Orchestral Works	Methods plus Selected Works
Bernard Romberg (1767–1841)	10 Concertos 3 Concertinos, Op. 51, 78, and without Op. no. Concertino for 2 cellos, Op. 72 Variations, op, 50, 61	Cello Method (c. 1840) 3 Sonatas, Op. 38 3 Sonatas, Op. 43
J. J. Friedrich Dotzauer (1783–1860)	9 Concertos 3 Concertinos	Cello Method (3 vols., more systematically arr. by Klingenberg) 113 Selected Studies (3 vols. arr. by Klingenberg)
Joseph Merk (1795–1852)	1 Concerto 1 Concertino Variations, Op. 4	20 Etudes, Op. 11
Friedrich August Kummer (1797–1879)	Concerto, Op. 10 3 Concertinos	Cello Method, Op. 60 c. 160 opus numbers for cello works
Sebastian Lee (1805–1887)		Cello Method, Op. 30 40 Etudes, Op. 31
Friedrich Grützmacher (1832–1903)	3 Concertos	Daily Exercises, Op.67 Technology of Cello Playing, Op. 38, vols. 1 and 2
Julius Klengel (1859–1933)	4 Concertos, Op. 10, 20, 31, 37 3 Concertinos, Op. 7, 41, 46 Concerto for 2 cellos, Op. 45	Chaconne for unaccomp. cello, Op. 43 Suite for unaccomp. cello, Op. 56 Suite for 2 cellos, Op. 22 Theme and Var. for 4 cellos, Op. 28 Hymmus for 12 Cellos, Op. 57 (altogether more than 50 works for cello)
Hugo Becker (1864–1941)	Concerto, Op. 10	Smaller pieces

Other Renowned Nineteenth-Century Cellists and Composers

Adrien François Servais (Belgian) (1807–1866)	Concerto, Op. 5 Concerto Militaire, Op. 18 Morceau de Concert, Op. 14 16 Fantasies for cello and orch. including *Souvenir de Spa*, Op. 2 and *O Cara memoria*, Op. 17	6 Caprices for 2 cellos, Op. 11 (i.e., Etudes)
Auguste Franchomme (French) (1808–1884)	Concerto, Op. 33 Many short pieces with orch.	12 Caprices, Op. 7 12 Etudes, Op. 35
Alfredo Piatti (Italian) 1822–1901)	2 Concertos, Op. 24, 26 Concertina, Op. 18	12 Caprices, Op. 25*
Karl Davidoff (Russian) (1838–1889)	4 Concertos, Op. 5, 14, 18, 31	Cello Method, At the Fountain, Op. 20, No. 2 Many other short pieces
David Popper (Bohemian) (1843–1913)	4 Concertos, Op. 8, 24, 59, 72 Suite 'Im Walde' for cello and orch., Op. 50	High School of Cello Playing, Op. 73 (40 Etudes) Suite for 2 cellos, Op. 16 Requiem for 3 cellos, Op. 66 Pieces: Chanson Villageoise, Op. 62, No. 2 Gavotte, No. 2, Op. 23 Hungarian Rhapsody, Op. 68 Concert Polonaise, Op. 14 Tarantelle, Op. 33

* The Luigi Silva edition to these is particularly helpful in that it provides introductory exercises for each caprice.

To this list should be added Bernhard Cossman (1822–1910), who was a great virtuoso but wrote little for his instrument; Georg Goltermann (1824–1898), who was not among the great virtuosi but wrote a great deal for his instrument, including seven concertos, three concert pieces, duos, sonatinas, and innumerable pieces; and Wilhelm Fitzenhagen (1848–?), who wrote more than 60 opus numbers devoted to cello, including four concertos.

All of the literature mentioned above is outmoded for recital use today although it will continue to interest the music historian. What survives of it includes a few concertos, especially of Goltermann (Nos. 4 and 5) and Romberg (including his concertinos) used for student teaching, a few pieces by Davidoff and Popper, and several of the exercise books, studies, and études indicated in the third column. These are very useful for laying a foundation for playing music written in traditional tonality, with its reiterated finger patterns, shaped to groups of notes, which recur frequently in the figurations found in music based on the major and minor scales. These cellists were all trained in composition, but not one had a true gift for composing. With various forms available to them, bolstered by their study of traditional harmony, they were able to write pieces with an understandable musical syntax, but they all lacked originality. The cello writing is idiomatic, and one can build from these works a technique that solves all the technical problems of tonal music, with emphasis on thirds, double-stops, or broken octaves, arpeggio figures, and the like. It is regrettable that there was no cellist comparable to Chopin, who wrote idiomatic music for the piano but at the same time wrote great music.

From the whole romantic concerto literature (more than 200 cello concertos) only three or four concertos remain in the current repertoire: the Robert Schumann Concerto in a minor, Op. 129 (1854), the Saint-Saëns Concerto in a minor, Op. 33 (1873), and the Antonin Dvořák Concerto in b minor, Op. 104 (1895), the latter being undoubtedly the greatest of all romantic cello concertos. The Edouard Lalo Concerto in d minor (1787), popular in the first part of this century, has dropped in its appeal to the present-day audience. Unfortunately it does not touch in musical worth his *Symphonie espagnole* for violin and orchestra, but it remains very useful as a learning piece for the student, and is still given an occasional performance.

The Schumann concerto survives because the musical ideas are so beautiful, but the composition is not put together with a first-class technical control; the orchestration is weak in spots, and some performers make cuts where the writing seems diffuse. In fact, it takes a performer of great eminence to render the concerto, unaltered, a convincing work of art. It is not a great masterpiece as is his concerto for piano in the same key.

The Saint-Saëns Concerto is delightful in every way. It is built with a perfect craftsmanship, a hallmark of Saint-Saëns' gift for composition. That it does not plumb the depths of emotional meaning is beside the point; it should simply be accepted on its own terms. The composition is in one continuous movement although it is sectional. It is not so difficult to perform as some, so that a player of fairly modest attainments can convey the work, but it does have its challenging moments. Saint-Saëns wrote a second cello concerto, Op. 119 (1903), but it has never become popular.

The Dvořák Concerto is a great masterpiece, and one of the great performances of it, by Pablo Casals and the Czech Philharmonic Orchestra on 28 April 1937, was eventually recorded on the Angel Records series of 'Great Recordings of the Century'. Dvořák composed his concerto in b minor, Op. 104, near the end of his three-year stay in America (1892–95), but he revised the last part of the last movement after he had returned to Czechoslovakia. The work is in three movements, the first Allegro in sonata form. It starts with a classical orchestral exposition that introduces both themes. A particularly beautiful spot is the horn announcement of the second theme. The soloist then enters, *Quasi improvisando*. A striking balance is maintained between the orchestra and the soloist, partly by a light orchestration during the solo parts and by much dialogue between cello and orchestra. The development, starting 'grandioso', is sectional, and there are some striking modulations. The recapitulation starts with a return of the second theme. That Dvořák was a violinist during part of his career must have given him a particular insight in sensing the difficulties of writing for a cello and orchestra. The balance is harder to maintain than between a violin and orchestra, partly on account of the lower register of the cello. The perfect balance between the two that Dvořák created in this concerto is one reason that it lives.

The second movement is a three-part form (ABA); the first section is very lyrical; the second section starts with a very solemn orchestral phrase, then the cello enters with literally a song, an actual quotation from one of Dvořák's songs (Op. 82, No. 1), entitled 'Leave me alone'. He quoted this song because he had heard that his sister-in-law had become ill. Dvořák had been in love with her when they were both young and she had been his pupil, and this song was one of her favourites. Her death shortly after his return to his native land caused him to rewrite the last part of the last movement. The new part starts at the Andante (Eulenburg score, m. 449). He turned the work into a cyclical work: about a dozen bars after the Andante he quotes the first theme of the first movement, followed by a varied version of the song theme of the second movement, which he put there in memory of his sister-in-law.[19] He then has more references to the first theme of the first movement before the final orchestral *Andante maestoso*. This last movement is a Rondo with a first theme of very infectious rhythm. The balance is maintained throughout. It is a well-known anecdote that when Brahms, a great supporter of Dvořák, first saw the score of this concerto, he said to the cellist Hausmann, 'Why on earth didn't I know that one could write a violoncello concerto like this? If I had only known, I would have written one long ago!'[20]

Dvořák wrote an earlier cello concerto in A major in 1865, which he had written out with only a sketchy piano accompaniment and never did orchestrate. It was rediscovered in 1925. Clapham, commenting on Günter Raphael's attempt to complete the work, which was then published, says in view of his extended alterations '. . . it would be more accurate to describe it as reshaped and newly composed'.[21]

Several other nineteenth-century works for cello and orchestra should be mentioned, especially the Tchaikovsky *Rococo Variations*, Op. 33 (1876), which are very difficult technically but give a charming effect (also, they do not suffer as much as most pieces for cello and orchestra when accompanied by the piano), and the Brahms *Double Concerto* for violin and cello, Op. 102 (1887), which perhaps does not represent Brahms' highest inspiration but is a very effective work. The Léon Boëllmann *Symphonic Variations*, Op. 23 (1893) for cello and orchestra, a work in one movement, popular earlier in this century, is scarcely played now except by students. Its extraordinary repetitiveness makes one wonder how it ever gained the popularity on the concert stage that it had. Richard Strauss' *Don Quixote*, Op. 35 (1897) is not exactly a cello concerto but a 'Symphonic Poem' with cello obbligato. It is in the form of a set of ten 'fantastic variations' preceded by an introduction and followed by a finale. The solo cello represents Don Quixote. It is highly programmatic. By the end of the introduction Don Quixote has lost his mind; the ten variations each represent an insane encounter, and the finale represents his death, shortly before which he has regained sanity. The programme of this symphonic poem is so extensive that one misses a great deal of the reasoning behind Strauss' choice of this or that effect if he is unfamiliar with the story and its sequence of events. When a piece of music depends to this extent on its programme, it becomes questionable whether its musical integrity is of the highest order. Nevertheless, it has been fairly popular and today still has its devotees.

Although the production of sonatas dropped in importance in comparison with other types of writing during the nineteenth century, there was a great flurry of writing pieces, such as fantasy pieces, fantasias, romances, variations, divertimentos, gavottes, mazurkas, polonaises, souvenirs, melodies, serenades, and others. There were, however, still a considerable number of sonatas written. A total of 322 cello sonatas are recorded as listed in the Cumulative Volumes of Hofmeister between the years *c.* 1800–1897.[22] This, of course, would not account for them all. Newman in his book *The Sonata since Beethoven* mentions or discusses in short detail 224 cello sonatas, of which about 60 are from the early twentieth century but show no break in style with late nineteenth-century sonatas. Of this whole number, many of which he has examined, he points to only one among those dropped from the current repertoire which he believes is worth reviving and reintroducing into our repertoire, the Hans Pfitzner sonata, Op. 1 (1892). It is above the interest of the run-of-the-mill romantic sonata, although it is the more interesting harmony (the piano part) that makes it so. The cello part is not particularly challenging.

The best sonatas of the post-Beethoven nineteenth century were by Felix Mendelssohn (2), Frédéric Chopin (1), Johannes Brahms (2), Edvard Grieg (1), and Richard Strauss (1).

The two sonatas by Mendelssohn, Op. 45 (1838) and Op. 58 (1843) are excellent examples of early romantic lyricism. They are filled with broad singing melodies and are optimistic, spirited works. The piano part especially calls for an extremely fluent technique, representing perhaps Mendelssohn's own style of command of the keyboard (he was a great piano virtuoso). In fact, these sonatas can be made or marred by the pianist. The first sonata, in B♭ major, is simply a pleasant work in three movements, written for his brother, who was a cellist. The second sonata, in D major, is much the more interesting of the two. It is in four movements, the first in sonata form and with more drive than the first movement of the first sonata; the second, a scherzo of the type only Mendelssohn could write; the third, a unique movement, opening with eleven measures of rolled chords on the piano that sound like an organ harmonizing a chorale-like melody. Then the cello enters with a long recitative, like a tenor voice in one of Mendelssohn's oratorios; the piano sounds again the organ-like chords, with which the cello has another recitative; the coda gives the piano the expressive recitative, while the cello has a long held pedal on G, with the strong beats marked by pizzicato on the open G string. The mood is one of religious tranquillity. The final movement, also in sonata form, abounds in a buoyancy that brings this excellent sonata to a close. This sonata is stylistically a good representation of Mendelssohn at his best. The sonatas are not much played today, Mendelssohn being out of fashion, but there is a fine recording (Vox, PL8500) by Nikolai Graudan (cellist) and his pianist wife, Joanna (who was a student of Schnabel), both of whom were obviously very sympathetic to these works.

The Frédéric Chopin sonata in g minor, Op. 65 (1847), in four movements, Allegro moderato, Scherzo, Largo, and Finale (Allegro), is another romantic sonata that is on the sidelines of the current repertoire but deserves more serious consideration. As with the Mendelssohn sonatas, it is the lovely music that counts, and here again the pianist holds the key to a successful performance of the work. This sonata requires great subtlety and control of technique on the part of the pianist, and on the part of both players a perfect sense of phrasing; otherwise the work sounds like a piano sonata with a cello obbligato. Chopin wrote this work for his friend, the French cellist Franchomme, from whom he undoubtedly got suggestions for the cello part. They played the work together first at a private concert in 1847 and again on the last concert in which Chopin appeared, in February, 1848, when he was already a sick man.

Next to Beethoven's, the two sonatas by Johannes Brahms are probably the most frequently performed cello sonatas. The first sonata in e minor, Op. 38 (1866), has a striking and dramatic first movement in sonata form. The cello opens with a beautiful, singing theme low on the instrument. The movement is filled with contrapuntal devices, such as imitation and double counterpoint, but because of its lyricism, the movement does not sound academic. The second movement is a charming, almost wistful Minuetto and Trio, the trio being more pensive. The last movement is a triple fugue, which turns out to be almost a battle between the two instruments. The cello fights hard to hold its own against the two hands of a pianist on a concert grand piano, and all but goes down to defeat. It is not a gracious movement to listen to, but it has its lyrical moments. One has to follow the imitation and the development of the fugue itself to get the most pleasure from listening to this movement.

The second sonata, in F major, Op. 99 (1886), has never been so popular with a general audience as Brahms' first sonata. In a way, it is a musician's sonata. It is a colossal work, but does not have the immediate charm of the first two movements of the first one. It starts off with what might be called a craggy theme, not beautiful but expressive. Since the movement is in sonata form, the theme is heard often and this cragginess therefore characterizes the first movement. It perhaps does take some musicianship to comprehend the nature of the ideas and their often contrapuntal working out. A novel device that Brahms uses in this movement, and with particularly telling effect in the middle of the development section, is the tremolos between two strings used as a background sound as the piano develops the first theme. The very beautiful second movement is a three-part form that opens with two themes, one in the piano and the other in the cello playing pizzicato. The pizzicato passage is higher and more extended with the return of the 'A' section, and it is heard also at the beginning of the coda. These are some of the most beautiful pizzicato notes in the literature and are unforgettable once one has heard them beautifully played. The scherzo and trio movement is likewise extremely effective. Neither of these movements is difficult to appreciate, and the last movement having a folk-like theme (the whole being a rondo setting), is simple indeed. It is a foil in the sense of setting off distinctly the previous three really profound movements.

The formerly popular Edvard Grieg Sonata in a minor, Op. 36, (Harold Bauer once told me that he had played it with Casals about 100 times all over Europe), has almost slipped from the current repertoire. It is a work in three movements, the first two of which are lovely romantic music. Unfortunately the third movement is not up to the level of the first two, being far too repetitious. It is a long sonata form without sufficient material to make it interesting. Furthermore, the main theme does not lend itself to development, only to repetition, and this theme in augmentation serves as the second theme instead of a contrasting theme. Is there any reason why either the first or the second movement might not be played alone on a programme? The beauty of them deserves some performance. The sonata was written for Grieg's only brother, John, who was an amateur cellist, with whom Grieg played it at its first performance in 1885.[23] The sonata is not difficult, perhaps tailored to his brother's technical capabilities, but neverless it is rewarding for both performer and listener.

The cello sonata in F major, Op. 6, by Richard Strauss is an early work, having been composed when he was 19 years old, in 1883. If one did not know that Strauss had written a cello sonata, and heard this piece, I doubt if he would be able to identify the composer since there is absolutely nothing that foreshadows the Strauss that most of us know. This sonata is a student work, and if nothing else, it testifies to the traditional, conservative training that laid the foundation for his future style. The sonata is eclectic with a bit of Beethoven, Mendelssohn, and Brahms, but no Wagner in its makeup. Perhaps Strauss' training as a violinist (as well as a pianist) gave him an understanding of all string instruments, because this sonata is grateful for the cello. It is a refreshing, attractive work demonstrating much talent in spite of some naïve writing. It is cast in three movements, and although not performed often, is worth a place beside the relatively few nineteenth-century sonatas still performed.

Anton Rubinstein (1830–1894) wrote two cello sonatas, Op. 18 in D major and Op. 39 in G major. At the beginning of this century the D major sonata still had a certain popularity, but it now has fallen by the wayside. It is a pleasant work that might be used with interest on a historical programme as an example of a typical romantic sonata, under the influence of the Mendelssohn style. He also wrote two cello concertos.

Camille Saint-Saëns (1835–1921) also wrote two cello sonatas, Op. 32 in c minor (1873) and Op. 123 in F major (1905), which are lost to the current repertoire. The c minor sonata is another pleasant sonata, well put together, and of historical interest. The sonata in F major suffers from a very disappointing first movement, but the other three movements are interesting. The second movement is the Scherzo and the third movement a slow one; these could be played with effect today, in reverse order, as Paul Bazelaire once recorded them. (Saint-Saëns' Suite in d minor, Op. 16, is salon music).

The reader may be surprised that so little of the nineteenth-century cello literature has passed the test of time, especially since it was the great century for piano music. The modern piano was perfected at the beginning of the nineteenth century, and indeed the modern concert grand piano is a formidable partner for the cello. It is actually harder to write a satisfactory sonata for cello and piano than for, say, violin and piano because the problem of balance is more difficult with the lower tessitura of the cello. It is for the same reason that it is more difficult to write a cello concerto with the larger romantic orchestra. This difficulty is reflected, I believe, in the relatively few really successful romantic works.

Since the main recital and concert fare for piano, violin, or cello is still basically classical and romantic music, the sparseness of this acceptable cello literature has led to an unusual activity on the part of the twentieth-century composers to fill in the gap for the cellist. We are very fortunate, at least, in this turn of events.

Twentieth-Century Literature to c. 1960

An enormous amount of literature for the cello has been written during the twentieth century, not only, perhaps, because of the relatively small amount of really distinguished literature available to cellists, but also because of the final perfection of cello technique in this century (see p. 194). There is almost a parallel between the spread of interest in the cello throughout most of Europe during the second half of the eighteenth century with the spread of interest in the instrument throughout the world in the twentieth century. Composers from countries scarcely heard of before in terms of the cello have sprung up during this century – from the Scandinavian countries, Finland, South Africa, South America, Mexico, Cuba, Turkey, Armenia, Australia, New Zealand, and even Japan.

In the early part of the century the majority of works were post-romantic, such as Dohnányi's Konzertstück in D major, Elgar's Concerto in e minor, Bloch's *Schelomo*, Rachmaninoff's Sonata in g minor, and Fauré's two sonatas. Debussy's sonata of 1915 is one of the first to make a real break in style from romantic form and harmony. Notably, Webern's Three Little Pieces, Op. 11 (1914), in an atonal, pointillistic style, are in a highly original vein.

After 1930 one may expect the more conservative works to come from Russian composers because of their political ideal of controlling art so that it is immediately comprehensible to the average audience. Thus works of Prokofiev or Shostakovitch offer no difficulty of comprehension. One senses in many works after *c.* 1930 an effort on the composer's part to find new sounds, new effects, new shapes, so that each work offers new problems to be solved by the performer. There is little carry-over from one work to another by way of clichés, or manners of speaking, characteristic of each of the former eras, baroque, classical, and the less-than-greatest romantic music.

I thought it might be useful to the cellist to have a list of about 100 (not more than a fifth) of the most famous composers who have written cello music during this century along with their works. (The order of the composers listed in the following charts is based on their birth date). After the charts of the major twentieth-century works that follow, we shall speak of certain particular compositions and attempt a few generalizations.

English Composers

Sir Edward Elgar
(1857–1934)

Cello Concerto in e minor, Op. 85 (1919)*

Frederick Delius
(1862–1934)

Cello Concerto (1921)
Caprice and Elegy for cello and orchestra (1925)
Sonata (1917)
Romance for cello and piano (1896)

Sir Granville Bantock
(1868–1946)

Elegiac Poem for cello and orchestra (1908)

Sapphic Poem for cello and orchestra (1909)
Celtic Poem for cello and orchestra (1914)
Dramatic Poem for cello and orchestra (1941)
Sonata No. 1 (1941)
Sonata No. 2 (1945)
Sonata for unaccompanied cello (1924)
Fantastic Poem for cello and piano (1924)
Dramatic Poem for cello and piano (1945)
Two pieces for harp or piano and cello:
    Hamabdil, Pribroch

* The dates on these lists are for the most part the dates of publication.

26 Cello of Thomas Dodd, 1790

27 Cello of Abraham Prescott, 1831–1845

Ralph Vaughan Williams (1872–1958)	Six Studies in English Folksong, for cello and piano (1927) (The *Fantasia on Sussex Folk Tunes* for cello and orchestra, sometimes listed, never appeared)
Gustav Holst (1874–1934)	Invocation for cello and orchestra (MS.) (1911)
Sir Donald Francis Tovey (1875–1940)	Cello Concerto, Op. 40 (1935) Sonata, Op. 4 (1900) Elegiac Variations for cello and piano, Op. 25 (1909) Sonata in D major for unaccompanied cello, Op. 30 (1914) Sonata for 2 cellos, unaccompanied (1912)
William Yeates Hurlstone (1876–1906)	Sonata, D major Lullaby for Cello and Piano
Joseph Holbrooke (1878–1958)	Sonata, Op. 19 (1914)

Frank Bridge (1879–1941)	Concerto elegiaco ('Oration') (1930)
	 Sonata (1917)
	 Pieces:
	     Cradle Song (1911)
	     Élégie (1911)
	     Mélodie (1911)
	     Spring Song (1912)
	     Meditation (1912)
	     Morning Song (1919)

John Ireland (1879–1962)	Sonata (1924)

Cyril Meir Scott (1879–1970)	Cello Concerto (1937)
	 Sonata (1949)
	 Pieces:
	     Pierrot amoureux (1912)
	     Poem, The Melodist and the Nightingale (1930)
	     Pastoral and Reel (1930)
	     Andante languido
	     Ballade
	     Vesperale

Sir Arnold Bax (1883–1953)	Cello Concerto (1932) Sonata (1923)

	Sonatina (1933)
	Legend Sonata (1943)
	Rhapsodic Ballad for unaccompanied cello (1968)
Arthur Benjamin (1893–1960)	Sonatina (1938)
Ernest John Moeran (1894–1950)	Cello Concerto (1947)
	Sonata (1948)
	Irish Lament
	Prelude
Gerald Finzi (1901–1956)	Cello Concerto (1956)
Edmund Rubbra (1901–)	Soliloquy for cello and orchestra, Op. 57 (1945)
	Sonata, Op. 60 (1947)
Sir William Walton (1902–)	Cello Concerto (1957)
Alan Rawsthorne (1905–1971)	Concerto (1966)
	Sonata (1949)
Benjamin Britten (1913–)	Cello Symphony for cello and orchestra, Op. 68 (1963; revised 1964)
	Sonata, Op. 65 (1961)
	Suite No. 1 for unaccompanied cello, Op. 72 (1966)
	Suite No. 2 for unaccompanied cello, Op. 80 (1969)

French Composers

Gabriel Fauré (1845–1924)	1st Sonata, Op. 109 (1918)
	2nd Sonata, Op. 117 (1922)
	Pieces for cello and piano:
	Élégie, Op. 24 (1883)
	Romance, Op. 69 (c. 1895)
	Papillon, Op. 77 (1898)
	Sicilienne, Op. 78 (1898)
	Sérénade, Op. 98 (1908)
	Lamento
Vincent d'Indy (1851–1931)	Lied for cello and orchestra (1885)
	Sonata, Op. 84 (1926)
Claude Debussy (1862–1918)	Sonata (1915)

	Intermezzo for cello and piano (found by Gregor Piatigorsky in Paris, 1938)
Guy Ropartz (1864–1955)	Rhapsodie, originally for cello and orchestra
	Sonata in g minor (1904)
	2nd Sonata
Albert Roussel (1869–1937)	Cello Concertino (1936)
Jean Huré (1877–1930)	Sonata in f♯
	Sonata in F
	Sonata in F♯
André Caplet (1878–1925)	Epiphanie d'apres une légende ethiopienne – a musical 'fresco' for cello and orchestra (1923)
Jacques Ibert (1890–1962)	Concerto for cello and wind instruments (1926)
	Étude – Caprice pour un tombeau de Chopin for unaccompanied cello (1949)
	Ghirlarzana for unaccompanied cello
Arthur Honegger (1892–1955) (Swiss parentage; b. Le Havre)	Cello Concerto (1931)
	Sonata (1920)
Darius Milhaud (1892–)	Concerto No. 1 (1935)
	Concerto No. 2 (1947)
	Élégie for cello and piano (1945)
	Sonata (1959)
	Suite Cisalpine, originally for cello and orchestra
Francis Poulenc (1899–1963)	Sonata No. 1
Henri Sauguet (1901–)	Mélodié Concertante for cello and orchestra (1964)
	Sonata
	Ballade for cello and piano
	Sonata for unaccompanied cello
André Jolivet (1905–)	Concerto
	Suite en Concert for cello unaccompanied (1966)
Jean Françaix (1912–)	Fantasie for cello and orchestra (1934)
	Variations sans thème for cello and piano (1951)

                        Mouvement perpétuel for cello and piano
                           (1944)
                        Berceuse
                        Nocturne
                        Rondino-Staccato
                        Serenade

Paul Tortelier (1914–)	Two Cello Concertos Concerto for two cellos Sonata (1946) Suite for unaccompanied cello (1944)

Russian Composers

There have been a great many Russians who have written literature for the cello in this century. The best known to the western world of these Russian composers are as follows:

Alexander Gretchaninov (1864–1956)	Sonata, Op. 113
Alexander Glazunov (1865–1936)	Concerto-Ballata, Op. 108 for cello and orchestra (1933) Two Pieces for cello and orchestra, Op. 20 (also for cello and piano) Mélodie Arabische Sérénade espagnole (1888) Chant du Ménestrel, Op. 71, for cello and orchestra (1901). Pensée à Liszt, Op. 17, for cello and piano
Sergei Rachmaninoff (1873–1943)	Sonata, Op. 19 (1901) 2 Pieces for cello and piano, Op. 2 (1892) Prelude Danse Orientale
Reinhold Glière (1875–1956)	Cello Concerto, Op. 87 (1946) Ballad for cello and piano, Op. 4 (1902) Twelve Pieces for cello and piano, Op. 51 (1910) Ten Duos for 2 cellos, Op. 53 (1910)
Nikolai Miaskovsky (1881–1950)	Cello Concerto, Op. 66 (1945) Sonata No. 1, Op. 12 (1911) for cello and piano Sonata No. 2, Op. 81 for cello and piano

Sergei Prokofiev (1891–1953)	Cello Concerto, No. 1, Op. 58 (1938) Sinfonia Concertante = Symphony-Concerto, Op. 125 (1952) Concertino for cello and orchestra, Op. 132 (pub. posth. 1955) Sonata, Op. 119 (1949) Ballade for cello and piano, Op. 15 (1912)
Alexander Tcherepnin (1899–)	Songs and Dances, Op. 84 Mystère for cello and chamber orchestra, Op. 37, No. 2 (1926) Rhapsodie Georgienne for cello and orchestra (1924) Ode for cello and piano (1919) Sonata in D Sonata No. 2 and No. 3 (Op. 30, No. 1 and 2) Le Violoncelle bien temperé: 12 preludes for cello and piano, 2 of them with drum, Op. 38 (1927) – (Pub. Durand Co. without drum part) Suite for cello unaccompanied (1945)
Alexander Mossolov (1900–)	Cello Concerto (1935)
Vissarion Shebalin (1902–1963)	Cello Concerto (1950) Sonata, Op. 51, No. 3
Aram Khatchaturian (1903–)	Cello Concerto (1946) Concerto-Rhapsody Sonata
Nikolai Lopatnikoff (1903–) (Estonian)	Sonata, Op. 11 (1928) Variations and Epilogue for cello and piano (1946)
Dmitri Kabalevsky (1904–)	Cello Concerto, Op. 49 (1949) Cello Concerto No. 2 (1964) Sonata, Op. 22 Sonata, Op. 71
Dmitri Shostakovitch (1906–)	Cello Concerto, Op. 107 (1959) Cello Concerto No. 2 (1966) Sonata, Op. 40 (1934) Three Pieces, Op. 9 (1924)

Pezzi (2) orig. for cello and orchestra
Adagio
Spring Waltz

United States of America

Walter Piston (1894–)	Variations for cello and orchestra; piano reduction by the composer (1966)
Leo Sowerby (1895–1968)	Cello Concerto (1917) Cello Concerto (1933) Sonata (1921)
Virgil Thomson (1896–)	Cello Concerto (1950)
Henry Cowell (1897–1965)	Four Declamations with Return Hymn and Fuguing Tune No. 9
Quincy Porter (1897–1966)	Fantasy for cello and small orchestra (1950) Poem (for cello or viola and piano)
Ross Lee Finney (1906–)	Sonata No. 2 (1950) [Sonata No. 1 (1941) withdrawn]
Elliott Carter (1908–)	Sonata (1948)
Samuel Barber (1910–)	Cello Concerto, Op. 22 (1946) Sonata, Op. 6 (1932)
William Schuman (1910–)	Song of Orpheus, for cello and orchestra (1963)
Alan Hovhaness (1911–)	Suite, Op. 193
Norman Dello Joio (1913–)	Sonatina (1943) Duo Concertante for cello and piano (1945)
David Diamond (1915–)	Cello Concerto (1938) Sonata (1938) Sonata for unaccompanied cello
Louis Mennini (1920–)	Sonatina for cello and piano (1952)
Peter Mennin (1923–)	Cello Concerto (1956)

Status Change to United States Citizenship

Arnold Schoenberg (1874–1951; born in Vienna; became U.S. citizen 1941)	M.G. Monn-Schoenberg Concertos in g minor (1913) and D major (1932)

Ernest Bloch
(1880–1959; born in
Switzerland, lived in
USA from 1917–1930
becoming a citizen; and
lived again in U.S.,
1939–59

Schelomo, Hebraic Rhapsody for cello and
orchestra (1916)
Voice in the Wilderness, symphonic poem
with cello obbligato (1936)
Méditation Hébraique for cello and piano
(1925)
From Jewish Life, 3 Sketches (1924)
Prayer
Supplication
Jewish Song
3 Suites Unaccompanied (1957–58)
Suite Italienne for cello and piano (1954)

Igor Stravinsky
(1882–1971; born in
Russia; became U.S.
citizen 1945)

Ernst Toch
(1887–1964; born in
Vienna; became U.S.
citizen 1940)

Cello Concerto with chamber orchestra,
Op. 35 (1925)
Sonata, Op. 50
Impromptu, Op. 90, for unaccompanied
cello

Paul Hindemith
(1895–1964; born in
Germany; became U.S.
citizen 1946)

Cello Concerto, Op. 3
Cello Concerto (1940)
Kammermusik No. 3 for cello and 10
instruments, Op. 36/2 (1925)
Sonata, Op. 11 (1922)
Sonata (1948)
Sonata for unaccompanied cello, Op. 25,
No. 3 (1923)
3 Pieces for cello and piano, Op. 8 (1917)
Capriccio
Phantasiestück
Scherzo
3 Easy Pieces (1938)
Variations, 'A Frog He Went A-Courting'
for cello and piano (1946)

Ernst Křenek
(1900–   ; born Vienna;
became U.S. citizen 1945)

Concerto
Capriccio for cello and orchestra
Suite for unaccompanied cello, Op. 84 (1939)

Vladimir Dukelsky,
pseudonym, Vernon
Duke, (1903–1969; born
in Russia; became U.S.
citizen *c.* 1929)

Cello Concerto (1946)

Other Countries

AUSTRIA

Anton von Webern
(1883–1945)

Two Pieces (1899)
Three Little Pieces for cello and piano,
   Op. 11 (1914)
Cello Sonata (one movement, 1914)

Egon Wellész
(1885–   )

Suite for unaccompanied cello, Op. 31
   (1921)
Suite for unaccompanied cello, Op. 39
   (1927)

CZECHOSLOVAKIA

Bohuslav Martinu
(1890–1959)

Cello Concerto, with chamber orchestra,
   (1931; rev. with full orchestra, 1939)
Cello Concerto No. 2 (1946)
Sonata da camera for cello and chamber
   orchestra (1940)
Sonata No. 1 (1940)
Sonata No. 2 (1941)
Sonata No. 3
Suite miniature
Variations on a Slovakian Theme
Études rhythmiques for unaccompanied
   cello (1931)
Pieces:
   Arabesques, 7 pieces (1930)
   Nocturnes, 4 studies (1930)
Variations on a Theme by Rossini
Pastorales, 6 pieces

FINLAND

Jean Sibelius
(1865–1957)

Solemn Melodies: for violin or cello and
   orchestra, Op. 77
     Laetare anima mea
     Ab imo pectore
Pieces with piano:
   Malinconia, Op. 20 (1901)
   4 pieces, Op. 78 (1915)
     Impromptu
     Romance
     Religioso
     Rigaudon

GERMANY
Hans Werner Henze
(1926–   )

Ode to the Westwind for cello and orchestra (1954)
Serenade for unaccompanied cello (1949)

HOLLAND
Willem Pijper
(1894–1947)

Cello Concerto (1936)
Sonata No. 1 (1919)
Sonata No. 2 (1924)

HUNGARY
Emanuel Moór
(1863–1931)

Concerto No. 1, Op. 61 (1905)
Concerto No. 2, Op. 64
Concerto for 2 cellos, Op. 69 (1908)
Rhapsody No. 1, Op. 78, for cello and orchestra
Rhapsody No. 2, for cello and orchestra (1911)
Ballade for cello and orchestra (1914)
Largo for cello and orchestra, Op. 105
7 Sonatas (Op. 22, 53, 55, 76, 148; 2 without op. no.)
2 Suites, Op. 117 (the second unfinished)
Suite, Op. 122, for unaccompanied cello
Suite for 4 cellos
Prelude, Op. 123

Ernst von Dohňanyi
(1877–1960)

Konzerstück, Op. 12 for cello and orchestra (1906)
Sonata, Op. 8 (1903)

Béla Bartók
(1881–1945)

Rhapsody No. 1 for cello and piano (Bartók's arrangement of his Rhapsody No. 1 for violin and piano) (1928)

Zoltán Kodály
(1882–1967)

Sonata, Op. 4 (1909/10)
Sonata, Op. 8 for unaccompanied cello (1915)
Capriccio for unaccompanied cello (1915)
Three Chorale Preludes by Bach arr. for cello and piano (1924)
Magyar Rondo for cello and piano (1917)

ITALY
Ildebrando Pizzetti
(1880–1968)

Cello Concerto (1934)
Sonata (1921)
Tre Canti (1st version) for cello and piano (1924)

Gian Francesco Malipiero   Cello Concerto (1937)
(1882–)   Sonata (1907/8)
   Sonatina (1942)
   Fantasie Concertanti: III

Alfredo Casella   Cello Concerto Op. 58 (1934/35)
   Sonata, No. 1 (1907)
   Sonata, No. 2 (1927)

Mario Castelnuovo-Tedesco   Cello Concerto (1935)
(1895–1968)   Sonata (1928)
   I nottambuli, Variozioni Fantastiche, for cello and piano (1928)

Luigi Dallapiccola   Dialoghi for cello and orchestra
(1904–)   Ciacconna, Intermezzo e Adagio for unaccompanied cello (originally for violin? 1945)

MEXICO

Carlos Chavez   Sonatina (1924)
(1899–)

NORWAY

Harald Saeverud   Cello Concerto (1930)
(1897–)

RUMANIA

Georges Enesco   Symphonie Concertante for cello and
(1881–1955)   orchestra (1909)

SOUTH AMERICA

Alberto Williams   Sonata, Op. 52
(1862–1952)

Uribe-Holguín, G.   Two Sonatas
(1880–)

Enrique Soro   Sonata
(1884–)

Heitor Villa-Lobos   Grand Concerto (1915)
(1887–1959)   Cello Concerto No. 2 (1955)
   Fantasia for cello and orchestra (1945)
   Two Cello Sonatas (1915, 1916)
   Pequena Sonata (1914)
   Bachianas Brasileiras No. 1 for 8 cellos (1932)
   Bachianas Brasileiras No. 5 for 8 cellos and soprano (1939)

	Song of the Black Swan
	Pieces:
	Peguena Suite (1913)
	Romancette
	Legendaria
	Harmonias Soltas
	Fugato a antiga
	Melodia
	Gavotte-Scherzo
	Ten Pieces (1914–30)
José Mariá Castro	Sonata for cello and piano
(1892–1968)	Sonata for 2 cellos
Alberto Ginastera	Cello Concerto (1968)
(1916–)	Pampeana No. 2 for cello and piano (1950)

SPAIN

Pablo Casals (1876–1973)	*La Sardana* for an ensemble of cellos (1951)
	Song of the Birds. Catalonian Folk Song, arr. for cello and orchestra
	(Other cello works may be published posthumously)
Gaspar Cassadó	Cello Concerto (*c.* 1927)
(1897–1966)	Catalonian Rhapsody for cello and orchestra (1928)
	Sonata, nello stile antico spagnolo (1925)
	Sonata
	Partita for cello and piano
	Suite for unaccompanied cello (1907)
	Pieces:
	Serenade
	Lamento de Boabdil
	Requiebros
	Danse du Diable Vert

SWEDEN

| Lars-Eric Larsson | Cello Concerto (1948) |
| (1908–   ) | Concertino, Op. 45, No. 10 |

Probably the first cello concerto of any importance published in this century (and one frequently performed earlier in the century) was Eugène d'Albert's cello concerto in C major, Op. 20 (1900). Although it has been dropped from the repertoire, it was given a revival, but without success, at the Edinburgh Festival of 1949.

Ernst von Dohnányi wrote his Cello Concerto in D major, Op. 12, called Konzertstück, in 1904. It is in one movement with three sections, and in an unabashed romantic vein. It has one novel feature: after the recapitulation a cadenza accompanied by the cello section of the orchestra makes a nice effect. The concerto is a pleasing piece and could be played more often to vary the small romantic diet that cellists present to the public.

Ernest Bloch's *Schelomo, A Hebraic Rhapsody for Cello and Orchestra* was written in Switzerland during 1915–16, before Bloch came to the United States. The composition was written during a period in his life when he was quite intentionally writing Jewish music, for about a decade, ending in 1923. *Schelomo* is based on some vocal sketches Bloch based on Ecclesiastes, but with which he was dissatisfied. ('Schelomo' refers to King Solomon. Although Ecclesiastes was written centuries after King Solomon actually lived, Bloch follows the older tradition associating him with that biblical book). A good preparation for listening to this piece is to read through Ecclesiastes – not that it is religious music in any sense, and not that there is any too specific programme to the music. But the preparation will put the listener in the general mood to receive the music. The music is strong emotional stuff, ranging from the ecstatic, not to say frenzied, to the solemn, to the despair of 'Vanity of vanities, all is vanity'.

The composition is a musical rhapsody in one movement without any special form. The solo cello has a number of moving soliloquies as it represents King Solomon. Although there are many tempo changes, there are only two main themes.

Bloch also wrote *A Voice in the Wilderness*, a symphonic poem with cello obbligato (1936), but it has never achieved the success of *Schelomo*, which is one of his best works.

Sir Edward Elgar's Cello Concerto in e minor, Op. 85, written in 1919, got off to a bad start, the reason being that insufficient rehearsal time was allowed for the concerto among other works on the programme. The fault was not that of the soloist, Felix Salmond, but the performance did the concerto no good. It took some time for the effects of that *première* to be overcome, but the concerto is now recognized for what it is, one of the most rewarding concertos in the repertoire. The score is written with British understatement, which perhaps also contributed to the long period before its complete acceptance. This is one concerto, by the way, that I think suffers less than most other concertos when accompanied by a piano reduction of the orchestral score. It is only a black-and-white reproduction of the coloured orchestral score, but the musical ideas come across very well in transcription. In so many concertos the very colouring of the orchestral score is the main point; when that is taken away, there is not much left, and they sound poor in transcription.

The concerto is composed of four movements: the first, Moderato, is introduced by a noble adagio recitative, referred to in the introduction of the second movement, and in the fourth movement near the end of the movement. The work therefore is cyclical. The two themes of the first movement exposition are connected by a bridge that presents its own theme. This bridge is repeated to serve as a substitute for a development section, and the recapitulation is of the first theme only. The movement ends attacca, the second movement starting with a pizzicato reference to the introduction of the first movement, interspersed with hints of the main theme of the second movement. This movement is a scherzo, without the classical shape of one. The main theme is given full expression (starting after the third light double bar) for 39 measures, when it is repeated in varied form, with a new harmonization. The coda hints at the first theme ten bars from the end. The third movement is a simple song based on only one idea, and certain passages have a Wagnerian flavour. The fourth movement, a rondo, is the most vigorous of the four movements.

Near the end of the movement there is an extended discussion of the theme of the third movement (from Poco piu lento to the Adagio come prima), then a four-measure repetition of the opening bars of the concerto, and a final reference to the theme of the rondo.

Sergei Prokofiev wrote three concertos: his first concerto, Op. 58 (1938), Symphony-Concerto, Op. 125 (1952), and Concertino for cello and orchestra, Op. 132 (published posthumously, 1955, having been completed by Rostropovitch and orchestrated by Kabalevsky). The unusual thing about the Op. 58 and Op. 125 is that they are based on the same themes. The Symphony-Concerto is actually a reworking of the material of the first concerto, but the works are quite different except for the themes themselves. Prokofiev uses traditional forms in both. In Op. 58 the three movements are rondo, sonata form, and theme and variations. The scheme of the variations movement is quite interesting: Theme-Interlude I (Theme 2), Variation I – Variation II – Variation III – Cadenza – Interlude II (Theme 2) – Variation IV – Reminiscence (Variation V) – Coda. The movement is long, running to 503 measures. In recording this work

Janos Starker cuts from measure 420 to 448 and from 454 to 474 (both cuts in the coda). In the new version, Op. 125, the movements are a three-part form (ABA) with coda, sonata form, and another three-part form with coda in which the 'A's' are theme and variation (the first 'A' taking two of the variations and the second 'A' Variations III–V). The 'B' part carries the second theme; there are two versions of the 'B' part, one being longer than the other. The themes of these works are notable, especially the second theme of the second movement, a long, flowing, beautiful melody, and help make these works attractive. Both concertos are effective, and a comparison of them will give the student insight into Prokofiev's musical imagination as it works over a span of more than a decade. Prokofiev's Concertino is altogether simpler; it is as if he wanted to write a cello concerto available to cellists with less than a consumate technique. Even this Concertino bases its final movement on a theme derived from the third movement of the Symphony-Concerto.

Dmitri Shostakovitch published his first concerto, Op. 107, in 1959. It is a spirited work in four movements, a novel feature being a third movement composed entirely of a cadenza 150 measures long. The first movement in sonata form is especially notable for its intense rhythmic drive; the second movement, the slow movement, is in a modified three-part form with an interesting feature starting near the end of the movement, where the cello plays harmonics for a long span with the celesta in a dialogue with the cello for most of the passage. The third movement, the cadenza, features, among other manners of writing, double stops, pizzicato, and accompanied melody. The cadenza is based for the most part on thematic material from the second movement, but there is one reference to the first theme of the first movement, as there is also late in the fourth movement, making this a cyclical work. The fourth movement, based on three main ideas, is brief; one is startled by the abrupt end of the movement. The orchestral colouring in the first section has an almost oriental sound. The third idea is the first theme of the first movement. Both the first and the third movements have a great deal of repetition. This concerto, as well as Shostakovitch's second concerto (1966), is dedicated to Rostropovitch.

One could hardly imagine two concertos more different than the first Shostakovitch concerto and Benjamin Britten's *Symphony* for cello and orchestra (1964). The latter is dramatic, evocative, often subtle, and highly original. After one has heard the Shostakovitch concerto several times, there is nothing new to be heard. With the Britten, one becomes more deeply involved at each hearing and new meanings keep presenting themselves. The music is anything but repetitious; and when Britten does return to material, it is always varied. Compare, for instance, the recapitulation in the first movement, which is in sonata form, with the exposition statement. The second movement, Presto inquieto, is muted throughout. A notable feature of the beautiful third movement, Adagio, is the timpani accompaniment in the first part of the long cadenza. The movement proceeds attacca into the fourth movement, an unusual example of a passacaglia.

The four cello sonatas by Max Reger fall on either side of the turn of the century: Op. 5 (1892), Op. 28 (1898), Op. 78 (1904), and Op. 116 (1911). It is hard to say just why these sonatas have failed to find a place in the permanent repertoire, since the workmanship is craftsmanlike; but they fail to hold the interest of the listener. They are heavy, serious works, somewhat under the shadow of Brahms (particularly the first sonata), and although there is no trouble with balance, they lack the spark of true inspiration. The third sonata contains an attractive variations movement, which though built on a less than memorable theme, offers much variety in the different styles of the several variations. Reger's particular type of chromaticism is one of the most interesting aspects of these sonatas.

Reger also wrote three suites for unaccompanied cello in G major, d minor, and a minor (1915). He may have had the Bach suites in mind in composing in this medium, since he was a Bach student, but these Reger suites are in no way an imitation of the Bach style. The suites are given occasional performance.

There have been a number of twentieth-century works written for unaccompanied cello. Kinney lists more than 160 written between 1900 and 1960 and discusses a number of them in his dissertation.[24] One of the most frequently performed of these is the Zoltan Kodály Sonata, Op. 8 (1915), a highly original and effective work. The sonata presents many new sounds and effects from the cello that only one who had studied the instrument would be likely to think of. The most obvious technical novelty is the scordatura tuning required. The two lower strings are each tuned down one-half step, but, for the convenience of the performer, the notes are written one-half step higher than they sound. New sounds are created by the way Kodály uses traditional techniques such as pizzicato (here both right and left hand pizzicato), harmonics, tremolo, pedal point, sul ponticello, and sul tasto. The great range of the work is notable, almost five octaves (not counting harmonics). Although the composition is ostensibly in b minor/B major, there are modal passages that lend harmonic interest. Certain melodic and rhythmic elements derive from true Hungarian folk music, a topic in which Kodály, as well as Bartok, was greatly interested. The work is in three movements, the outer ones in sonata form and the middle one in a three-part form.

Hindemith's Sonata, Op. 25, No. 3, for unaccompanied cello is one of his best works for cello. It is in five movements, the whole being in arch form, that is, parallels linking movements one and five, and linking two and four, with the third movement being the peak of the arch. The Ernest Bloch three unaccompanied suites (1956–57) may also be mentioned as effective pieces in this category, especially Suite No. 1.

Sergei Rachmaninoff's Sonata in g minor (1901) is still holding its place in the current repertoire. It was the next work composed after his most popular work, the Piano Concerto No. 2. There is a certain affinity between the works, the second theme of the first movement being particularly reminiscent of the concerto. His cello sonata is a long work, taking slightly more than a half-hour to perform. It is filled with melodies that are worked out in a leisurely way. The melodies, particularly of the first three movements, all have a similar cast, that of the Rachmaninoff type of melancholy, though I would scarcely call the work cyclical. The melodies are well suited to the cello, mostly in its middle range, and sound well. The piano part is a virtuoso part and takes most of the action, so to speak, but it also introduces several of the themes. Of the four movements, the outer ones are in sonata form, the first preceded by a Lento introduction that furnishes some of the material for the development section; the second a scherzo combined with two slower themes in the scheme: S (scherzo) – Theme I – S – Theme II – S – Theme I – S. The second theme is especially beautiful. The third movement is rhapsodic, dwelling mostly on the theme with which it starts, though there is a subordinate idea starting with the first 'a tempo'. The whole work is typical Rachmaninoff, written at the height of his creative inspiration in his late twenties, and though some will find it too long, others will feel that the many hauntingly beautiful passages make it a uniquely rewarding work. It is for those who still love lyrical, romantic melody.

28 (*left*) 5-stringed cello
(*Courtesy Museum of Fine Arts,*
Boston)

29 (*right*) 5-stringed
violoncello piccolo
by Jacobus Stainer

31 (*left*) Copper Cello
(*Courtesy Museum of Fine Arts, Boston*)

The Claude Debussy sonata of 1915 was original in every way for its time: the nature of the themes, the unique form, the harmony, and the new effects of the devices of pizzicato, portando, sul tasto (flautendo), and ponticello. Whether the theory that this sonata reflects Debussy's 'preoccupation with the symbolic figure of Harlequin'[25] in his later life throws light on the meaning of this sonata will probably depend on the listener. The music is filled with nuances, and Debussy has been careful to indicate as much as possible exactly what he wants. The second movement, Sérénade, is marked 'Fantasque et léger' and through part of it the cello is made to sound like a guitar. Even at one place he indicates 'ironique'. If it is not inherent in the notes, how is one to interpret such a direction? The third movement, Finale, is marked 'Animé, Léger et nerveux' but there is a Lento passage in the middle 'molto rubato con morbidezza', which according to the Harlequin theory represents the final unmasking of him, the final disillusionment. Although the sonata was considered superficial and bizarre at the time it was written, it has largely overcome that prejudice (often shown towards anything really original) and today is firmly accepted in the standard repertoire.

The two sonatas of Gabriel Fauré, Op. 109 (1918) and Op. 117 (1922) are beautiful works, greatly neglected. They are written in pastel shades, with great discretion, subtlety, and sensitivity. The second sonata offers more variety of mood, and is, I think, the better of the two. The sonatas do not show off the performer (the piano part especially is restrained) but are for that part of an audience who have come to hear the music. They should be heard more often.

Of the sonatas written after 1930, among the more successful are the Samuel Barber Sonata (1932), the Dmitri Shostakovitch Sonata (1934), the Bohuslav Martinu Sonata No. 2 (1941), the Elliott Carter Sonata (1948), (the Sergei Prokofiev Sonata, Op. 119 [1949], a little disappointing in spite of beautiful themes in each movement, and some very effective spots), the Ross Lee Finney Sonata No. 2 (1950), and the Benjamin Britten Sonata, Op. 65 (1961).

The Barber sonata is an early work in a lyrical romantic vein and very appealing to an audience. Its three movements offer considerable contrast, and the writing throughout has solved the balance between cello and piano by careful handling of the accompaniment when the cello has the important material. The sonata is affirmative, strong, and passionate; in other words, it is eloquent.

The Shostakovitch sonata is effective, and the second movement is actually riotous and a great deal of fun. The third movement is a deeply felt Largo (where has Shostakovitch written more beautiful music?), and the last movement is gay, in a very measured rhythm.

Bohuslav Martinu's Sonata No. 2 is an engrossing work in three movements. It is rather short, taking only 18 minutes to perform. The first movement, Allegro, has a pervasive syncopation (many metre changes) that gives the movement much forward drive and vitality. It is fairly contrapuntal. The second movement, in contrast is very chordal, with beautiful Slavic-sounding harmonies and an effective piano interlude. The third movement has great motion and drive, but is interrupted by a cello cadenza, most unusual in a sonata. The balance between the instruments that Martinu achieves is splendid, and the cello really 'sounds' in this work.

The Ross Lee Finney sonata is a fine work, one that deserves more performances. (Mrs Inga Borgstrom Morgan, pianist, and I gave the world *première* of this sonata, by default, in the spring of 1952, a circumstance that may have added to my partiality towards it). It is in five movements, in arch form. The Introduction is hinted at in the fifth movement, the Conclusion. The second and fourth movements are fast, Allegro/con Brio and Prestissimo (with a mean spot in it for the pianist), and the peak of the arch, the Adagio Arioso. The cello part, as well as the piano part, is effective throughout. That Finney played the cello in his earlier days undoubtedly gave him the insight for writing effectively for the instrument. The work exploits the range of the cello and is altogether idiomatic in its writing. This composition has also achieved a fine balance between the instruments.

The Benjamin Britten sonata, planned in 1960 and published in 1961, is a fascinating addition to the cello repertoire. It is in five movements: Dialogo, Scherzo-pizzicato, Elegia, Marcia, and Moto Perpetuo.

The first movement is most unusual. There seems to be much gesture in it; the cello is almost humanized as it takes its part of the dialogue. An animato passage employs bariolage and there are many other nameless new effects in this movement, the most difficult of the five to understand. The second movement is pizzicato throughout, and the cello is made to sound something like a guitar or some Balinesian string instrument. The third movement is strikingly beautiful, with long cello lines; the fourth movement is a unique march that exploits ponticello and harmonics. The fifth movement is notable for its drive. The sonata was most effective in the performance of it which I heard at the Aldeburgh Festival in the summer of 1968, with Rostropovitch as cellist, and the composer at the piano.

The generalizations about the innovations in recent writing for the cello approximate those for innovations in music generally. There is no doubt the composer is striving for new and original effects: string-crossing figures (often taking two staves to notate, because of the wide range) that create new sounds; various pedals used with new effect (notably in Britten's Suite No. 1, for unaccompanied cello, 3rd Movement, where the 'd' pedal is sustained throughout); glissandos; pizzicatos (left- and right-hand pizzicatos, as well as pizzicatos in combinations with bowed notes), and harmonics exploited to their highest degree. Such effects as col legno (i.e., merely effect and very hard on a good bow) are also used.

The melody line has changed considerably. Instead of beautiful, flowing melodies (so suited to the cello, but romantic in their effect, like those in the Rachmaninoff sonata), melodies become more disjunct (with less of a stepwise motion and more skips in the melody) as well as many that have a meandering quality. This quality stems from the break with functional harmony. Not being rooted in traditional harmony, the melodies seem haphazard in tonal space, without too much logic, and they are hard to keep in the memory. Indeed, many compositions have little melody at all. Take the interesting but relatively mild *Rhapsodic Ballad* by Arnold Bax (copyright in 1968, although he died in 1953). It is a good piece (I think), but one looks in vain for anything more than a melodic phrase or snatches of a melodic line.

The rhythmic revolution has also affected cello composition. Rapid changes of metre, difficult and irregular rhythmic groupings that defy the bar line of the measures, and cross rhythms with the piano part abound in recent cello music. In the first movement of Gaspar Cassadó's *Partita* for cello and piano, there are no bar lines at all. (He uses the designation 'partita' in the sense of a suite, rather than a set of variations; the second movement of his work is a particularly beautiful recitative-like movement, followed by two dances). The most interesting experiment in the rhythm of a piece is in Elliott Carter's sonata, in which he is experimenting with 'metrical modulation' (perhaps most noticeable in the third movement, the Adagio). The following example may give an idea of this new experimental device:

Example 26: Carter. Sonata (corrected edition, 1966), 3rd Movement

Carter has more than 50 of these equations in his sonata. The sonata is very difficult, particularly rhythmically. At first it was thought to be impossible to perform, but this contention is given the lie in the effective recording by Joel Krosnick, cello, and Paul Jacobs, piano. The sonata is dedicated to Bernard Greenhouse.

Composers of cello music have experimented with various kinds of harmony, some of it resulting in extremely dissonant music: elaborate chromaticism, modal writing, series of tonal centres (Hindemith), atonal music (without the row), and even 12-tone music. For an example of the latter, the Ernest Křenek Suite for unaccompanied cello, Op. 84, offers a good example. The first four measures present the row:

Example 27: Křenek. Suite for Violoncello Solo, Op. 84. 1st Movement

This row is used throughout the suite in the usual positions of basic row, inversion, retrograde, and retrograde inversion, all of which are used in the fifth movement.

The form varies a great deal, from fairly close patterning on the traditional sonata form and cycle to the principle of constant variation. The marvellous architectural form of the classical sonata, having done duty for two hundred years, and more, may have spent its force. The comparison of this classic form with the plan of the Gothic cathedral, as a product of the human mind, offers many likenesses, but the building of those cathedrals ceased with changes in society, and so, probably, will this musical architectural plan.

Even the notation of music is changing. A simple example is the use of two staves for cello chords with so wide a range it is impossible to contain them within one staff. But when one looks at a score like Iannis Xenakis's *Nomos* for unaccompanied cello, one is quite bewildered:

Example 28: Xenakis. Nomos, Violoncello Solo. p. 5, l. 6

Reprinted by permission of Boosey & Hawkes Music Publishers Ltd.

Maybe someone will be brave enough to record this work one day so the rest of us may hear what the eye does not convey.

William Schuman's *A Song of Orpheus, Fantasy for Cello and Orchestra* quotes words in the score for the first 38 measures 'to enable the soloist to perform the melody with the clarity of a singer's projection'.[26]

When a composer combines cello music with electronic media, such as tape, he is almost admitting that it is easier to find new sounds thus than finding unexplored ways of writing for the cello alone or with a traditional accompaniment. In Kenneth Heller's *Labyrinth*, one finds such an experiment.

Cello music, so far as I know, has not yet arrived at the place where the music has no meaning, i.e., complete chance music or music of indeterminacy. Although lack of meaning in music seems to appeal to a certain type of mentality that has surfaced in our society, the medium of the cello does not, fortunately, seem to lend itself to this genre. Why have music with no principle of order, music that has no meaning?*

* Since writing this paragraph, I have learned of one piece of chance music for cello and piano. Having examined it (Morton Feldman's *Durations 2*) I find no reason to change the basic conclusion of this paragraph.

Chapter 4

A Selective Group of Twentieth-Century Cellists

The four cellists in the twentieth century who have had the most stunning careers and the greatest influence on the music world and may therefore be accounted the greatest of the century to date are Pablo Casals (1876–1973), Emanuel Feuermann (1902–1942), Gregor Piatigorsky (1903–   ), and Mstislav Rostropovitch (1927–   ).

Casals is a towering figure among cellists. Not only was he an eminent cellist, but he revolutionized cello technique and his influence in this respect has been pervasive. It is, however, his stature as a great humanitarian that has made such a mark on this century.

With Casals the cellist, not only were the mechanics of his performance perfect, but his interpretations have been widely accepted. There are many, many fine cellists in the sense that they have excellent technical control over their instrument, but they are not able to convey so profound an interpretation of the literature they perform. Undoubtedly one's interpretive abilities are bound up with one's intellectual and personal traits. It is true that Casals has been criticized for his interpretations of the Bach suites for unaccompanied cello. There simply are two schools of thought in interpreting music. The classical, objective view, in which the performer attempts to perform music as closely as possible to the manner in which it would have originally been performed, presents particular problems in the performance of eighteenth-century music, and all music before that time, and involves knowledge of the performance practices of earlier times. Such performance can be only approximate at best, because nobody now living has ever heard the music performed. On the other hand, the romantic view, in which the performer attempts to perform the music in a manner that will make the music live and appeal most to the present-day audience reinterprets the music through the personality of the performer. I daresay that both points of view are legitimate, and the one you prefer depends upon who you are. Casals was an out-and-out romanticist, and his interpretations of the Bach suites were unconvincing to the classical mind, especially his use of rubato and his romantic shadings of tone. The more classical interpretation of these suites makes them seem dry, mechanical, and uninteresting to the romantic mind. In fairness one will have to admit that Casals achieved a supreme expression of his intentions in his interpretation of these suites. He was the first one, by the way, who played the suites as a whole in public. Before his time, a cellist might include a movement or two from one of the suites on his programme, but never a whole suite. Casals 'discovered' a copy of these suites in a music store in Barcelona when he was 12 years old – he had not known they existed – and practised them every day for 12 years before he dared to play them in public. Besides his performance of the Bach suites, Casals was best known for his performances of romantic music, the Schumann, Dvořák, and Elgar Concertos and many small pieces, each one of which he turned into a gem. He had no sympathy for contemporary music.

Casals' concert career started with his *début* in 1899, when he played the Lalo concerto with the Lamoureux orchestra in Paris. It was a huge success, and from then on he made numerous successful tours all over western Europe, England particularly, but also in South America and several tours of the United States (1901–2; 1903–4; 1914–17; 1927, 1929). He said: 'I lost track of the number of concerts I gave. I do know it was often around two hundred and fifty a year'.[1] This extraordinary schedule went on until he moved back to Spain (he had been making his home in Paris) in 1919 and became conductor of the Orquestra Pau Casals, when he had less time to give performances as cellist.

Besides being a great performer, Casals revolutionized cello technique. He freed the arms. He had been taught to play with his elbows close to his sides, but this did not seem natural to him. In his bowing, the hand is not far forward at the nut, nor does it change positions much throughout the whole bow. In bow changes there is a slight motion of the wrist and fingers, but it is minimal. His bow fingers were very flexible, and their action accounted for many subtleties of gradation of tone and changes in tone colour. He knew the place on the bow where each note was to be played, the speed with which it was to be played, and where on the string the bow would be, as well as analysing the precise articulation of each phrase. Nothing was left to chance.

Casals also made many innovations in fingering and left-hand technique. One of the most important was introducing the shift in substitution of the slide. Violinists had long used shifts, and it is strange that cellists did not adopt this technique before Casals. In playing two notes too far apart to be reached by the extended hand, these notes can be connected by either shifting or sliding. In shifting, two fingers are involved; in sliding, one. The distance of the actual glide is shorter in the shift, and the passage is cleaner. An over-use of the slide can give a too sentimental effect, and it is now used only for special effects. To avoid too many changes of hand position, Casals introduced over-extension and under-extension to interlock positions.

Because of the large distances between notes on the cello, it is an advantage to have long fingers. But this can be compensated for by developing through exercises large stretches between the fingers. Casals did not have a large hand, but he developed its flexibility and could stretch a perfect fourth (an octave between two strings) between first and fourth fingers or a minor third between the first and second fingers. This gave a wider choice of fingering with which to achieve a musical effect. He also developed percussion and pluck-ing of the string in making notes. He advocated a percussive finger action (with no effort, though) when putting the finger on the string to make a note, and a slight plucking (side-wise, not up and down) of the string on descending from a note.

Casals believed that there are many cellists whose technical com-mand of the instrument is as great as his (he never cultivated the sautille bowing, by the way), but that the essential difference between his and other interpretations rests in the concept of intonation. He played in what he called 'expressive intonation', which involves the idea of 'note attraction'. This is difficult to explain because it really is not a system. To give only a few examples: the major third and the major seventh of the scale are to be played very slightly higher, the distance some call the comma, (in contrast to notes in the equal-tempered system of tuning, even when one is playing with the piano which is tuned in the equal-tempered scale). The relatively constant degrees of the scale are 1, 2, 4, 5, and 8 except when these are subject to 'note attraction'. These scale degrees change if there is a modula-tion, i.e., 'a' in the key of D major is a perfect fifth (constant) while the same note in B♮ major, for example, is a major seventh and therefore slightly higher. Between minor seconds the principle operates so: in the note series a-b-c, the 'b' will be played slightly higher because it is going up and is attracted to the 'c'. In the progression c-c♯-d as compared with the c-d-d♭, the 'd' is lower in the latter case because it is going down a half step; d♭ is lower than c♯. All major thirds are wider, minor thirds smaller; major and minor sixths are variable, depending on their direction; whole tones are wider going up; vice versa, down. The extreme sensitivity with which Casals perceived the pitch of every single note accounted for his 'expressive intonation', which was, he believed, the single most important element in bringing out the expressiveness of the music he played.

The favourite 'instrument' of Casals was the orchestra rather than the cello. The cello simply has more limited possibilities. He conducted widely as well as organized his own orchestra in Barcelona, the Orquestra Pau Casals, which was formed in 1919 and existed until 1936, when the political situation in Spain forced him to disband it. The forming of this orchestra was not, however, to give him the opportunity to conduct. It was formed in order not only to create a first-class orchestra in Spain, but even more so that concerts could be available at prices the working man could afford. He paid many of the expenses himself out of his own earnings in order to give music to his fellow Catalan citizens. The founding of this orchestra was an early, conspicuous demonstration of his concern and care for others.

As a teacher, Casals coached many of the fine performers of this century. He helped found the École Normale de Musique in Paris with the violinist, Thibaud, and the pianist, Cortot, and taught master classes there for some years. These three musicians formed one of the famous trios of this century. He taught master classes also in Berlin, Zermatt (Switzerland), Tokyo, the University of California at Berkeley, and Marlboro, Vermont. An International Concours, a competition for cellists, was set up in Casals' honour, starting in 1957. He received countless honours of various kinds.

During and after World War II Casals' role as cellist was almost eclipsed by his role of great humanitarian. He began his voluntary exile from Spain in 1938 in protest against its fascist government. He went first to Paris, where he became very ill, suffering because of the tragedies that were happening to his people, and finally went to Prades in the spring of 1939, in the Pyrènées Mountains, where there were many Spanish refugees whom he could help. He spent the next years in organizing and, literally, himself helping to distribute aid to the refugee camps in the Pyrénées for the Spaniards who escaped their country, amidst appalling conditions. He also gave benefit concerts until 1945, when he gave up playing the cello in public as a further gesture of protest, since when World War II ended, the democracies would not intervene through the United Nations to liberate Spain from its fascist rule. It was not until the summer of 1950 that Casals' cello was heard again, at the first Prades Festival. It was a Bach centennial festival, and Casals not only played his cello (all six Bach suites), but conducted. From then on these festivals took place for 17 years. In the meantime, in 1956 he moved to Puerto Rico, and in the spring of 1957 conducted the Puerto Rico Festival, which continues.

It was Casals' personal philosophy, however, and the actions that sprang from it, that rank him among the great spiritual forces of our times, to be compared with Albert Schweitzer or Mahatma Ghandi. '. . . to work for peace based on justice, understanding and freedom for all mankind. These ideals have always been my ideals, and have determined the most important decisions – and the most important renunciations – in my life'.[2] In October 1958 he accepted an invitation to play at the United Nations over a world network. He may have been the first person ever to play to a worldwide audience, and he was then past 80. He accepted the invitation because he believed the United Nations was the best hope for world peace. His written message for peace was distributed among the delegates; he played the Bach D Major Sonata (originally written for viola da gamba) and then the Catalonian folk song, *El Cant del Ocells* (Song of the Birds), now so closely associated with him. For the same reason of peace he accepted an invitation to play at the White House in 1961, and also had a conversation with President Kennedy. (This concert was recorded). He began his 'peace crusade' in 1962, travelling over the world conducting his oratorio, *El Pessebre* (The Manger), when he was almost 85, and continued this tour for several years. The message of his oratorio is somewhat that of Beethoven's ninth symphony, the brotherhood of mankind. Casals' passion for world peace and human freedom, and his respect for the worth of every person, 'For me the life of a single child is worth more than all my music', are what transformed this cellist into a compassionate and great human being.

Emanuel Feuermann was one of the great virtuosos of this century, and it was a terrible loss to the musical world when he died unexpectedly six months short of his fortieth birthday. (He had gone into the hospital for a minor operation but was apparently allergic to the anaesthetic). Although born at Kolomyya in East Galicia (Galicia was a former Austrian crownland; now most of East Galicia belongs to the Ukraine), his family moved to Vienna when he was seven. He was already giving performances at only nine years old. His teachers included Julius Klengel. He began his teaching at the Cologne Conservatory at 16, and in 1929 he was appointed Hugo Becker's successor at the Königliche Hochschule für Musik in Berlin, where he remained until 1934, when he left because of the political situation. He settled in the United States, giving his New York *début* on 2 January 1935. In the spring of 1938 he gave a series of four concerts with the National Orchestra at Carnegie Hall, representing much of the important cello concert literature from the late eighteenth century until 1925. The programmes were as follows:[3]

C. P. E. Bach — Concerto No. 3 in A major
Bloch — Schelomo, Hebrew Rhapsody
Haydn — Concerto in D major

Schoenberg — G. M. Monn – Cello Concerto [Adaptation of a harpsichord concerto of 1746]
Schumann — Concerto in a minor
Boccherini — Concerto in B♭ major

Saint-Saëns — Concerto, Op. 33
? — Konzerstück in F major, Op. 75
Dvořák — Concerto in b minor, Op. 104

Strauss — Don Quixote
Tartini — Concerto in D major
Toch — Concerto

It is hard to put in words the quality of Feuermann's playing. It had everything: it was natural, and the ease with which he played the most technically difficult and brilliant passages was stunning. His tone and intonation were pure and very beautiful, having a gorgeous singing quality; his phrasing was impeccable; his total style had *élan*. His tribute to Casals could be applied to himself except for the first sentence.

. . . Nobody who ever heard him play can doubt that with him a new period for the 'cello began. He has shown that the 'cello can sing without becoming overly sentimental, that phrasing on the 'cello can be of highest quality. He adopted a technique according to the musical requirements. The enormous reaches seem to have disappeared; so have the ugly noises theretofore considered an integral part of 'cello playing. He has set an example for us younger 'cellists and demonstrated what can be done on it . . . that listening to the 'cello can be an extraordinary artistic enjoyment.[4]

A biography of Emanuel Feuermann by Professor Seymour Itzkoff of Smith College is now in progress, and should be a welcomed addition to the sparse literature about cellists.

Gregor Piatigorsky (1903–   ) has done a vast service towards making the cello more popular. His giant physique (being almost 6 ft. 4 inches tall, at one time he had his picture taken holding the cello like a violin), his ingratiating stage manner, and his consummate command of his instrument combine to make an indelible impression on audiences everywhere. On hearing Piatigorsky play, one has the impression that he wants the audience to like the cello as well as the music. In America, at least on his Community Concerts programmes, he has not been above including short pieces, often transcriptions, often flashy, just to coax the audience to a greater interest in the instrument. Through the organization, Community Concerts, he pioneered for the cello in many smaller communities which had never heard a cello recital before his appearance, and in his spirited, anecdotal biography, *Cellist*, he acknowledges his gratitude for having been able to do this.

Piatigorsky was born in Russia, trained first by his father, an aspiring violinist, and later at the Moscow Conservatory. His early playing career was very chequered, but included being first cellist of the Bolshoi Theatre before he was 17. He escaped from Russia in 1921 and went to Warsaw, where he eventually became a member of the Warsaw Philharmonic; then on to Berlin. Here he was unsatisfied with his half-dozen or so lessons with Hugo Becker and went to Leipzig for lessons with Julius Klengel, about which he said in his book (pp. 64–65); 'I marvelled at Klengel's art of teaching by not really teaching. At lessons one seldom heard suggestions or discourses on music from him. He let a student play a piece to the end and said, "Fine" or in a severe case, "Watch your left arm, young man!"' Piatigorsky mentions they studied music of the following composers: Volkmann, Lindner, Romberg, Popper, Davidov, Duport, Klengel, and Grützmacher.

In 1924 Piatigorsky became first cellist of the Berlin Philharmonic under Furtwängler, playing with them until 1928, when he began to devote his life to that of a touring virtuoso. His *début* in the United States was in 1929, and since then his travels have taken him around the world, including Japan. He has twice played at the White House, the first time for President Hoover and the second for President Roosevelt. His musical sympathies for much contemporary music have found him giving *première* performances, for instance, of concertos by Castelnuovo-Tedesco, Hindemith, Dukelsky, Pizzetti, the *Concerto Lyrico* by Nicolai Berezowsky, *Schelomo* by Bloch, among others. Several of these are dedicated to him as well as pieces by Cassadó and Mainardi.

Not only has Piatigorsky been active as soloist but also as chamber music player and as teacher. Among the chamber groups he has performed with are the trio combinations with Flesch and Schnabel Milstein and Horowitz, and Heifetz and Rubinstein. His teaching activities have taken place at the Curtis Institute of Music, Boston University, Tanglewood (Berkshire Music Festival), and now in Los Angeles.

Two beautiful Stradivari cellos, the Baudiot (1725) and the Batta (1714), are owned by Piatigorsky. He has this to say of the 'Batta' cello:

> While all other instruments I had played prior to the 'Batta' differed one from the other in character and range, I knew their qualities, shortcomings, or their capriciousness enough to exploit their good capabilities to full advantage. Not so with the 'Batta,' whose prowess had no limitations. Bottomless in its resources, it spurred me on to try to reach its depths, and I have never worked harder or desired anything more fervently than to draw out of this superior instrument all that it has to give. Only then will I deserve to be its equal.[5]

Mstislav Rostropovitch was born in Baku, Soviet Union, in 1927. He graduated from the Moscow Conservatory, where he is now professor of cello. His artistry is so consummate that he is becoming a legend in his own time. Reading reviews of his concerts, one comes across the words 'extraordinary', 'magnificent', 'colossal', 'astounding', 'wizard-like', or 'dazzling'. It seems that Rostropovitch possesses a technique that must be the *ne plus ultra*. He has become a champion of contemporary cello music; in this way, he picks up where Casals left off. Indeed he has inspired some of the best known contemporary composers to write for the cello and has even collaborated with some of them. Prokofiev wrote his second cello concerto, Op. 125 (called Sinfonia Concertante or Symphony-Concerto), for Rostropovitch and dedicated it to him. The cellist must have inspired him, because shortly after completing that work, Prokofiev started to write his Concertino, Op. 132, for cello and orchestra. He died before he completed this work, but because of their collaboration, Rostropovitch was able to complete it. Another collaboration was with Shostakovitch and his cello concerto, Op. 107, dedicated to Rostropovitch. Perhaps Rostropovitch's most famous collaboration is with Benjamin Britten, who has written all of his cello works for him, his sonata, Op. 65, his symphony for cello and orchestra, Op. 68, and his two unaccompanied suites, Op. 72 and Op. 80 (the dedication for the suites reads 'For Slava'). Many other composers have been inspired to write for Rostropovitch such as Khatchaturian (Rhapsody Concerto) and André Jolivet (second cello concerto). Although Rostropovitch commissioned Henri Sauguet to write the *Mélodie concertante*, he was obviously the inspiration for it, too.

It is somewhat in the role of musical ambassador from Russia that Rostropovitch takes his place in the world. In spite of this he was publicly reprimanded by the Soviet government in 1970 for defending his friend, the novelist, Aleksandr Solzhenitsyn. He was not allowed to travel abroad for six months and was declared a 'nonperson' (whatever that means) during his seclusion.

His first American tour was in 1956, and he has had many since then. His feat of 1967 will go down in cello annals: a series of eight concerto concerts in Carnegie Hall, New York, given within two and a half weeks in which he performed 34 works by 20 composers. His interests range over the complete literature.

Rostropovitch is not only a cellist but a composer and a fine pianist, who accompanies his wife, Galina Vishnevskaya, the Bolshoi Opera soprano.

In addition to the four cellists spoken of above, there are a number of cellists, all with flawless technique, all possessing great musicianship, all playing gloriously, but for one reason or another they do not quite take the same place as the four in the public esteem. I refer to (in the order of their birth dates) Maurice Eisenberg (1900–1972), Pierre Fournier (1906–   ), Gabor Rejto (1916–   ), Antonio Janigro (1918–   ), Leonard Rose (1918–   ), and Janos Starker (1924–   ). All of these cellists have had or are having distinguished teaching careers, Eisenberg at the École Normale de Musique, Paris (he succeeded Diran Alexanian), the International Cello Centre in London, the Longy School of Music (Cambridge, Massachusetts), Juilliard, and the summer master classes at Estoril, Portugal; Rejto at Eastman School of Music (Rochester, New York) and since 1954 at the University of Southern California; Janigro, at the Zagreb Conservatory since 1939; Rose, at the Juilliard School of Music and the Curtis Institute (Philadelphia); and Starker at Indiana University. Fournier gave up his teaching (Paris Conservatory) in 1949 because of the heavy schedule of his concert engagements.

Maurice Eisenberg, a Casals pupil and a lifetime friend of his, was particularly known for the nobility of his playing, its beautiful tone, the warmth of his interpretation, the command of his technique, and his rhythmic vitality. He studied with Hugo Becker, Julius Klengel, Alexanian, and Casals and became a standard bearer for the Casals innovations. He had an extensive concert career. Always interested in teaching, he published a book setting forth his interpretations of musical problems for cellists, *'Cello Playing of Today* (1957).

The French cellist, Pierre Fournier, made his *début* in 1925; since that time he has played with all the major European orchestras and several times in around-the-world concert tours. He has frequently been invited to play at the summer music festivals such as Lucerne, Edinburgh, Aix-en-Provence, and Puerto Rico. Poulenc's sonata and Martinu's Sonata No. 1 as well as his Concerto No. 1 have been dedicated to Fournier. A small booklet on Pierre Fournier by Bernard Gavoty in the series 'Great Concert Artists' was published by Rene Kister, Geneva, in 1956.

Gabor Rejto was born in Budapest. After graduation from the Royal Academy there, he became a student of Casals. His concert career included performing with many of the European orchestras before he went to the United States in 1939. Rejto is not only known as a soloist, but is the only original member still playing in the Alma

Trio. His performances as soloist and chamber musician have taken him all over the world – Australia, New Zealand, Japan, Africa, as well as Europe and the United States. He is a great teacher and much in demand for cello workshops, holding them at numerous colleges and universities. He was chosen as cellist for the cello workshop of the twenty-fifth anniversary of the American String Teachers Conference in March 1972. He is known for his exquisite musical taste, magnificent phrasing, and beauty of tone.

Antonio Janigro was born in Milan, and trained in the conservatory there. Later he went to the École Normale in Paris and studied with Alexanian. He has not only toured over the world as soloist – South America, North Africa, Indonesia included – but became conductor and soloist with the chamber orchestra of 14 string players known as Solisti Di Zagreb. The American *début* of this organization was triumphant, as were its successive appearances. He has been called a cellist of 'commanding strength and virtuosity', 'an artist of the first order'. His tone is haunting in its purity and beauty.

Leonard Rose, the great American cellist, was a student of Felix Salmond at the Curtis Institute. His tenure as orchestral player was climaxed by his being first cellist of the New York Philharmonic, which career he gave up after 1951 to create a career as soloist. He has steadily climbed to the top and now draws superb reviews. He plays a Nicolo Amati cello (1662), and with it has become famous for his luminous tone. It may be likened to a ribbon of spun gold. Mr Rose's technique enables him to produce a magically even quality of that tone which is exceptionally enchanting. It is not only his tone, of course, but his complete technical mastery, his refined phrasing, and the significance of his interpretations that make him a great cellist. He is also a great teacher of the cello. In a questionnaire that I sent to all the cello teachers in the colleges and universities in the United States (with about a 37% response), the three teachers who had by far the greatest number of students in these positions were Leonard Rose, Gabor Rejto, and Luigi Silva.

Janos Starker was born in Budapest and graduated from the Royal Academy there. A public career starting when he was ten years old was interrupted by the war but resumed after it, when he appeared with major European orchestras. He went to the United States in 1948 as first cellist of (successively) the Dallas Symphony, the Metropolitan Opera Orchestra, and the Chicago Symphony, after which he joined the Indiana University School of Music faculty, where he is

'Il virtuoso del
ʒr. de Bacqueville'

34 Excerpt from
Giorgio Antoniotti,
XII Sonate, op. 1, 1736

35 Excerpt from
J. P. Duport,
Six Sonates pour la Violoncelle, 1788

teaching today. He continues, however, to give performances extensively over the United States and Europe.

Mr. Starker has recorded a great deal. In the *Schwann Artist Issue*, 1970, he and Rostropovitch are listed as having the greatest number of currently available cello recordings. His pedagogical interests are reflected in a recent recording, 'The Road to Cello Playing' which is a recording of traditional exercises by Sebastian Lee, Friedrich Dotzauer, and others, which should be helpful to the student. He has also recently made his own edition of the Bach cello suites.

In an interview with Stephen E. Rubin which appeared in the *New York Times* of 15 October 1972, Starker comments on his attitude towards cello tone:

My sound is clean and centered, therefore it has a certain lean quality. That leanness does not coincide with the cello sound that people get accustomed to. When you achieve a clear, focused sound, it eliminates that mushiness which you get by vibrating so widely the playing becomes basically out of tune. People think my playing is cold because it is not what they expect to hear from a cello.

A number of cellists are better known for their association with chamber music groups. The Belgian Robert Maas, a member of the famous original Pro Arte Quartet (1913–1940), later founded the Paganini Quartet, which made its American *début* in 1946. Mr Maas died in July 1948. He told me when the Paganini Quartet was in Greensboro, North Carolina, on 15 December 1947, that he had played in more than 2,000 chamber music concerts. The Paganini Quartet took its name from the instruments they played on, all Stradivari instruments and all once owned by Paganini. The viola is the one for which Berlioz wrote *Harold in Italy*. The cello is the last cello Stradivari made, dated 1736. It is partly from the inscription on this cello, 'D'anni 92' that Stradivari's birth year is estimated as 1644. At present this quartet of instruments is on indefinite loan to the quartet-in-residence at the University of Iowa, who have named themselves the Stradivari Quartet. Charles Wendt, a student of Luigi Silva, is the cellist of this group. In the earlier part of the century the Flonzaley Quartet with d'Archambeau as cellist, was the most famous quartet. They disbanded in 1929.

The English cellist C. Warwick Evans made a name as cellist with the London String Quartet, Mischa Schneider with the Budapest String Quartet, David Soyer with the Guarneri Quartet, Claus Adams with the Juilliard String Quartet, Martin Lovett with the Amadeus Quartet, and Colin Hampton with the Griller Quartet.

There have been fewer trio groups (violin, cello, and piano), probably because the literature for this combination is not so extensive. We have already mentioned Gabor Rejto as the only remaining original member of the Alma Trio. Benar Heifetz was the great cellist in the Albeneri Trio. A recent trio group made up of solo virtuoso who have not made a career of chamber music playing might be mentioned, the Isaac Stern (violin)-Leonard Rose (cello)-Eugene Istomin (piano) combination. Jascha Heifetz (violin) and Gregor Piatigorsky have joined in playing duos (Kodály and Martinu), as well as inviting various other artists to join them for playing chamber music from trios to sextets.

Janos Scholz, a fifth generation cellist, is a man of broad interests. He was born in Hungary and trained at the Royal Hungarian Academy of Music in Budapest. Before obtaining his music degree, however, he was graduated from the Royal Hungarian College of Agriculture. At the beginning of his musical career he was first cellist of the Budapest Symphony Orchestra, and later became the original cellist of the Roth String Quartet, with which group he first went to the United States in 1933, remaining there. He has played with various chamber groups and at present is the first cellist in the New York String Sextet. Mr Scholz was one of the first exponents of the viola da gamba in America. He holds the bow of the gamba in cello fashion, which many of the early performers did in the revival of this family of instruments. He is the first to record the three Bach sonatas for viola da gamba on that instrument.

Mr Scholz took a lively interest in the formation of the Violoncello Society, which was founded in 1956 (see p. 195). He became its second president (1962–67) and has remained on the Board of Directors since then. He is much respected for his generous help to this organization and to many cellists in it. He is also president of the Stradivarius Association (see p. 33).

Having an interest in the music of the past, Scholz has a fine collection of eighteenth-century cello music, and his cello bow collection (see p. 51) is probably the largest owned by any individual. His interests go beyond music into the field of the fine arts. He has one of the foremost collections of early Italian drawings (the picture of Il virtuoso del Sigr. De Bacqueville, Plate 33, is from Scholtz' private collection). He lectures and writes on art and at present is Adjunct Professor of Art History, Columbia University, also lecturing at New York University. He has written numerous articles on art and has edited two books, *Theatrical Designs from the Baroque through Neoclassicism* (1940) and *Baroque and Romantic Stage Design* (1962). In 1972 he was honoured when the Italian government gave him the Great Cross of Commander of the Order of Merit.

There were no women cellists in the early history of the cello because of the manner of holding the instrument. It will be recalled that the cello lacked an end pin until the latter part of the nineteenth century. This lack, combined with the fact that it was considered unladylike for a woman to straddle the cello (as it was to straddle a horse), precluded her playing. It is clear that it is impossible to hold a cello 'side-saddle' without an end pin except by placing the body of the instrument on the floor (see Plate 33 for the manner in which Sigr. De Bacqueville is holding his cello) and that it would be impossible to play very much with an instrument held so insecurely.

As late as 1915, in the third edition of van der Straeton's *The Techniques of Violoncello Playing*, the author describes several possible positions in which some women were still holding the cello:

Ladies hold the violoncello in different ways. Some place the instrument in the ordinary way between the knees. This has now been almost universally adopted, because it brings the instrument under more complete control. The other methods, which were considered more graceful, have become almost obsolete on account of the obvious disadvantages.

The first and better of these ways of holding the instrument is to turn both legs to the left, bending the right knee and placing it under the left one. The left edge of the back should rest against the left knee, and the instrument against the chest, in a slanting position.

The second is to rest the right knee on a cushion or stool concealed by the back of the instrument, the latter leaning against the left knee.

Some ladies cross the right leg over the left, and rest the instrument against the right leg. This is, however, not to be recommended, as it necessitates a forced and unnatural position of the whole body in handling the instrument.[6]

In spite of the impediment of no end pin and social conventions about women holding the instrument, one woman cello virtuoso presents herself in the annals of early nineteenth-century cello history. Her name was Lisa Barbier Cristiani, and we know her through two particular associations. She played on a Stradivari cello of 1700, which cello is now known as the Cristiani cello; and Mendelssohn dedicated his *Song without Words*, Op. 109, to her. She was born in Paris in 1827 and died during a concert tour at Tolbolsk, Siberia, in 1853 at the young age of 26. I think we may assume that she was a woman's libertarian of her day and straddled her cello.

At the end of the nineteenth century (with the adoption of the end pin) and about the turn of the twentieth, women cellists begin to appear, and with increasing frequency. In the anonymous book *Violoncellisten der Gegenwart in Wort und Bild*, 1903,[7] there are five women included among the 100 cellists pictured and discussed: Josefine Donat, Viennese; Agga Fritsche, Danish; Kato van der Hoeven (1874–?) Dutch; Lucy Müller-Campbell, born in Louisville, Kentucky, but trained in Germany; and Elsa Ruegger (1881–?), Swiss. Although obviously several of the women hesitated to give their birth-dates, we may assume they were trained on a cello with an end pin. The picture of Kate van der Hoeven shows her with her cello equipped with end pin. The pictures of Agga Fritsche and Elsa Ruegger show them seated, each with her cello, which is obviously supported by an end pin although only the upper half of the cello is pictured.

More famous than the above-named cellists was the pioneer woman cellist, May Mukle (1880–1963). Born in England of gypsy parents (she said), she began her concert career at the age of nine. Not realizing she was still giving performances or indeed even living in 1959, I was surprised to read in the paper an announcement of her recital in Burlington, North Carolina, in the spring of that year. Of course, I went to the recital. It was fascinating in several ways, one of which was that she and her accompanist, Mrs. Pearl Sutherland Ideler, were touring in the old manner of 'barnstorming', that is, they found their own place to play in, in this instance a church, mimeographed their own programmes, and put a plate at the back of the room for contributions. (There was no charge for the concert).

Another way was her programme. It started out with a baroque suite, but according to the early custom of choosing the various dances from different works instead of playing a complete suite by one composer. Her suite was as follows:

Gavotte	—	Geminiani *Mukle*
Allemande	—	Lully *Mukle*
Courante	—	Galliard *Salmon*
Sarabande	—	Galliard *Salmon*
Gigue	—	Galuppi *Moffat*

This was followed by the Elgar Concerto in e minor, which was simply beautifully played. Miss Mukle's last group was composed of 'Nautilus' by MacDowell-Mukle and 'Reel' by Thomas Pittfield.

Still another way in which this recital was particularly fascinating was that her technique was of the pre-Casals era. Her eminent musicality, however, over-rode the old-fashioned fingering techniques with its many slides. Her arms were free, however, and not held close to the body, as apparently was sometimes the manner in the pre-Casals day.

In her long career of playing Miss Mukle had toured over most of the world – throughout Europe and in the United States, including Hawaii, Canada, Australia, China, Japan, Burma, India, and Africa.

A much-admired contemporary, not to say rival, of May Mukle's was the English cellist Beatrice Harrison (1892–1965). Among her teachers was Hugo Becker. She is known, among other ways, for her dedication to the then contemporary cello literature: the Elgar concerto, the Delius concerto, and the Kodály sonata for unaccompanied cello. She also made many European tours, mostly as cellist in a trio with her sisters, May, the violinist, and Margaret, the pianist. Although according to *Baker's Biographical Dictionary*, she toured the United States twice, in 1913 and 1932, there is no review of any recital in the *New York Times*, but the 22 May 1931 issue (p. 28) carries the following quaint item:

London. May 21. Nightly attempts to broadcast the song of a nightingale from the woods near Miss Beatrice Harrison's home in Surrey to distant countries were rewarded tonight with reports from Australia that the wonderful notes have been distinctly heard there.

The famous musician who originated the nightingale broadcasts by encouraging a timid bird to sing as she played her 'cello in the hushed woods, was unable to assist in tonight's broadcast owing to bad weather, and the fact that scores of motorists were attracted by the attempt convinced her that a satisfactory relay was almost impossible.

'I think that the romance of broadcasting the nightingale's song is one of my most thrilling experiences, bringing us in contact with nature' she said tonight. 'I have broadcast him with my 'cello often from my Old World garden since I enticed him here for the first relay in 1924. As he had not been heard here for fifty years, I am sure it was the voice of my 'cello which lured him back to these parts. . . .'

The next day's paper confirmed that the radio listeners over WABC's network clearly heard 'with remarkable clarity and sweetness' in the United States the nightingale's song, which lasted five minutes.

Guilhermina Suggia (1888–1950), the famous Portuguese cellist, studied with Julius Klengel and Casals, whose first wife she became. (The marriage lasted only from 1906 to 1912). Her famous portrait by Augustus John hangs in the Tate Gallery, London. When I visited that gallery in 1970 to look once again at the portrait, it was on indefinite loan to Athens, Greece. Suggia made her home in London until the late 1940s, when she returned to Portugal, where she died. While in London she became its leading cellist and was known particularly for bringing the Casals innovations to England through her playing and teaching.

Marie Roemaet Rosanoff (1896?–1967), who also studied with Casals, was perhaps best known for her rôle as cellist in the Musical Art Quartet from 1926 to 1947. She taught at the Peabody School of Music (Baltimore), the Third Street Music School in New York, and (in the summers) at Blue Hill in Maine. She was known for her 'magnificent cello playing'. With her cellist husband she edited the Bach cello suites according to the interpretation she learned from Casals. She is known, also, for bringing the Casals style to the United States through her playing.

Eva Heinitz (1907–   ) was born in Berlin, where she was trained at the State Academy for Music under Hugo Becker. Later she studied with Diran Alexanian. When she went to the United States in 1940, she gave concerts before becoming assistant first cellist with the Pittsburgh Symphony (1942–46), followed by her appointment to the music faculty of the University of Washington at Seattle from 1948 to the present. Although she has performed as a cellist in Europe and the Americas, she early became interested in the viola da gamba and has become one of the most distinguished gambists in the world today. She often gives recitals on both instruments. As a gambist she has played the famous gamba solos in the Bach literature under Wilhelm Furtwängler and Otto Klemperer, and as an ensemble player has been associated with Alice Ehlers and Ralph Kirkpatrick, both famous harpsichordists.

Raya Garbousova (1906–   ), famed woman cellist, was born in Tiflis, Russia, and trained in the conservatory of that city. Later she studied with Hugo Becker and Pablo Casals. Before making her *début* in the United States on 4 December 1934 she was well known in Europe, having played in recital and with major orchestras throughout that continent. Following her successful American *début* she has given performances widely over the United States, including the Civic Music circuit. A particularly important occasion of her playing was in 1946, when she gave the *première* of the Samuel Barber cello concerto with the Boston Symphony Orchestra under Koussevitsky.

For anyone who has heard Mme Garbousova play, it is hard not to remark on the fact that she is a petite and very charming lady. It bears home the point that in playing the cello, it is not one's height or even the length of the fingers that counts, but the flexibility of the left hand and the extent to which one is able to develop the stretch between the fingers that is the crucial factor in developing a technique.

Mme Garbousova's repertoire not only includes the standard repertoire, but twentieth-century works as well. Her programmes have included not only the Barber concerto, but also his sonata, the Debussy sonata, the Stravinsky Italian suite, the Hindemith sonatas and his chamber concerto, Op. 36/2. She has owned from time to time a number of great cellos, a Seraphin, a Matteo Gofriller, a Nicolas Lupot, a Stradivari, and at present she is playing a G. B. Guadagnini about which she is very enthusiastic.

Zara Nelsova (?–   ) was born in Winnipeg, Canada, and lived there until her family moved to London when she was ten. She gave her *début* at the age of twelve, playing the Lalo concerto under Sir Malcolm Sargent. During the war she returned to Canada, but in 1956 became an American citizen. She has performed extensively throughout the Americas and Europe with all the major orchestras as well as giving solo recitals and has taught at the Juilliard School of Music. She plays the Marquis de Corberon Strad of 1717, a gift to her.

Sadly, the career of the most promising young woman cellist, Jacqueline Du Pré, pupil of Casals, was interrupted in 1973 owing to a serious illness.

Some very great cellists are simply better known in their capacity as teachers of cello. Many of them have had significant concert careers which were crowded out by their teaching but others are continuing such careers. At the beginning of the century Julius Klengel (d. 1933) in Leipzig and Hugo Becker (d. 1941) in Berlin were the two most famous cello teachers. They were quite different in their approach to teaching. Becker was the intellectual and had a very analytical mind, as can be appreciated today by reading his *Mechanik und Ästhetik des Violoncellspiels* (1929; reprinted 1971). Klengel had a more inspirational approach. He would encourage and cajole and gave pieces that were too hard for the students to spur them on. Becker was best known in performance for his chamber music playing, whereas Klengel was cellist in the Gewandhaus Orchestra, Leipzig (1874; first cellist, 1881–1924).

In the earlier part of this century in Paris the two leading centres of cello teaching were at the Conservatoire de Musique (which had been founded in 1795 and had been a centre all through the nineteenth century), with Paul Bazelaire as one of the main cello teachers, and the École Normale de Musique founded in this century by Casals, Thibaut and Cortot, with Diran Alexanian as the teacher in residence, but with Casals giving master classes from time to time. The association of Casals' name with the École attracted the former favour of the Conservatoire to the École, certainly so with English students.[8] When Alexanian published his *Theoretical and Practical Treatise of the Violoncello*, 1922, his name became famous as that of one of the great cello pedagogues. This is a most stimulating manual though, I think, much more useful to the teacher than to the young student. It is highly analytical and provocative. The main defect in Alexanian's approach to cello playing was the position he recommended for the left hand:

In the following exercises the outside fingers (1–4) should maintain between each other the correct distances for the execution of a minor third. The space between the 2nd and 3rd (bent) fingers should be fairly wide. In the beginning this will call for a considerable permanent effort.[9]

A wide space between the second and third fingers tightens the hand so much that it tires too easily. I knew of at least one of Alexanian's students whose hand got into such knots that he sent her to Bazelaire, but as soon as Bazelaire got her playing again, she went right back to Alexanian. She claimed there were others in the same situation. When he left the École in 1930, he came to the United States, where he taught at the Peabody Conservatory, being succeeded at the École by Maurice Eisenberg.

In England William Whitehouse (1859–1895), student of Piatti, held sway, teaching for years at both the Royal Academy of Music and the Royal College of Music, and also in Cambridge. An autobiography, *Recollections of a Violoncellist* was published by Whitehouse in 1930.

In America one of the early twentieth-century centres was the Institute of Musical Art, which was absorbed by the Juilliard School of Music in 1926. Willem Willeke (1879–1950), a Dutch-born and -trained cellist who came to the United States in 1907 to become cellist of the famous Kneisel Quartet until it broke up in 1917, was the main teacher of cello at the Institute of Musical Art. His edition of *Thirty Solo Pieces for Violoncello With Piano Accompaniment*, 2 vols., 1909, was one of the popular collections of cello solos earlier in the century.

In Philadelphia the Curtis Institute was founded in 1924. The unique feature about this Institute is that it is free to those selected to attend. Felix Salmond (1888–1952) was head of the cello department from 1925 to 1942; he also had a long tenure at the Juilliard Graduate School. It was due to the fiasco of the *première* of Elgar's cello concerto, with Salmond as soloist, that Salmond migrated to the United States. According to the English writer S. Dale, the account is so: 'As I have said, the first performance was a disaster unmitigated by any saving grace. Let it be clearly understood that the fault was not that of Felix Salmond, a most brilliant cellist, with a powerful tone, a remarkable range of dynamic gradations, and acute and penetrating intellect, and a most accomplished technique. It does not speak much for English audiences that Salmond never had his due in England; and to be recognized at his true worth he had to emigrate to the United States'.[10]

Leonard Rose has distinguished himself most among Salmond's students, but other students include Orlando Cole (presently teacher at the Curtis Institute), Bernard Greenhouse, Samuel Mayes, and Daniel Saidenberg, among many others.

Joachim Stutschewsky (1891–) born and trained in the Ukraine, also studied with Klengel. He lived in Zürich, Switzerland (1914–1924) and Vienna (1924–1938), and finally settled in Israel, where he now lives. It is rather through his published pedagogical works that he has become teacher to many cellists. His most ambitious work, *The Art of Playing the Violoncello*, in six parts (2 vols, 1929) deserves study. Janos Scholz has this to say in his tribute to Stutschewsky:

> ... Any cellist who delves into this work, and into Stutschewsky's subsequent technical writings, must admit that this master created a novel approach to attacking the technical problems of both hands. In the beginning it is rather difficult to grasp the explanations of his preparatory technical studies, and to execute these studies properly. I have found from my own experience that this can be done only by approaching the problem with a curious, willing, and absorbing mind. ... I started to read the studies and became fascinated with his approach which was so utterly different from anything I had experienced during my own formative years. It took time and effort to understand the basic reasons behind his exercises. It soon became clear, however, that they not only made sense, but also worked in practice and performance.[11]

Stutschewsky's subsequent publications are *New Collection of Studies for Violoncello Playing* (Books I and II). The folder I have announcing these works carries very appreciative comments from Luigi Silva, Diran Alexanian, Emanuel Feuermann, Richard Sturzenegger, and Fritz Reitz. Speaking of a further work, *New Technic of Playing the Violoncello*, Feuermann says: 'To my mind, this work should become an integral part of the practice repertoire, not only of every cello student, but also of the virtuoso'.

Luigi Silva (1903–1961) was above all else a great teacher of the cello. He had taught in his native Italy and performed in Europe before going to the United States in 1939. His tenure as cello teacher at the Eastman School of Music was from 1941 to 1949, after which he taught at the Juilliard School of Music, the Mannes College of Music, the Peabody Conservatory, the Hartt School of Music, and Yale University, some years commuting to all of them in the same year. After his death in November 1961, 50 of his students were moved to present a concert (on 11 April 1962) in memory of their teacher. The programme consisted of multi-cello groups, from the Popper *Requiem*, Op. 66, for three cellos, to works for the whole group making up an orchestra of 50 cellos.

To say that Luigi Silva was a great teacher of the cello in his case means a teacher of technique rather than a coach of its literature. He was fascinated with cello technique, and his mind was constantly at work devising ways to overcome or make simpler the formidable problems of a fluent left hand. He had a great understanding of the cello and a gift for conveying enthusiastically what he knew. Because of his own astonishing technique he was often called the 'Paganini of the cello' (as others have been).

Luigi Silva arranged a number of works for the cello. Among his transcriptions are numerous pieces as well as several technical studies – the 24 violin caprices by Paganini, the 42 violin études by Kreutzer, 13 studies for the piano by Guerrini, and 12 caprices for viola by Lillian Fuchs. He also published his own editions of the six caprices for cello by Servais and 12 caprices for cello by Piatti. At the time of his death he had others in preparation. Silva was particularly interested in Boccherini and had published two of the concertos. He was also planning an edition of the six Bach suites for unaccompanied cello in which the score would contain the original three contemporary copies with his own compilation, all lined up together. He believed, probably correctly, that in Bach's time in Germany the cello bow was held in gamba fashion (palm up, where the strong stroke is up-bow) and that that manner of bowing should be taken into consideration in any modern edition of the Bach suites.

At the time of his death Silva was also writing a *History of Violoncello Technique*. His library contains many notes for such a book, which someone one day might well put together. He had started and planned to do much more publishing, but his time was cut short by his unexpected death. One testimony to his teaching is the large number of his cello students, now performers and teachers, who are members of various orchestras and teachers in many colleges and universities of the United States today.

Luigi Silva's library was purchased by the Friends of the Library of the University of North Carolina at Greensboro and donated to the Jackson Library on that campus in the autumn of 1963. The dedication of the library took place on 5 April 1964, with Janos Scholz, then president of the Violoncello Society, giving the memorial address.

Rudolf Matz (1901–   ) was born and trained in Zagreb and subsequently taught cello at the Zagreb Conservatory. Again, it is through his quantity of publications, both technical and musical, that he has become known to us. His exhaustive method is divided into six parts: Part I (3 vols), Part II (5 vols), Part III (4 vols), Part IV (1 vol), Part V (2 vols), and Part VI (2 vols). (There are two suites, a sonata da camera, and a sonata in the old style included in Part II). In addition he has published three sonatinas, a Sonata in e minor, a Suite in G major, a concertino and a baroque concerto, smaller pieces for cello and piano, a classical Concerto in D major for cello and orchestra, an elegy, a 'Humorous Sketch' for cello and string orchestra, a duet for two cellos, a cello quartet in d minor, and a suite for solos and violoncello ensemble. I have been unable to obtain all of this material, but I have a sufficient amount of it to recommend it as valuable teaching material. If the teacher finds there is too much material or too many exercises for some of the problems presented, he can be selective.

Two cellists have become specialists in the viola da gamba: the German cellist, Paul Grümmer (1879–1965) and the Swiss cellist, August Wenzinger (1905–   ). Grümmer's cello career included being cellist at Covent Garden, member of the Adolf Busch quartet, and teaching at music schools in Cologne, Berlin, and Vienna. He published one of the first contemporary methods for gamba, *Viola da Gamba Schule* (1928), with explanatory columns in three languages. This was near the beginning of the revival of interest in this family of instruments in this century.

August Wenzinger has made himself an international reputation as performer on the viola da gamba and gives workshops on the instrument in Europe and in America. In the summer of 1973, for instance, he was in residence at Oberlin College, Oberlin, Ohio. He has a gamba method *Gambenübung* (2 vols, 1935 and 1938) and *Gambenfibel* (joint authorship with Marianne Majer, 1943).

A brief mention follows of a number of other fine cellists:

Horace Britt (1881–1971), a Belgian cellist, toured extensively in a trio with Georges Barrère (flutist; he played on a gold flute) and Carlos

Salzedo (harp). He became professor of cello at the University of Texas at Austin.

Gaspar Cassadó (1897–1966), Spanish cellist and student of Casals, had a distinguished concert career. He is well known to cellists through many interesting compositions for his instrument (see p. 155) as well as many transcriptions, the most famous being the Frescobaldi *Toccata* (see p. 214, *note*).

Maurice Gendron (1920–   ), was born in Nice. He won first prize at the age of 14 at the Nice Conservatory, as he did later at the Conservatoire National Supérieur de Musique in Paris where he now teaches. He also teaches at the Yehudi Menuhin School in England. Mr. Gendron is an accomplished conductor, participating in international festivals as both cellist and conductor. Among his well-known recordings are the Boccherini and Haydn concertos in their authentic versions, performed with the Lamoureux Orchestra conducted by Pablo Casals. He has received in Amsterdam the Edison Prize and in Paris the Grand Prix du Disque. Among his honours are that of Knight of the Légion d'Honneur and Officer of the Ordre National du Mérité.

Bernard Greenhouse (?   –   ) was trained at Juilliard and was accepted as a pupil of Casals in 1946. He performed extensively and was later on the faculty of Juilliard for some years. He became a present-day expert as a continuo player, as anyone who heard him with the Bach Aria Group could testify. At the present time he is teaching privately at his home in New York.

Ludwig Hoelscher (1907–   ) studied with Klengel and Becker. He has performed in almost all the European countries with the most famous orchestras and conductors, also in Japan. He has given first performances of more than two dozen contemporary cello works, mostly by German composers, including Hans Werner Henze, *Ode an den Westwind*.

Edmund Kurtz (1908–   ) was born in Leningrad. He was a pupil of Klengel, Alexanian, and Leo Weiner (Budapest). His numerous tours (in the season 1949–50, he played 112 concerts) have taken him all over the world, including Australia, New Zealand, India, Indonesia, and Japan. His *début* was in Rome in 1923, his American *début* under Toscanini in 1945. He has *premièred* a number of works, including Milhaud's first cello concerto, dedicated to him. He is at present living in London.

Fritz Magg (1914–   ) was born and educated in Vienna. His studies further included attendance at the State Academy of Cologne and study with Diran Alexanian in Paris. He has made his residence in the United States since 1938. He held the first cello chair with the New Friends of Music and the Metropolitan Opera Orchestra and was cellist in the Gordon and Berkshire Quartets until 1948, when he became Professor of Cello and Chamber Music at the School of Music, Indiana University. He is now chairman of the string department there. He has written *Cello Exercises*, an excellent, comprehensive survey of essential cello technique.

Enrico Mainardi (1897–), is an Italian cellist who studied with Hugo Becker. In 1933 he became professor of cello at the Academy of Santa Cecilia in Rome. His compositions for cello include a concerto (1947) and a suite for cello and piano (1940). His edition of the Bach suites for unaccompanied cello is interesting as an attempt at a visually contrapuntal interpretation of them (as in Alexanian's).

Maurice Maréchal (1892–1964), French cellist, had a concert career including concerts in the Orient. From 1942 he was professor at the Paris Conservatory.

Dimitry Markevitch (1929–), studied with Eisenberg at the École Normale, from which he was graduated at the age of 12; he also studied with Piatigorsky. He has toured all over the world, including the Orient and Africa. In 1969 he founded the Institute for Advanced Musical Studies at Sion, Switzerland, a training school for students looking forward to a professional performing career. Mr Markevitch's edition of the Bach suites for unaccompanied cello was made after consulting the three earliest manuscript copies of these suites.

André Navarra (1911–), a French cellist, was trained in his younger years at the Conservatory of Toulouse, later at the Conservatoire National Superieur in Paris. After winning a First Prize in the International Competition for cellists in Vienna, his career was established. He has played extensively all over Europe, the USA, Canada, India, Japan, the USSR, Australia, etc. Since 1949 Navarra has been Professor of the cello at the Conservatoire in Paris and regularly gives courses in interpretation in Siena, Italy: St. Jean-de-Luz, France; Detwold, Germany; and Skopje, Yugoslavia.

Aldo Parisot (? –), a Brazilian-born cellist, has performed with many major orchestras in the United States and in Europe. He played with the world *première* with the New York Philharmonic of the Villa-Lobos Cello Concerto No. 2, dedicated to him. The composition with which his name will be permanently linked is *Parisonatina Al' Dodecafonia* for unaccompanied cello by Donald Martino, written for him, the title using a play on words based on his name. He gave a sensational performance of this most bravura piece at Tanglewood in the summer of 1966, with repetitions since. He is sympathetic to contemporary music and frequently performs it. At present Mr Parisot is on the Yale University School of Music faculty.

Leslie Parnas (? –) American cellist, was a student of Gregor Piatigorsky at the Curtis Institute of Music in Philadelphia. In 1957 he was the winner of the Prix Pablo Casals in the Paris International Cello Competition and in 1962 he won the second prize in the Tchaikovsky International Competition in Moscow. Since then he has appeared in numerous recitals and orchestral appearances throughout the United States, Europe and South America. He is professor of music at Boston University and Director of the Kneisel Hall Summer Music School in Blue Hill, Maine.

Daniel Saidenberg (*1906–*), was born in Winnipeg, Canada. He studied with André Hekking (Paris Conservatoire) and with Felix Salmond (Juilliard), and coached with Emanuel Feuermann. He was cellist in the Kroll String Quartet, and second cello for the Budapest String Quartet and the Juilliard Quartet. His orchestral experience includes the Philadelphia Orchestra (1925–1929), Chicago Symphony (solo cellist, 1930–1936), and the Casals Festival at Prades and Perpignan (1950–1951). His conducting career somewhat eclipsed his cello performing. He formed his own group, the Saidenberg Little Symphony, which toured for some years, and also conducted the Illinois Symphony and the Connecticut Symphony.

Joseph Schuster (*1903–1969*) was born in Constantinople and educated at St. Petersburg Conservatory and the Hochschule für Musik in Berlin. He emigrated to America in 1934. From 1936 to 1944 he was first cellist of the New York Philharmonic, after which he performed widely in Europe and South and North America.

Paul Tortelier, French cellist, was graduated from the Paris Conservatory; he also studied with Casals. He was first cellist of the Boston Symphony from 1935 to 1939, when he returned to France. In 1950 he made his New York *début* and has performed widely, including the Orient, North Africa, and Israel, where he now lives.

Needless to say, there are hundreds of other excellent cellists in the United States and around the world who cannot be named individually here. A special study should be made of the whole picture of twentieth-century cellists, including the many fine players who have made or are making their main careers that of orchestral playing.

Chapter 5

Conclusions and Reflections

The cello has now been in existence for about 450 years. It began, along with the violin, as a social outcast among instruments. There was no solo music for the instrument, nor were there any known performers until some time after the middle of the seventeenth century, that is for about 150 years of its early existence. Then slowly it started making its way until today it is one of the leading solo instruments.

In the section in this book on instrument makers, I gave figures (whenever I could find any) on the number of known instruments of certain makers. It seems to me significant how comparatively few cellos were made by the great makers in the seventeenth and eighteenth centuries. Of course it is more expensive to make a cello than a violin, but perhaps the small number reflects most of all a small demand. As the cello soloists first rose in the second half of the seventeenth century, it would seem plausible that they would create the demand for the fine instruments, while performers who made a profession of continuo playing might settle for the cheaper instruments by lesser-known makers.

In the eighteenth century there was a great surge of interest in the instrument. In the first half of the century most of the performers came from Italy. In the second half of the century, the interest in the cello spread widely over Europe. Remembering that the bow was not yet perfected, it is hard to imagine exactly how the cello sounded, but there is no doubt about the virtuosity of the cellist's left hand, i.e., the music of the Duports, the Krafts, Bréval, and perhaps especially of Boccherini. The virtuosity is attested by the fact that some difficult violin scores were to be played alternately by the cello (an octave lower) or some cellists were even known to play violin music *not* composed alternately for the cello.

In spite of all the activity, even in the nineteenth century, cello recitals or concerto performances were far from equal in popularity to those of the violin. It is believed that even during the nineteenth century, cello playing was rough, that a great amount of bowing noise was accepted as inevitable, and that the left hand slides with the overdose of glissandos marred a performance. Feuermann commented on his views of nineteenth-century performance: 'The technique, therefore, remained perfected . . . only to the extent that one could play vigorously and rapidly but without taking into consideration the finesse of performance. . . . The cellists had not succeeded in creating for themselves a mechanism, a technique which would have made pure artistic enjoyment for the listener. One took it for granted that scratching, lack of clarity, bad phrasing, ugly glissandi, and even bad intonation simply belonged to a 'cello'.[1]

Fournier describes the practising of Joseph Hollmann (Hollmann was a well-known travelling virtuoso at the end of the nineteenth century and dedicatee of Saint-Saëns Cello Concerto No. 2). The Hollmanns lived on the ground floor of the house the Fourniers lived in in Paris during Pierre Fournier's younger days: 'The instrument grated, blew, boomed, whistled, wheezed, coughed and sometimes even sneezed. In short, all the symptoms of a head cold were accurately parodied by the bow of "Monsieur Hollmann"'.[2]

If it had not been for Monsieur Hollmann, we might not know how Bernard Shaw felt about the cello, perhaps expressing a typical late nineteenth-century attitude towards the instrument: 'Hollmann . . . played an aria of Bach's as only a great artist can play that great composer's music. I am not fond of the violoncello: ordinarily I had as soon hear a bee buzzing in a stone jug; but if all 'cellists played like Hollmann, I should probably have taken more kindly to it'.[3]

As Feuermann said, and everyone has since acknowledged, a one-man revolution changed all this. The reforms of Casals have staged a new era for the cello. He was the first to transform the technique of the cello so that the beauty of a fine cello performance is equal to that of the violin. The great twentieth-century cellists all play with noiseless bowing, clear, articulate musical sounds, substituting the shift for the slide, thus minimizing the glissandos, and with beautiful phrasing and intonation. For the first time a cellist, Rostropovitch, can sell out Carnegie Hall. The best cellists, in other words, can now present a performance equally satisfying as that of the violin (though it is more difficult because the instrument is larger), and there is no reason for the past prejudice to linger any longer. Because of its wider practical range and the appeal of the sonority of its lower tones, it may in time build an audience that may prefer this instrument. The increased interest in the cello in this century is evidenced by the development of a number of special enterprises in behalf of the cello. In England the development went from the founding of the London Violoncello School by Herbert Walenn, which was closed at his death in 1953, to the enlargement at that time of the London Violoncello Club, founded as an offshoot of the school. This was succeeded by the International Cello Centre (ICC) established specifically to teach Casals' 'precepts', with Maurice Eisenberg as its director. It is my understanding that at present the Centre is still in existence, but other string players are now also admitted. The stimulation of the interest in the cello in England resulting from these successive enterprises was so great that it turned the tide, and instead of the English cellists going abroad for their training as they had earlier in the century, they remained in England, and foreigners began coming to London for their training.[4]

In the United States the Violoncello Society was founded in New York in 1956. Its stated aims are the following:

... [to] promote the art of 'cello playing in this country; to provide a common meeting ground for professional and amateur 'cellists; to promote interest in the 'cello as a solo instrument; to provide opportunity of performances for artist and composer; to develop a broader and more mature understanding of the art of the 'cello, and to further the members' artistic development.[5]

The society has five meetings a year in each of which a cello programme is presented by a visiting artist or a member of the Society. To choose a programme at random, on 1 February 1973, Paul Tobias, cellist and Elizabeth Moschetti, pianist, gave the following programme:

Ginastera	— Pampeano No. 2, for Cello and Piano
Mozart	— Adagio
Schumann	— Fantasiestücke, Op. 73
Servais	— Grand Fantasy 'Barber of Seville'

Thirty-two members of the Violoncello Society gave a recital on 10 December 1958, presenting the world *première* of Villa-Lobos'

Fantasia Concertante, with Villa-Lobos conducting. It was written for the Society at the request of Bernard Greenhouse, then its first president. The recital was given in Town Hall, New York; the *Fantasia Concertante* was later recorded by the group.

The Society also sponsors young cellists in New York recitals to help them in establishing their careers. Attention to young promising cellists has been focused by the Gregor Piatigorsky Triennial Artist Award, established in 1962 for the Violoncello Society by Piatigorsky. The recipient is helped for three years. The Emanuel Feuermann Memorial Scholarship Fund was also established in 1972. The Society issued a record, 'The Art of Emanuel Feuermann', (Haydn Concerto in D; Schubert, Arpeggione Sonata) in the early 1960s when his performance of these works was not otherwise available.

The Society publishes a very valuable *Newsletter*, which carries articles of great interest as well as information on new books, records, and related matters.

Recently an interesting new group of eight cellos, 'I Cellisti', has been founded and is directed by Jerome Kessler, who 'became interested in the multiple cello literature as a member of the Violoncello Society, in New York, during the 1950s'.[6] This group has begun to record.

Other evidence of special activity is the master classes in cello, for example, Casals at the École Normale de Musique early in the century; later at Zermatt, Switzerland, the University of California at Berkeley, and Marlboro, Vermont (from 1960); Eisenberg at Estoril, Portugal; Piatigorsky at Tanglewood, Massachusetts; and Rostropovitch at Oxford, England (1968).

The American String Teachers Association (A.S.T.A.), which is a non-profit educational organization, was founded in 1946. Increasingly it has been sponsoring string workshops during the summer until now they are held in every region of the United States. Each one has a specialist in cello, in addition to the special cello workshop during the A.S.T.A. annual convention. Special attention was given to the cello during the meeting in March 1965, when the association honoured Casals with its annual award, 'Outstanding Teacher of the Year'. Sixty-four cellists were invited to go to Dallas, Texas, to compose a cello choir; they came from 30 states. They performed *The Three Kings*, arranged by Rudolf von Tobel from the *Christmas Oratorio* by Casals and the *Sardana* by Casals. The balance of the programme included otherwise two eight-cello works, the world *première* of *Dithyramb* by Robert Linn, and *Bachianas Brasilieras* No. 5 for Soprano Solo and Eight Celli by Villa-Lobos, the soprano part being sung by Norma Newton (from the Statsoper, Kiel, Germany). Casals had been invited to come from Puerto Rico and conduct the group, but the weather was so bad in Dallas that his doctor advised against it. Instead, after the programme, which he listened to at long distance, he spoke to the group over the telephone, amplified; and after his remarks he played, unaccompanied, his *El Cant del Ocells*.

In addition many colleges and universities in the United States are now giving independent string workshops during the summer. In recent years they have multiplied tremendously; Milly Stanfield reports in addition that in England, 'There are youth orchestras, summer schools and music camps of all kinds'.[7]

One of the phenomena in the United States in the training of musicians in this century has been the absorption of the typical conservatory of music into a college or university structure and the consequent transformation of the conservatory into a department of music or a school of music in which the student must meet certain general liberal arts requirements set up by the college or university. This inevitably cuts down on practice time. A few music conservatories, with or without that name, are still independent, such as Juilliard, Curtis, or Peabody. There has been a slight reaction to this trend as evidenced by the extension of the summer music camp at Interlochen, Michigan, into a year-round high school of music and the formation of the School of the Arts in Winston-Salem, North Carolina, recently incorporated as one of the 16 state schools administered within the University of North Carolina and financed by the state of North Carolina. In Europe the conservatory training is still functioning, and the universities do not offer applied music, but restrict their music teaching to the training of music historians or musicologists.

Which is the better system for training a cellist who wants to become a performing artist? I think there is no doubt that if the student is to become a top-flight performer with the chance of an international career (and there is a large element of chance in creating this kind of career), he will have to be trained at the conservatory type of school and from an early age. Joseph Knitzer (deceased, but formerly head of the violin department at the Eastman School and the University of Michigan) said that to make the grade one must have his complete technique by the age of 16. (There are always exceptions to such generalizations). The trouble is that there never are enough students at any one time who have the potential of making it to the top, so that the conservatory, in order to survive financially, has to admit students (it turns out to be most of them), who have less than that potential. It is my belief that these students would be better off in a music school, or even in a department of music which offers a Bachelor of Arts degree, because these students will, for the most part, become the teachers of music, and in the world today a teacher needs to be an informed citizen just as much as a competent musician. There are some superb music schools and departments of music that give excellent applied training, sufficient for assuming every music position except that of world virtuoso. Indeed, many of the majors in applied music from the music schools or departments of music become performing artists. Furthermore, the chances of getting a substantial job are better for graduates of the music school or department of music than they are from the conservatory, because the broader training is recognized as almost a prerequisite today. (The world virtuoso accumulates his education through his extensive travels and his meeting with a multitude of different peoples).

I would like to comment on the misconception that many parents have that any teacher will do as a beginning teacher for their child and that he can go to a better teacher after he has learned to play a bit. Nothing could be further from the truth. The foundation must be solid, as the foundation of a building must be. The best teacher possible should be obtained from the very beginning. If the child is set right to begin with, his chances are infinitely better for developing his capacities. Above all, no violinist or violist should attempt to instruct a beginner in cello.

The whole purpose of learning to play an instrument, of course, is to play its literature. Performing on an instrument is a means to an end, and that end is the performance of its literature. In this sense, the study of music (and in this case cello music) is like the study of language. One must know its literature.

Probably because the standard of cello playing has been raised so much in this century and because there are numbers of first-class cellists, many of the best twentieth-century composers have been interested to write for the cello, which the charts on pp. 144–5, I hope, illustrate. There is a whole new literature for the instrument if only the cellists will dare to play it. Some do, of course. (I sometimes think we should declare a moratorium of a decade or so on the Boccherini, Haydn, Saint-Saëns and Dvořák concertos, and the Beethoven and Brahms sonatas).

To convey the meaning of this literature is the purpose of concerts and recitals, and today our cellists are able to convey cello music to an audience in as enjoyable a manner as violinists have been able to do for some time past. The cello is now on a par with the violin as never before.

A university colleague of mine in the English department in the early 'fifties, Robie Macauley, had just published his novel, *The Disguises of Love*, about the time I gave a cello recital. In my copy of the just-published novel his inscription reads, 'To Betty, with thanks for her recital – which I still think is a greater occasion [than publishing a book]'. He may have been right: for both the joy of performing music and listening to it are experiences finally beyond words.

References

CHAPTER I

1 Illustration from Edmund S. J. van der Straeten, *The Technic of Violoncello Playing*, 3rd ed. (London: 'The Strad' Office, 1915), facing p. 143.

2 The awkward date 11 January 1581 is given because it is positively known that A. Amati was dead by then (*Grove's Dictionary*, I, 131; 1580 is the year by the old calendar; 1581 by our calendar).

3 Olga Racster talked about this cello in *Chats on Violoncellos* (London: T. Werner Laurie, *c.* 1907), pp. 110–115. Although there are two plates, back and side, facing pp. 110 and 114, the details do not show up sufficiently. She apparently did not know the cello had been cut down.

4 David D. Boyden, *The History of Violin Playing* (London: Oxford University Press, 1965), p. 19.

5 Robert Haven Schauffler, *Fiddler's Folly and Encores* (New York: Henry Holt and Co., 1942), pp. 46–51.

6 Margaret L. Huggins, *Gio. Paolo Maggini: His Life and Work* (London: Hill & Sons, 1892), p. 67.

7 W. Henry Hill, Arthur F. Hill and Alfred E. Hill, *Antonio Stradivari, His Life and Work (1644–1737)* (New York: Dover Publications, Reprint of 1902 edition, 1963), pp. 297–298.

8 Ernest N. Doring, ed., *Violins and Violinists*, January 1950, p. 15.

9 *Grove's Dictionary*, v, 114.

10 Ernest N. Doring, *op. cit.*, pp. 14–15 and February, 1950, p. 57.

11 The corrected information was given by Gaetano II to Count Cozio di Salabue, recorded in Antonio Cordani, *Cozio de Salabue-Carteggio* and reported in *Violins and Violinists*, October, 1952, pp. 245–247.

12 Walter Hamma, *Italian Violin Makers* (Stuttgart: Schuler Verlagsgellschaft, MBH, 1964), p. 327.

13 Ernest Doring, *The Guadagnini Family* (Chicago: William Lewis & Son, 1949), pp. 287–289; 299.

14 *Violins and Violinists*, October, 1952, p. 245.

15 *Ibid.*, February, 1950, pp. 58, 60.
16 These prices are taken from John H. Fairfield, *Known Violin Makers* (New York: The Bradford Press, 1942).
17 *Ibid.*, p. 50.
18 Roger Millant, *J. B. Vuillaume, Sa Vie et son Oeuvre* (London: W. E. Hill & Sons, 1972), p. 93.
19 There is one biography in English, William Alexander Silverman, *The Violin Hunter* (New York: The John Day Company, 1957).
20 Edmund S. J. van der Straeten, *History of the Violoncello, the Viola da Gamba, Their Precursors and Collateral Instruments* . . . 2 vols (London: William Reeves, 1915), p. 653.
21 Nicholas Bessaraboff, *Ancient European Musical Instruments: An Organological Study of the Musical Instruments in the Leslie Lindsey Mason Collection at the Museum of Fine Arts, Boston* (Cambridge: Harvard University Press, 1941), p. 307 and Plate XIV.
22 Germaine de Rothschild, *Luigi Boccherini, His Life and Work*, trans. A. Mayor (London: Oxford University Press, 1965), p. 37.
23 Sibyl Marcuse, *Musical Instruments* (New York: Doubleday & Co., 1964), p. 579.
24 Van der Straeten, *op. cit.*, p. 660.
25 *Ibid.*, pp. 238–239.
26 *Ibid.*, p. 638.
27 *Ibid.*, pp. 638–639.
28 Marcuse, *op. cit.*, p. 338.
29 Robert Taylor, 'The Porta Cello Reconsidered', in *American String Teacher*, Spring, 1972, p. 37.
30 Robert Crome, *The Compleat Tutor for the Violoncello* (London: C. & S. Thompson, *c.* 1765), p. 1.
31 Marin Mersenne, *Harmonie Universelle. The Book on Instruments*, trans. by Roger E. Chapman (originally published 1636–1637; The Hague: M. Nyhoff, 1957), Figure 35, p. 243.
32 Henry Saint-George, *The Bow, Its History, Manufacture, and Use* (London: Horace Marshall & Son, 1922), p. 26.
33 *Ibid.*, opposite p. 32.

CHAPTER 2

1 *Grove's Dictionary*, v, 432.
2 Emanuel Winternitz, *Gaudenzio Ferrari, His School, and the Early History of the Violin* (Valsesia: Varallo Sesia, 1967), p. 9.
3 David D. Boyden, *The History of Violin Playing from Its Origins to 1761*. (London: Oxford University Press, 1965), p. 10.
4 Jambe de Fer, *Epitome musical* (Lyon, 1556), p. 63.
5 Claudio Sartori, *Bibliografia della Musica Strumentale Italiana Stampata in*

References

Italia Fino al 1700 (Florence: Leo S. Alschki, 1952; Supplement, 1968). A study of this book is the source of my information about score titles referred to in this chapter.

6 Gordon James Kinney, *The Musical Literature for Unaccompanied Violoncello* (Doctoral dissertation, Florida State University, 1962), I, 120.

7 W. Henry Hill, Arthur F. Hill, and Alfred E. Hill, *Antonio Stradivari, His Life and Work (1644–1737)* (Reprint of 1902 Edition, New York: Dover Publications, 1963), pp. 110n–111n.

8 Anon., 'On the Rise and Progress of the Violoncello', *Quarterly Musical Magazine and Review* (1824) VI, 352.

9 John Gunn, *The Theory and Practice of Fingering the Violoncello* (London: Printed by the author, 1793), p. 21.

10 Francisco Vatielli, *Primordi dell' Arte del Violoncello* (Bologna: Pizzi & Co., 1918), pp. 19–20.

11 Johann Joachim Quantz, *On Playing the Flute*, 1752; trans. E. R. Reilly (New York: The Free Press, 1969), p. 241.

12 Marc Pincherle, *Corelli, His Life, His Music*. trans. H. E. M. Russell (New York: W. W. Norton, 1956), p. 121.

13 Charles Burney, *A General History of Music From the Earliest Ages to the Present Period* (1789) . . . with critical and historical notes by Franck Mercer (New York: Harcourt Brace, 1935), II, 439.

14 Kinney, *op. cit.*, pp. 81–83. This table is the most useful I have seen for cello measurements and tunings and is the source for the figures in this section.

15 Henry Burnett, 'The Bowed String Instruments of the Baroque Basso Continuo (*ca.* 1680–*ca.* 1752) in Italy and France' in *Journal of the Viola Da Gamba Society of America*, VIII (1971), 47.

16 This name means Francis (Italian, Francesco), cellist. This was a fairly common way to identify performers in the Renaissance, i.e., Alfonso della Viola, Leonardo dell'Arpa, Antonio degl' Organi, Antonio da Cornetto or Bartolomeo Trombone. (See Gustave Reese, *Music in the Renaissance*, p. 546).

17 *Dizionario Ricordi della Musica e Dei Musicisti* (Milan: G. Ricordi, 1959), pp. 486–487.

18 I am indebted to Nona Pyron of California for a copy of these sonatas.

19 Charles Burney, *op. cit.*, p. 629.

20 Paul Nettl, *Forgotten Musicians* (New York: Philosophical Library, 1951), p. 303.

21 *Ibid.*, p. 304.

22 *Ibid.*, p. 213.

23 Charles Burney, *op. cit.*, p. 1005.

24 Edmund S. J. van der Straeten, *History of the Violoncello, the Viola da Gamba . . .* 2 Vols (London: William Reeves, 1915), p. 179.

25 Percy A. Scholes (ed.), *Dr. Burney's Musical Tours in Europe*. Vol. II:

An Eighteenth-Century Musical Tour in Central Europe and the Nether-lands. (London: Oxford University Press, 1959), p. 135.

26 Van der Straeten, *op. cit.*, pp. 181–231, *passim.*

27 Oscar George Theodore Sonneck, *Early Concert-Life in America, 1731–1800* (New York: Musurgia Publishers, 1949), p. 85.

28 Oscar George Theodore Sonneck, *A Bibliography of Early Secular American Music* (Washington, D.C.: The Library of Congress, 1945), p. 87.

29 *Grove's Dictionary*, III, 447.

30 Hubert Le Blanc, 'Défense de la basse de viole contre les entreprises du violon et les prétentions du violoncel', in *La Revue Musicale* IX (1927–28), 54.

31 *Grove's Dictionary*, V, 244.

CHAPTER 3

1 Gordon James Kinney, *The Musical Literature for Unaccompanied Violon-cello* (Doctoral dissertation, Florida State University, 1962), I, p. 196.

2 Francesco Vatielli, *Primordi dell'Arte del Violoncello* (Bologna: Pizzi & C., 1918), p. 23.

3 The authenticity of the whole body of Pergolesi's instrumental works has been under question in the past. (See *Music and Letters,* XXXIV, October 1949, pp. 321–328). However, that Pergolesi's patron, the Duke of Maddaloni, was an amateur cellist would seem to have offered him a particular incentive to write a cello sonata.

4 William S. Newman, *The Sonata in the Classic Era* (Chapel Hill: The University of North Carolina Press, 1963), p. 365.

5 Henry G. Mishkin, 'The Published Instrumental Works of Giovanni Battista Sammartini: A Bibliographical Reappraisal', in *Musical Quarterly*, XLV (July 1959), p. 361.

6 *Ibid.*, p. 364.

7 Marc Pincherle, *Vivaldi, Genius of the Baroque*, trans., C. Hatch (New York: W. W. Norton, 1957), p. 68.

8 David D. Boyden, *The History of Violin Playing from Its Origins to 1761* (London: Oxford University Press, 1965), p. 263.

9 A xerox copy of both the Kellner and Westphal manuscripts, with notations in Silva's hand, came with the Silva Library, now housed in the UNC-G Jackson Library.

10 Gordon James Kinney, in *op. cit.*, pp. 315–414, discusses the Bach suites in detail and offers a complete analysis of each one.

11 *Grove's Dictionary*, IX, 31–32.

12 Hans Weber, *Das Violoncellkonzert des 18. und Beginnenden 19. Jahr-hunderts* (Berlin-Wilmersdorf: published by the author, 1932), pp. 39–52.

References

13 *Ibid.*, pp. 53-54.
14 *Ibid.*, pp. 57-72, *passim*.
15 Alfred Wotquenne, *Thematisches Verzeichnis der Werke von Carl Philipp Emmanuel Bach* (Leipzig: Breitkopf & Härtel, 1905), a minor concerto (♯166, flute version, ♯170, cello version; B♭ major concerto ♯28, cembalo version, ♯167, flute version, ♯171, cello version; A major concerto, ♯168, flute version, ♯172, cello version.
16 Alexander Wheelock Thayer, *The Life of Ludwig van Beethoven*, rev. H. E. Krehbiel (New York: The Beethoven Association, 1921), p. 205.
17 Benjamin Britten, *On Receiving the First Aspen Award* (London: Faber and Faber, 1964), p. 18.
18 William S. Newman, *The Sonata Since Beethoven* (Chapel Hill: The University of North Carolina Press, 1969), p. 220.
19 John Clapham, *Antonin Dvořák* (New York: St. Martin's Press, 1966), p. 103.
20 Donald F. Tovey, *Essays in Musical Analysis*, Vol. III (London: Oxford University Press, Fifth Impression, 1943), p. 148.
21 John Clapham, *op. cit.*, p. 94.
22 William S. Newman, *op. cit.*, p. 94.
23 David Monrad-Johansen, *Edvard Grieg*, trans. M. Robertson (New York: Tudor Publishing Company, 1945), p. 271.
24 Gordon James Kinney, *op. cit.*, II, pp. 422-567.
25 Edward Lockspeiser, *Debussy* (New York: Pellegrini and Cudsby, 1949), pp. 176-177.
26 William Schuman, *A Song of Orpheus*, Fantasy for Cello and Orchestra (Bryn Mawr, Pennsylvania: Merion Music, Inc., 1963), pp. 3-4 of piano reduction score.

CHAPTER 4

1 Albert E. Kahn, editor, *Joys and Sorrows, Reflections by Pablo Casals* (New York: Simon and Schuster, 1970), p. 110.
2 *Ibid.*, pp. 289-290.
3 The programmes were reported in the *New York Times*, 1938, 6 Feb. and 6 March. All reviews in Section 2, p. 2.
4 Emanuel Feuermann, 'Cello Playing: A Contemporary Revolution', *Violoncello Society Newsletter* (Spring, 1972), p. 2.
5 Gregor Piatigorsky, *Cellist* (Garden City, New York: Doubleday & Co., 1965), pp. 259-260.
6 E. van der Straeten, *The Technics of Violoncello Playing* (London: 'The Strad', 1915), p. 19.
7 Anon., *Violoncellisten der Gegenwart in Wort und Bild* (Hamburg: A. G. Vormals, J. F. Richter, 1903). (The pictures in this book would offer a

primary source for a study of moustaches and beard in the nineteenth century).
8 Milly B. Stanfield, 'The Other Half' in the Violoncello Society *Newsletter* (May, 1968), pp. 5–6.
9 Diran Alexanian, *Theoretical and Practical Treatise of the Violoncello* (Paris: A. Z. Mathot, 1922), p. 25. The footnote indicated by* within the quotation reads, 'Except in case one of the notes they are playing should be "attracted" by the other'.
10 S. Dale, 'A Great Masterpiece: Elgar's Cello Concerto' in the Violoncello Society *Newsletter* (Winter, 1970–71), p. 2.
11 Janos Scholz, 'A Tribute to Joachim Stutschewsky' in the Violoncello Society *Newsletter* (Spring, 1971), p. 2.

CHAPTER 5

1 Emanuel Feuermann, ''Cello Playing: A Contemporary Revolution', Violoncello Society *Newsletter* (Spring, 1972), p. 2.
2 Bernard Gavoty, *Pierre Fournier* (Geneva, Switzerland: Réné Kister, 1956), p. 10.
3 Ayot St. Lawrence Edition, *The Collected Works of Bernard Shaw*, (New York: Wm. H. Wise & Co., 1931), pp. 36–37.
4 Milly B. Stanfield, 'The Other Half', Violoncello Society *Newsletter* (May, 1968), p. 5.
5 As stated on its stationery.
6 Record jacket, 'Introducing I Cellisti', Orion Records 7037 (1971).
7 Milly B. Stanfield, *op. cit.*, p. 6.

Key to Library Abbreviations

BCB Bologna, Biblioteca Communale annessa al Conservatorio Musicale
(Name changed to Civico Museo Bibliografico Musicale)
BCM Milan, Biblioteca Conservatorio G. Verdi
BCR Brussels, Bibliothèque du Conservatoire Royal de Musique
BEM Modena, Biblioteca Estense
BM London, British Museum
BNP Paris, Bibliothèque Nationale
BSM Venice, Biblioteca di San Marco
CMN Naples, Conservatorio di Musica S. Pietro a Majella
CMV Venice, Conservatorio Musicale Benedetto Marcello
GMV Vienna, Gesellschaft der Musikfreunde
HGA Antwerp, Haags Gemeentemuseum
KBS Stockholm, Kungliga Musikaliska Akadamien
MLG Glasgow, Mitchell Library
MPL Manchester, Manchester Public Library
NBV Vienna, Nationalbibliothek
(housing the Estensian Collection)
NMP Prague, National Museum Library
SKB Berlin, Staatsbibliothek d. Stiftung Preussischer Kulturbesitz
UBR Rostock, Universitätsbibliothek
UFU Berlin, Universitätsbibliothek, Freie Universitat
W Wiesentheid, Musikbibliothek der Grafen von Schönborn
WBM Marburg/Lahn, Westdeutsche Bibliothek

Appendix A

Cello Continuo Sonatas[1]

ITALIAN BAROQUE COMPOSERS

	Number of Sonatas	Number of Duets	Date	Where Located
*1. F. Amadei	MS. (1)			W
2. Giorgio Antoniotti	Op. 1 (5)	Op. 1 (7)	1736	BNP
3. Pietro Antonio (or G.B.A.?) Avondano	MS. (2)	MS. (1)		SKB
4. Fillippo Banner	MS. (2)		c. 1700	NBV
*5. Giovanni Battista Bassani	MS. (6)			W
6. Domenico Dalla Bella	MS. (3)		c. 1700	NBV
7. Gaetano Boni	Op. 1 (12)		1717	BM
8. Giovanni Bononcini		1	1746/8	BM, BCR
9. M. A. Bononcini	MS. (1)			NBV
*10. Antonio Caldara	MS. (17)			NBV, W
11. Alexandre Canavas, L'Ane	Op. 1 (6) Op. 2 (6)		c. 1746	Op. 1, BM Op. 2, BNP
12. Andrea Caporale	6	1 (in Bononcini collection)	1746/8	BM, BCR

[1] For editions currently available see Margaret K. Farish, *String Music in Print*, (New York: R. R. Bowker, 1965), pp. 156–201; Supplement, 1968, pp. 34–43.
*Sonatas in the Schönborn Castle library at Wiesentheid were first located in print by Ute Zingler in *Studien zur Entwicklung der italienischen Violoncellsonate von den Anfängen bis zur Mitte des 18. Jahrhunderts* (Oberhausen im Rheinland: dissertation published by the author, 1967).

	Number of Sonatas	Number of Duets	Date	Where Located
*13. Antonio Caputi	MS. (1)			W
14. Giacomo Cattaneo	1		1700	BCB
15. Cervetto, L'Aîné (pseud. for Giacomo Basevi or Bassevi)	Op. 2 (12) Op. 3 (6)	Op. 4 (6)		BM
16. Fortunato Chelleri	MS. (1)		*c.* 1725?	CMV
17. Giuseppe Chinzer	Op. 1 (6)		1745	BM
*18. Abbate de Cinque	MS. (3)			W
19. Quirino Colombani	MS. (1)		*c.* 1735?	BCM
*20. Giovanni Battista Costanzi	MS. (9)		*c.* 1750?	GMV, UFU & W
21. Angelo Maria Fioré	MS. (5) 3 pub. in *Trattenimenti*		1698– *c.* 1701	BEM
22. Franciscello (i.e., Francesco Alborea)	MS. (2)			NMP
23. Domenico Gabrielli	MS. (2)		1689–90	BEM
24. Francesco Geminiani	Op. 5 (6)		1740s	MPL, BM
25. Giovanni Pietro Guignon		Op. 2 (6) (alternate viols or bassoons)	1737	BNP
26. Giuseppe Maria Jacchini	Op. 1 (2) Op. 3 (2)		*c.* 1695–97	BCB
27. Salvatore Lanzetti	Op. 1 (12) Op. 5 (6) Op. 6 (6) MS. 10 1 addl. sonata in Cook Edition		*c.* 1736–50	BNP, BM, WBM, MLG
*28. Laurenti	MS. (2)			W
*29. Leonci	MS. (1)			W
30. Benedetto Marcello	Op. 2 Walsh Ed. (6); same sonatas as Op. 1, LeClerc Ed.		1732?	BCR, BM
31. Antonio Martinelli	MS. (1)		*c.* 1750?	CMV

* See footnote on p. 207

	Number of Sonatas	Number of Duets	Date	Where Located
32. Martino	Op. 1 (5)		c. 1745	BCB, BM
33. Pasqualini de Marzis		Op. 1? (6) Op. 2 (6) 1 Sonata (Bononcini coll.)	c. 1745–48	BM, BCR
*34. P. Orio	MS. (1)			W
35. Niccolo Pasqualli		6 (for cello or violin)		BNP
36. Carlo Passionei	12		c. 1710–17?	BNP
37. Giovanni Battista Pergolesi	MS. (1)			CMN
38. Carlo Perroni[2]	1			UBR
39. Giuseppe Maria Perroni	MS. (3)			BCM
40. Felice Maria Picinetti	MS. (1)		c. 1700	NBV
41. Giovanni Benedetto Platti	MS. (12)		1725	W
42. Nicola Antonio Porpora	MS. (1)		c. 1730	BM
43. Porta		1 (in Bononcini coll.)	1746/8	BM, BCR
44. Quarsieri	MS. (1)			NBV
45. Guilio de Ruvo	MS. (4)		1703	BCM
46. G. B. Sacchi (Giovanni Battista Sammartini)[3]	MS. (1)			NBV
47. Giuseppe Sammartini		1 (in Bononcini coll.)	1746/8	BM, BCR
48. Fideli Saggione		6 (alternate viols or bassoons)		BNP
49. Alessandro or Domenico Scarlatti	MS. (3)			BCM, BCB

[2] The solo part only: the basso continuo part is missing.
[3] One sonata is attributed to G. B. Sammartini in the Bibliothèque Nationale in Paris; the other sonatas usually attributed to him are found under Martino and Giuseppe Sammartini.
* See footnote on p. 207

		Number of Sonatas	Number of Duets	Date	Where Located
50.	Francesco Scipriani	MS. (1)			CMN
51.	Giovanni Battista Somis	12			KBS
52.	Giuseppe Torelli (Giuseppe Valentini)[4]	MS. (1)			—
53.	Antonio Vandini	MS. (4)		1717	BNP, BSM
54.	Antonio Vivaldi	MS. (8)		*c.* 1740	BNP, CMN
55.	Matteo Zocarini	Op. 1 (6)		*c.* 1740?	HGA
56.	Carlo Zuccari	MS. (1) (alternate viola da gamba)		1730	BNP

[4] The *XII/Solos/for the/Violin/or/Violoncello/with a/Thorough Bass/for the Harpsichord* by Giuseppe Valentini were definitely written for the violin, and I would agree with the correction in *The British Union Catalogue of Early Music*, ed. Edith B. Schnapper (London: Butterworths Scientific Publications, 1957), Vol. II, p. 1032, 'or rather: for the violin with a thorough bass for the violoncello or harpsichord'.

Appendix B

A Short List of Effective Pieces for Cello and Piano

NINETEENTH CENTURY

1–3.	Ludwig van Beethoven	Twelve Variations, on a Handel theme
		Twelve Variations on a theme of Mozart, Op. 66
		'Ein Mädchen oder Weibchen'
		Seven Variations on a theme of Mozart,
		'Bei Männern, welche Liebe fühlen'
4.	Max Bruch	Kol Nidrei, Op. 47 (originally for cello and orchestra)
5.	Frédéric Chopin	Introduction and Polonaise, Op. 3
6.	Karl Davidoff	At the Fountain, Op. 20, No. 2
7–8.	Antonin Dvořák	Waldesruhe (Adagio), Op. 68
		(originally for cello and orchestra)
		Rondo, Op. 94
		(originally for cello and orchestra)
9.	Gabriel Fauré	Élégie, Op. 24
10.	Felix Mendelssohn	Variations concertantes, Op. 17
11.	David Popper	Gavotte in D Major, Op. 23*
12–13.	Sergei Rachmaninoff	2 Pieces, Op. 2*
		Prelude
		Danse Orientale
14–15.	Camille Saint-Saëns	Allegro Appassionata*
		The Swan*
		(originally from *Le Carnaval des animaux* for small orchestra)
16–19.	Robert Schumann	Fünf Stëcke im Volksten, Op. 102
		Adagio and Allegro, Op. 70 (alternate horn)

* Easy pieces for the young student.

Appendix B

Appendix C

A Short List of Effective Transcriptions

SONATAS

1.	Ludwig van Beethoven	Horn Sonata, Op. 17 (transcribed by the composer)
2.	Henry Eccles-Moffat	Sonata in g minor
3.	César Franck-Delsart	Violin Sonata in A major*
4.	Georg Friedrich Handel-Lindner	Sonata in g minor
5.	Joseph Haydn-Piatti	Sonata in C major
6.	Francesco Maria Veracini-Salmon	Sonata in d minor

CONCERTO

1.	Johann Christian Bach-H. Casadesus	Concerto in c minor

PIECES

1.	Béla Bartók	Rhapsody No. 1 (transcribed by the composer)
2.	J. S. Bach-Siloti	Adagio
3.	J. S. Bach-Siloti	Andante
4.	J. S. Bach-Franko	Arioso
5.	Luigi Boccherini-Bazelaire	Rondo
6.	Frédéric Chopin-Skalmer	Nocturne, Op. 9, No. 2
7.	Frédéric Chopin-Piatigorsky	Nocturne in c♯ minor, Op. posthumous

* In all probability Franck did not make a cello version of this sonata. However, in a *New York Times* article (17 November 1968, Section 11, pp. 25 and 39) about Zara Nelsova it states:
  Miss Nelsova has a letter from Casals in which he recalls that Ysaye, for whom the sonata was written, once told him that Franck had said that the work could be played on either the violin or cello. Miss Nelsova thinks it sounds particularly beautiful on the larger instrument.

Appendix C

8.	Frédéric Chopin-Glazounow	Étude, Op. 10, No. 6
9.	Frédéric Chopin-Glazounow	Étude, Op. 25, No. 7
10.	Arcangelo Corelli-Schuster	Adagio
11.	François Couperin-Bazelaire	Pièces en concert
12.	Claude Debussy-Gurt	Minuet
13.	Azzolino B. Della Ciaja-Silva	Toccata and Canzona
14.	Gabriel Fauré-Casals	Après un Rêve
15.	Girolamo Frescobaldi-Cassadó	Toccata*
16.	Enrique Granados-Cassadó	Intermezzo from the Opera *Goyescas*
17.	Maurice Ravel-Bazelaire	Pièce en Forme de Habanera
18.	Giuseppe Tartini-Stutschewsky	Variations on a theme of Corelli
19.	Tomaso Vitali-Silva	Ciaccona
20.	Carl Maria von Weber-Piatigorsky	Adagio and Rondo

* Cassadó's transcription of Frescobaldi's *Toccata*, presumably from a keyboard work, offers a problem. The piece is very effective, very cellistic, and a welcome addition to the literature. But the question is of what work of Frescobaldi's it is an arrangement. (I have looked in vain through Frescobaldi's published works, but of course not all his works are published.) Could Cassado have paralleled the Pugnani-Kreisler act? Pugnani was a famous eighteenth-century Italian violinist and composer. Fritz Kreisler wrote an original work, *Preludio e Allegro* and published it as Pugnani's. He later confessed that it was his own composition.

A Brief List of Useful Books

The source references will provide the reader with a certain bibliography in themselves. In addition to the usual dictionaries and encyclopedias, such as Baker's *Biographical Dictionary of Musicians* with 1971 Supplement, Eitner, *Quellen-Lexikon*, Fétis, *Biographie Universelle* and Grove's *Dictionary of Music and Musicians*, I have found *Cobbett's Cyclopedic Survey of Chamber Music* particularly useful. The useful catalogues for this study were the following:

British Union-Catalogue of Early Music. Printed before 1801. 2 vols. Edited by Edith B. Schnapper. London: Butterworth's Scientific Publications, 1957.

Ecorchville, Jules. *Catalogue du Fonds de Musique Ancienne de la Bibliothèque Nationale.* 8 vols. Paris: Société Internationale de Musique, 1910–14.

Fairfield, John H. *Known Violin Makers.* New York: The Bradford Press, Inc., 1942.

Farish, Margaret K. *String Music in Print.* New York: R. R. Bowker, 1965; Supplement, 1968.

Gaspari, Gaetano. *Catalogo della Biblioteca Musicale G. B. Martini di Bologna.* 4 vols. Revised Edition. Bologna: A. Foni, 1961.

Gérard, Yves. *Thematic, Bibliographical and Critical Catalogue of the Works of Luigi Boccherini* compiled by Yves Gérard under the auspices of Germaine De Rothschild, translated by Andreas Mayor. London: Oxford University Press, 1969.

Haas, Robert. *Die Estensischen Musikalien.* Regensburg: Gustav Bosse Verlag, 1927.

Hamma, Walter. *Meister Italienischer Geigenbaukunst.* Stuttgart: Schuler Verlagsgesellschaft, 1964. (Text in three languages.)

Laurencie, Lionel de La. *Catalogue des Livres de Musique (Manuscrits et Imprimé) de la Bibliothèque de l'Arsenal à Paris.* Paris: E. Droz, 1936.

Pubblicazioni dell' Associazione dei Musicologi Italiani. Parma: Zerbini e Fresching, 1911–1942.

Bologna, *Biblioteca del Liceo Musicale,* and *Archivo Musicale della Basilica di S. Petronio* (Series II);
Milan, *Biblioteca Conservatorio 'G. Verdi'* (Series III);
Modena, *Biblioteca Estense* (Series VIII);
Naples, *Conservatorio di Musica S. Pietro a Majella* (Series X);
Venice, *Biblioteca di San Marco* and *Conservatorio Musicale 'Benedetto Marcello'* (Series VII).

Sartori, Claudio. *Bibliografia della Musica Strumentale Italiana Stampata in Italia Fino al 1700.* Florence: Leo S. Olschki, 1952; Supplement, 1968.

Weigl, Bruno. *Handbuch der Violoncell-Literatur,* 3rd Edition. Vienna: Universal-Edition, 1929.

Wotquenne, Alfred. *Catalogue de la Bibliothèque du Conservatoire Royal de Musique de Bruxelles.* 4 vols. Brussels: J. J. Coosemans, 1898–1912.

The books that are particularly recommended are as follows:

Bessaraboff, Nicholas. *Ancient European Musical Instruments*; an Organological Study of the Musical Instruments in the Leslie Lindsey Mason Collection at the Museum of Fine Arts, Boston. Cambridge: Harvard University Press, 1941.

Boyden, David D. *The History of Violin Playing from Its Origins to 1761.* London: Oxford University Press, 1965.

Broadley, Arthur. *The Violoncello: Its History, Selection and Adjustment* ('The Strad Library', No. XXI). New York: Charles Scribner's Sons, 1921.

Burney, Charles. *A General History of Music* From the Earliest Ages to the Present Period (1789) . . . 2 vols, with Critical and Historical Notes by Franck Mercer. New York: Harcourt, Brace, 1935.

Casals, Pablo. *Joys and Sorrows.* Reflections by Pablo Casals as Told to Albert E. Kahn. New York: Simon and Schuster, 1970.

Duport, Jean Louis. *Essay on Fingering the Violoncello and on the Conduct of the Bow.* Translated by John Bishop (*c.* 1806; translation, 1878).

Goodkind, Herbert K. *Violin Iconography of Antonio Stradivari, 1644–1737,* Treatise on the Life and Work of the Patriarch of the Violin–Makers. Larchmont, New York: by the author, 1972.

Hayes, Gerald R. *Musical Instruments and Their Music. 1500–1750.* 2 vols. London: Humphrey Milford for Oxford University Press, 1928–30.

Heron-Allen, Edward. *De Fidiculis Bibliographie:* being an attempt towards a Bibliography of the Violin and all other instruments played with a bow in ancient and modern times. (First published in 1890–1894.) London: The Holland Press, 1961.

Hill, William Henry, Arthur F. and Alfred Ebsworth. *The Violin-Makers of the Guarneri Family* (1626–1762). London: W. E. Hill & Sons, 1931.

Hill, W. Henry, Arthur F. and Alfred E. *Antonio Stradivari, His Life and Work (1644–1737).* New York: Dover Publications, Reprint of 1902 edition, 1963.

Kinney, Gordon James. 'The Musical Literature for Unaccompanied Violoncello.' 3 Vols. Doctoral dissertation, Florida State University, 1962.

Newman, William S. *The Sonata in the Baroque Era*. Chapel Hill: University of North Carolina Press, 1959, rev. ed., 1966.

——. *The Sonata in the Classic Era*. Chapel Hill: University of North Carolina Press, 1963.

——. *The Sonata Since Beethoven*. Chapel Hill: University of North Carolina Press, 1969.

Pincherle, Marc. *Vivaldi: Genius of the Baroque*. Translation by Christopher Hatch. New York: W. W. Norton, 1956.

Praetorius, Michael. *Syntagma Musicum*. 3 vols. Wolfenbüttel, 1615-20. English translation by Harold Blumenfeld, vol. ii, Parts 1 and 2 New Haven: The Chinese Printing Office, 1949.

Quantz, Johann Joachim. *On Playing the Flute*. Translation and notes by Edward R. Reilly. New York: Free Press, 1966.

Shaw, Gertrude Jean. 'The Violoncello Sonata Literature in France During the Eighteenth Century'. Doctoral dissertation, Catholic University of America, 1963.

Tovey, Donald Francis. *Essays in Musical Analysis*, Vol. iii. London: Oxford University Press, 1936.

Straeten, Edmund S. J. van der. *History of the Violoncello, the Viol da Gamba, Their Precursors and Collateral Instruments . . .* 2 vols. London: William Reeves, 1915. Reprint by Reeves, 1971.

Weber, Hans. *Das Violoncellkonzert des 18. und Beginnenden 19. Jahrhunderts*. Berlin-Wilmersdorf: published by the author, 1932.

Zingler, Ute. *Studien zur Entwicklung der italienischen Violoncellsonate von den Anfängen bis zur Mitte des 18. Jahrhunderts*. Oberhausen im Rheinland: dissertation published by the author, 1967.

Index

Names given in the Appendices have not been included in the Index

Index

Index

Taylor, Raynor, 70
  sonatas, 123–4
Tchaikovsky, Peter Ilyich,
  Rococo Variations, 138
Tcherepnin, Alexander, 149
Tecchler, David, 35, 39
Thibaud, Jacques, 169, 184
Thomson, Virgil, 150
Tillière, Joseph Bonaventure, 76, 125
Toccata, 80
Toch, Ernst, 151
Tononi family, 35
Torelli, Giuseppe, 58, 64, 210
Tortelier, Paul, 148, 191
Toscanini, Arturo, 14
Tourte, François, 50–1
Tovey, Sir Donald Francis, 145
Trattenimento, 78, 80
Triemer, Johann Sebald, 73, 93

Uccellini, Marco, 64, 78
Uribe-Holguin, Guillermo, 154

Valentini, Giuseppe, n. 210
Vandini, Antonio, 69, 104, 210
Vatielli, Francesco, 58, 65, 79, 81
Vaughan Williams, Ralph, 145
Venice, 32, 35, 36, 38, 101
Vibrato, 25
Vienna, 63, 66, 73, 104, 108, 110, 111, 112
Villa-Lobos, Heitor, 14, 154–5
Viola pomposa, 43
Violoncello:
  see Cello
Violoncello alto, 45
Violoncello d'amore, 45
Violoncello da spalla, 45
Violoncello piccolo, 43, 44

Violoncello portatile, 46
Violoncello tenor, 45
Violone, 56–60, 78
Virdung, Sebastian, 53, 54
Virtuosi, 61, 65
Vitali, Giovanni Battista, 58, 64, 65, 81
  Partite, 78–9
Vivaldi, Antonio, 64–5, 84, 210
  concertos, 99–100
  sonatas, 91–2
  example 11, 103
Vuillaume, Jean Baptiste, 41–2

Washington, D. C.
  Library of Congress, 33, 34, 108, 123
Wagenseil, Georg Christoph, 110
  example 21, 111
Wahl Collection, 36
Walton, Sir William, 146
Wasielewski, Wilhelm Joseph von, 13, 71, 97
Weber, Carl Maria von, 132, 214
Webern, Anton von, 143, 152, 212
Wellész, Egon, 152
Wenzinger, August, 97, 188
Whitehall, Gertrude Clarke, 34
Whitehouse, William, 185
Wiesentheid, Germany, 84, 101, 104, n. 207
Willeke, Willem, 185
Williams, Alberto, 154
Winternitz, Emanuel, 52, 54
Witten II, Laurence C., 28–9
Wölfl, Joseph, 132
Women cellists, 179–184

Xenakis, Iannis,
  Nomos, 165
  example 28, 165

224